FROM THE COMPANY OF SHADOWS

Kevin Shipp
From The Company of Shadows

Other publications by this author:
In From The Cold - CIA Secrecy and Operations

Library of Congress Control Number: ....
ISBN13: 978-0-692-01796-8

Published by
Ascent Publishing, LLC
13046 Racetrack Road, Suite 260
Tampa, Florida 33626

www. KevinMShipp.com

Publisher's Cataloging-in-Publication
(Provided by Quality Books, Inc.)

Shipp, Kevin,
     From The Company of Shadows : including excerpts from
     In From The Cold : CIA Secrecy and Operations / Kevin
     Shipp.
     p. cm.
     LCCN 2012909271
     ISBN 978-0-692-01796-8

     1. United States. Central Intelligence Agency.
     2. History, Modern--21st century. I. Shipp, Kevin, 1956-
     In from the cold. II. Title.

     UB271.U5S55 2012   327.1273
                QBI12-600125

Photographs in this publication are used by permission.
Editor: Lisa Rowan
Cover Design and Text Layout by Caroline Blochlinger - www.cbAdvertising.com

FROM THE COMPANY OF SHADOWS

with Excerpts from
"IN FROM THE COLD - CIA Secrecy and Operations"

Kevin Shipp

To Sue.
Without you this book would not have been possible.
Thank you for your unselfish love and support.

To Lorena, Joey, Bobby and Carly.
I hope this book somehow explains all the months I was
gone and the difficult times you endured because of my
career. I hope it also brings you some measure of comfort
from the agonizing events you suffered. I love you all.

To Nell Murphy.
Thanks for all your loving support during our family's
crisis.

To Clint and Geep.
Thank you for your unbending courage in defending our
family.

Contents

Contents

Disclaimer

All statements of fact, opinion, or analysis expressed are those of the author and do not reflect the official positions or views of the CIA or any other US Government agency. Nothing in the contents should be construed as asserting or implying US Government authentication of information or Agency endorsement of the author's views. This material has been reviewed by the CIA to prevent the disclosure of classified information.

Acknowledgments

I would like to thank the dedicated CIA officers who stood alongside me during difficult and sometimes life threatening assignments. I hope this account brings you fulfillment knowing the story has finally been told.

I would also like to thank the courageous and dedicated attorneys who fought to defend our family against government tyranny and cover up.

I would like to express my appreciation to Steve Emerson. Steve has literally risked his life to expose the covert Jihad movement in America.

Author's Note

During my career at the CIA, I functioned as an internal CIA staff security officer, federal investigator, protective agent for the Director of Central Intelligence, chief of training for the CIA police force, assistant counter assault team leader, operational security team leader, counterintelligence investigator, Counter Terrorism Center officer, international information systems security officer, polygraph examiner and federal police officer. I was a Category I employee.

Because of my previous employment with the CIA, I must abide by my duty to protect CIA sources and methods. I have been careful to protect the true names of CIA employees, locations and any other information that could jeopardize the Agency or my former co-workers. Thus, I do not discuss my employment status (during my career I have also been assigned to several other government agencies), specific locations, true names of individuals or any other organizations involved. I use pseudonyms for individuals discussed in this book, and the names of all locations involved.

What you will read is a full expose' of CIA operations. I will also describe the Agency's use of secrecy ███████████████ .This will provide, in detail, internal CIA operations, sometimes humorous, I was a part of; revealed to the public for the first time. It details the CIA's role in the war on terror and results of the author's experience and research on this subject. The book follows my career as a CIA officer through the many experiences I had while conducting internal security investigations and overseas covert operations. It finishes with a shocking story of the CIA's misuse of the power of secrecy; I witnessed personally. This event changed my entire view of the Agency I loved, and revealed the Constitutional parameters routinely breached by the CIA.

I am a former intelligence officer. My expertise is in collecting and reporting intelligence. I am not a journalist. I ask the reader to forgive me for my tendency to write in analytical and technical fashion. Overcoming this tendency is a work in progress. This book contains multiple topics on CIA operations, intelligence and terrorism. I welcome the reader to read the entire book, or skip the technical sections and read those describing actual operations. Although there is no specific theme in this work, the overall theme is intended to be a multifaceted description of the internal workings of the CIA and related information regarding the war on terror.

This is, in many ways, the most fulfilling, and the most difficult document I have ever written. The CIA has an important role in protecting our national security. I owe much of my operational training and analytical skills to the organization I loved and served. I have many close friends there and fond memories of several of my assignments.

It is my hope that this book enables Americans to better understand the CIA, inspires them to hold dear our Constitution, never to be intimidated by corrupt, powerful and deceptive assertions of "secrecy," and motivates them to hold those in power accountable to the American people for their actions.

"There is something about the way the CIA has been functioning that is casting a shadow over our historic position [of freedom] and I feel that we need to correct it."

Harry S. Truman, December 22, 1963, op-ed, *The Washington Post*
(*The Post* later mysteriously excised the entire article)

Introduction

The CIA is a unique federal organization. It operates under a thick canopy of secrecy. Covert agents killed in the line of duty become lonely stars etched into the wall of CIA headquarters. Those officers who live must remain seated at ceremonies recognizing patriots serving openly in the military; sacrificing the recognition they so often deserve. This can be a lonely experience. I know this feeling. The sacrifices CIA officers have made, including risking their lives, remain hidden; locked away in their memories. For many officers, it is a unique brand of courage that will never be known.

CIA officers face a plethora of challenges in the field. They are held to the highest standards of any federal agency and undergo the most stringent clearance process in the world. Many times they are assigned to countries where torture is a real option if they are discovered. There is simply no room for mistakes or negligence. The environments they are routinely sent to are toxic, hellish war zones; where death has become a way of life. This kind of exposure, sometimes over long periods of time, can only be handled by vetted, seasoned men and women who will not bend under pressure. This pressure could include the loss of their life. They must tolerate the real possibility of illness from what they are forced to eat or drink to ensure they blend in to the culture. Long separations from their family are common. And many families do not survive the absence of a husband and father. Due to solitude and loneliness, some make moral mistakes while overseas, then try to cover up their moral failures so their husband or wife does not find out what they have done. But these flaws usually come out in the end and the state of their marriage is never the same again. Trained to keep secrets, they will sometimes leak to the ones closest to them. Significant others have an uncanny way of reading the behavior of those they love. These officers' rank and duties are a distinct privilege. They have worked and studied hard to earn them. They must continually live their cover, even in the US, so others do not expose their operations. The CIA will hold them accountable if they fail. There is no loyalty among spies.

In this book I stress Congress must continually hold the CIA accountable and provide oversight; ensuring it functions under the restraints of the Constitution and protects the freedom of the Americans it serves. This has not always been the case, and in the past Congress has been forced to take action and rein the CIA in. The Agency does not operate by popular vote and the majority of its action takes place in the darkness of secrecy.

This book is about that Agency. It is written to provide a three hundred and sixty degree view of the CIA and its function. It reveals the good, the bad and the ugly of the Agency I loved and served for so many years.

Chapter 1

CIA Operations

The night was dark and still; no movement, not even the sound of a dog barking. The atmosphere seemed unnatural, tense and quiet. I could feel the Asian air, moist and heavy brushing against my face as we moved in tandem up the dark, deserted street. Dressed in black, we moved slowly, paralleling each other, concealing our advance behind parked cars. My right hand gripped the handle of a black Colt AR 15 automatic rifle; my left hand cradled the stock. I held it in the ready position, shooting finger off the trigger, thumb on the firing selector switch ready to make the decision; single-shot or fully automatic. There were two of us. Darkness had become our companion, our most valuable protection. We were part of it. A dangerous meeting was about to go down. The leader of a major terrorist group was to meet us in a deserted office building. There was a possibility we could turn him and gather precious information regarding the organization's plan for its next attack. Four Americans had been killed, as many as eight local police a day were being gunned down and employees at the American embassy were being followed. Another attack was imminent.

Trained to use adrenalin to our advantage, we maintained a heightened state of alertness; a controlled cocktail of fear and courage motivated by mission. This operation could be a valiant success, or this street would be the site where we give our lives for our country. Was it a set up? They had the advantage. Knowing the time and place, they had the element of surprise. If they were going to turn on us, we had no control over the timing, the weapons or explosives they would use - and their numbers. We had trained for this and trained hard. Crouched low, the butt of my rifle pulled hard in the gap between my shoulder muscle and collar bone, we were ready for the worst. The AR 15 was almost invisible in the dark, its black smooth coating non-reflective. Feeling the unique surface of the weapon had become a familiar sensation, and brought a peculiar sense of comfort. We could trust this weapon.

Our minds focused on one set of actions; judge properly, shoot to kill - disappear. Being wounded or, even worse, captured and facing torture, beating or being skinned alive, was not an option. It was all or nothing. Staying alive was not part of the equation, unless we won.

Before we deployed from the vehicle to move, my mind flashed back to the months of training necessary for this operation; day and night. Officers were eliminated based on their inability to ignore death. Graduating from the training program was an accomplishment we all held dear. It was not easy. As an elite team, we had gone through five different performance cuts, leaving only a handful of us to deploy. Images jumped in my mind of driving in total darkness, lights off, 120 miles an hour, a vehicle ramming me from behind as we approached a 90 degree turn, while the instructor screamed obscenities at me from the passenger seat, "upping the adrenalin." Night after night we went through dark training scenarios, advancing towards our targets amidst live automatic fire, flash grenades and night flares.

Just weeks before during training I had come in last during speed plate shooting. It was embarrassing. Granted, I was shooting against the best, but we had to be the best to make the mission. I was despondent and upset at myself. I got very little sleep that night. The next night we were thrown into a real life, dark, live fire exercise in which we had to engage multiple terrorist targets in rapid succession. Something kicked in. I finished in first place, hitting all the targets center mass in a matter of eight seconds. After the jubilant cursing was over, the instructor rewarded me with a compliment, slap on the back and a cold beer.

"Good shooting son, damn good shooting."

I kept the beer can for months to remind myself to stay focused.

The Tail

I was assigned to several of these assignments during my early years with the Agency. They included intense moments, embarrassing moments and some humorous ones. I wish I could relate them all, but the majority can never be told. On one such assignment, I was deployed to ███████████████████████████████████. There were more KGB agents per capita in ███████████████████ than any city in the world. During our movements throughout the city, going out to dinner, to the gym or to the shopping mall, we regularly had our "shadow" following behind us. A young, blond KGB agent, always wearing his walkman "headphones," was our constant companion. After a couple of weeks, we nicknamed him "Boris." Wherever we went, Boris was always a part of the scenery. Although it was a little frustrating, as CIA officers we knew that you never, NEVER, confront or harasses your "tail." Doing so, especially with the Soviets, meant swift retribution, such as broken antennas on your car, key scrapes on the paint, or human feces in places you didn't appreciate. So, we just tolerated Boris and took him with us wherever we went. When it was work time, we employed our usual counter surveillance tactics and lost him; letting him find us again when we came "out."

Late one evening Brett, my co-worker, and I went out for a cold beer at the Irish pub, just a few doors down from the hotel. The establishment was packed. It was a small place, about the size of a shoe store, walled with walnut paneling and a short, polished cherry bar with a brass rail. The place was in an "L" shape with a room with tables in front of the bar area and one around the corner to the right. The tables themselves were tall, round, made of dark wood, no more than three feet across and were pushed so close together they almost touched each other. The bar was alive with the mixed sound of talking, laughter and emotional arguments about soccer. Brett and I took a table shoved next to the table of four young women. I guess someone had to take that table. It turned out the women were Irish school teachers visiting ▮▮▮▮▮▮▮▮ for a teacher's convention. We engaged them in small talk as we sipped on a Guinness beer. They were very curious about Brett and me, because we were obviously Americans. This evening we were "out" and our clothing and accent clearly showed everyone what country we were from. ▮▮▮▮▮▮▮▮ people are wonderful people and for the most part are very friendly to Americans. A ▮▮▮▮▮▮▮ local could immediately tell an American by his or her shoes. ▮▮▮▮▮▮▮people wear Levis and khakis like Americans, but never with tennis shoes. They wear leather loafers, or nice casual leather shoes. The ▮▮▮▮▮▮▮▮ would laugh at Americans who thought they were blending in, but were wearing their habitual tennis shoes. They stuck out like a sore thumb.

As we sat having a pleasant conversation with the ladies, Brett and I both married and wearing our wedding rings, one of the teachers turned to me, and with sincere curiosity said,

"Why do Americans hate the Soviet Union so much?"

"Americans don't hate the Soviet Union," I responded.

"Then why does your President Regan call them the "Evil Empire" and fight against them in Afghanistan? Why doesn't he just leave them alone? That is why people don't like Americans."

"It is really because our President is against what is happening in Afghanistan. They are leaving toy bombs on the ground, intentionally, so Afghan children will pick them up. The children do, and get their heads blown off. That is why our President says those things."

Just then, our friend "Boris," who was sitting around the corner where we could not see him, burst out of this chair and began yelling at the top of his lungs. Apparently, Boris had too much Vodka on the job. He was blowing his cover.

"Americans! Baby killers in Vietnam!" He shrieked.

"Americans! Baby killers in Vietnam!" He yelled again as he came around the corner where we were sitting.

We were surprised; we didn't know he was there. The Irish teachers were terrified. Knowing who "Boris" was and what our profile was supposed to be, Brett and I were trying to figure out how to stop an international incident.

Boris came over to our table, still yelling and obviously "schnokered." I stood up.

The entire bar went stone dead. Every face was looking at me and Boris, eyes wide open, mouths dropped. The bar tender, a large dark haired man with a handle bar mustache, was frozen in shock. This was not a good thing for someone who was supposed to be taking a low profile.

Boris got in my face, wreaking of Smirnoff and yelled at the top of his lungs,

"Americans! Baby killers in Vietnam!"

It was pretty clear Boris, who by some technical means had been picking up our conversation from around the corner in a noisy crowd, did not like my comment about his motherland dropping toy bombs for Afghan children to pick up.

My little table was now a stage, and the entire bar was the audience. I responded calmly to Boris as Brett began to stand up,

"Just calm down, why don't we both go outside, and we can talk about this together?"

"Americans! Baby killers in Vietnam!" He had his face right in mine.

At this point Boris' brain was powered only by its limbic system, the rest swimming in alcohol.

It appeared Boris was about to take things to a physical level. So, I, with Brett at my side and fully prepared to knock this fellow into the boutique next door, responded a little stronger,

"Let's go outside and we can talk about this as friends."

Boris must have gotten the message our body language was conveying. He turned around and ran out of the bar, full of petrified patrons, still yelling,

"Americans, baby killers!"

Brett and I, knowing this is the last thing you want to happen on assignment, kindly apologized to the, now red-faced, bar manager and gracefully made our exit. After making sure we were not being followed, we made haste back to our hotel for the night.

The next day as Brett and I went to the shopping mall for supplies, there was Boris, back again; our friendly Soviet caboose. We went back to the Irish pub two nights later. As soon as we walked in the bartender ordered,

"No more Vietnam, OK? No more Vietnam!"

"You don't have to worry about us sir. We promise, no more Vietnam."

Room Service

During another assignment, I was sent to the Middle East as a protective agent to advance the visit of a high level agency official. It was obvious the local government knew who I was. The foreign intelligence service harassed me the entire time I was there. First, I found a microphone concealed behind the curtains in my room. When I returned from my assignment during the day, my luggage had been gone through and my room searched. When I ordered room service (a big mistake), the hotel would bring food I had not ordered. One evening, I ordered steak and potatoes. I waited for forty minutes; and no dinner. Finally, I called room service to ask them where my dinner was.

"Do you speak English?"

"Little bit."

"I ordered dinner forty minutes ago."

"Heh?'

"Can you understand what I am saying?"

"Little bit."

"Is my dinner coming?"

"Yes, dinner coming."

Ten minutes later, there was knock on the door. It was room service. I opened the door and standing there was a tall Middle Eastern man in his thirties dressed in black pants and a blue dress shirt. He handed me a large tin of pipe tobacco.

"This is not what I ordered," I said.

"You take it," the man said in a thick Arabic accent.

"I am not going to take it; this is not what I ordered."

"You take it."

"No, I am not taking it."

Now, I was getting flustered. I knew I had to control myself, because if I made the intelligence service mad, they would just escalate the situation. I also knew I had to make sure I maintained diplomacy - at all costs.

"Thank you very much. But I ordered dinner. Please take that back."

"OK, OK," the man said.

Twenty minutes later, there was another knock at the door. It was room service. I opened the door to find a different Middle Eastern man dressed in business casual attire with a covered dinner plate in his hand.

"Dinner for you," he said.

"Thank you very much."

I tipped the man. He looked at me as if he was offended, then left. I wasn't sure if I tipped him properly or should not have tipped him at all. Brushing it off, I removed the cover from the dinner plate. On the plate lay two strips of meat; green meat. It was quite disgusting. I threw the dinner in the trash. This was the last time I ordered room service.

Finally, I was ready to go to bed. I had to get as much sleep as possible to prepare myself for the long days I would work when the Agency official arrived. I turned out the light at eleven p.m. As I began to doze off, I was jolted out of sleep by music so loud it shook the walls of my hotel room. I had been placed in the room directly above a Middle Eastern discothèque. The blasting Arabic music lasted into the early hours of the morning. It sounded like some kind of Middle Eastern Karaoke. Whoever put me in that room must have gotten a real kick out of it. I got very little sleep that night.

During my assignments overseas (and in the US in some cases) I learned there were several peculiar perks involved in being a CIA officer. These perks included receiving pre-opened mail, constantly having someone following behind you; so if you got lost you had someone to tell you where you were going, free clothing rearrangement in your luggage while you were out of the hotel, and being a video star in your room with or without you knowing it. One pesky "perk" was the fact that the local intelligence service constantly ran women at us. On the friendly side, some of this was an attempt to provide a service foreigners think every American man wants and, unfortunately some do. Others were attempts by the foreign intelligence service to exploit US government employees with female agents. Some officers were trapped, embarrassed and exploited by this; and paid a heavy price. Others partook of the service's offers quite regularly. This was a constant source of frustration for those of us who had families and did not want to partake of these particular "perks."

Evening Out

I began my time with the CIA as an internal Staff Security Officer. In the CIA, a Security Officer is one of the most heavily screened, vetted and trained career officers in the Agency. The CIA Office of Security is responsible for protecting the Director of the CIA, the Deputy Director of the CIA, performing internal counterintelligence and security investigations, conducting polygraph investigations, doing employee and applicant background investigations and protecting defectors from assassination. We went through months of grueling training on conducting investigations, surveillance and counter surveillance, high risk personal protection and covert operational security procedures. A good bit of our training took place at "The Farm," the affectionate name for the Agency's covert training facility.

During a long training stint at the Farm, all of us were relaxing in the student center enjoying a few beers and talking about the day's training. Unfortunately, this was also the last day of training for a colorful group of operational "soldiers." The group of twenty-five or so battle trained students burst into the student lounge and, essentially, took the place over. Before we knew it, the group had surrounded us, taken one of the female security officers, placed her on top of one of the bar tables and demanded she dance for them. With the exception of me, my closest friend Dan and a former Marine by the name of Kurt, all the security officers scattered like confetti in the wind. My fellow female student, terrified and embarrassed, looked down from the bar table and yelled "Help me!" This was a pretty tall order considering Dan, Kurt and I were surrounded by a group of heavily intoxicated men twice our size.

In an inebriated, stupid, night-in-shinning-armor moment, I walked up to the large fellow that had placed my associate on the table (the man's neck was so large it was hard to tell where his head ended and his shoulders began) and said,

"Why don't you just leave the lady alone, Face Lift?"

The words walked themselves right out of my mouth before I even knew they were free.

"What did you just say to me?" the burly fellow responded.

Dark haired and with a fu-man-chu mustache, the expression on his face looked like someone had just told him his mother was really a man. I had never seen a fellow with back muscles as wide as his. He looked like a turtle.

"Why don't you just leave the lady alone, Face Lift," I again responded with no real thought of surviving the evening.

The entire lounge went quiet. Slowly, the group of "soldiers" gathered around me, leaving Dan and Kurt outside of the circle, thankfully (for them). At least two of us would not wind up being mashed potatoes that evening. They could have all my personal effects.

"I daaaaare youuuuu to saaaaaay that again," my unwanted adversary said slowly, playing to the jeers of "kill him" and "crush the punk" coming from his teammates.

I was kind of like the lamb at a Gyro feast, I was committed and there was no going back. I could see my fellow security officers peeking at us from the doorway of the adjoining pool room. My female co-worker had secretly climbed down off the table and escaped into the pool room with the others.

"Who do you think you are? You guys outnumber us all, and you think that makes you tough? You need to leave the lady alone," I responded again in suicidal fashion.

The group closed in, and my large friend moved in for the kill. I thought to myself,

"We'll I am pretty hammered, maybe I won't feel anything."

Just as my ominous ring mate was about to pound my head into my feet like a cartoon figure, the door to the lounge flung open, and in walked an older, distinguished looking gentleman. The entire group of rowdy "soldiers" immediately froze. No one in the place moved, including me. I thought he may have been the chief of the base and I was now in even more hot water, albeit with a sense of relief that, at least, becoming mashed potatoes may have become less of a possibility.

The gentleman walked through the ring, up to my new "friend" and me and, in an authoritative tone, asked,

"What is going on here?"

"Sir," I responded, "I am attempting to prevent these fellows from embarrassing my lady associate over there."

The gentleman motioned to the lady. She sheepishly began walking over. He met her halfway across the open lounge floor. Quietly, he asked her what had happened and she related the preceding events. He returned to me and my larger companion and said to me,

"I would like to apologize on behalf of this entire group for this. Mark my words; I will take care of it."

"Thank you sir," I replied, feeling like I was observing some kind of life saving miracle.

"You, come over here with me," he sternly said to the still angry, but now somewhat afraid gladiator.

"The rest of you, back off, NOW and leave these people alone. Got it?"

"Yes sir!" The group responded in unison.

The gentleman then took the angry fellow and what appeared to be the group leader over to the bar. I could see he was having a stern talk with them. Perhaps, he was telling them someday a few of us may be doing their polygraph test and security reinvestigation.

As far as Dan, Kurt and I were concerned, the event was over. We were still breathing. The rest of the security officers were still huddled in the pool room.

Then, a line of the "soldiers" formed from the back of the lounge, leading up to me, Dan and Kurt. Every member of the large limbed group had joined the line, with my previous ring mate first. We had no idea what was coming next. He came close to me and said,

"I....don't....want to do this. I....reaaalllly....don't want to do this. But....I have to. So....I'll do it. I apologize for what I did....and for embarrassing the lady. I....am....sorry."

He looked like he was undergoing surgery with no anesthetic. I stuck out my hand and said,

"Hey guy no problem, no problem at all." I felt like Alfalfa on the Little Rascals.

I was thinking, "I can't believe this is happening. I just went from certain broken bones to an apology. I am going to live tonight."

Each member of the group came up in the line, one by one, and apologized for their behavior and for embarrassing the lady. Most of them, only spectators with no ego in the affair, were quite friendly and jovial. My friend glared at me the rest of the time we were there, which was not very long. I never saw him again, a fact I cherish to this day.

The Author with the ███████████ Training Team.
(Photo courtesy of the Author)

The Author during tactical firearms instruction.
(Photo courtesy of the Author)

Chapter 2

Entering on Duty

I was raised in Falls Church, Virginia in a typical middle class family. I earned my undergraduate degree in Biology from Virginia Tech in Blacksburg, Virginia. My parents, Bob and Caroline Shipp, worked hard to support their six kids. My father was brought to Washington, DC from Utah to work for the CIA, a fact none of us knew until we were older. I never knew what Dad did until I was inside the Agency in 1985. He did not even know I had applied until I was in process. When I was finally in, we had many rich days together in CIA headquarters, having lunch and discussing our respective challenges working for the organization. Dad received the career intelligence medal at his retirement. He was presented with the medal at a ceremony in CIA headquarters. During his acceptance speech, Dad thanked the Director of the Office of Information Technology (D/OIT) for the award. He told the group he wished he could say his thirty-one years with the agency had all been fulfilling, but unfortunately, he could not do that. He had seen the internal inequities that went on for far too long. Dad has always been about loyal, unfailing service to his country. His integrity stood out against that of those who would do anything to get promoted. I was so proud of him that day.

The Shipp family the day Bob Shipp received the career intelligence medal at CIA headquarters.
(Photo courtesy of the Author)

Because we had such a large family, living on one modest government income, and with Dad's help I took out a college loan to attend Virginia Tech. Since I invested all I had in the enrollment, I had no car to travel the two hundred and fifty-three miles to and from the college. I routinely hitch hiked from school to home and back on holidays; something I would not recommend anyone do these days. I spent an average of six hours, standing on the highway, day and sometimes night, at times in the rain getting muddy water splashed on my pants by passing eighteen wheelers. There were times it was late, I was exhausted and I slept in the woods by the side of the road, using my poncho as a tent. But, I knew what I wanted. I had a goal and I was determined to reach it. I had looked death in the face with a terminal illness, been given six weeks to live; then experienced a medical miracle and fully recovered. I was given a second chance. Every day was precious and I took nothing for granted.

In my early college days, I was somewhat (probably an understatement) of a wild young man. I had come so close to death, I lived life to the fullest; albeit in the wrong direction. I did not put the pieces of my life together until I was a junior in college, finally understanding what happened in the hospital when I was healed. I lived life hard. I was known for my relentless partying and fearless risk taking. Drugs, alcohol and loose intimate encounters were my weekend activities. It was not until the fall of 1976, that I finally decided to clean up my life and head in a positive direction.

I applied to the CIA in the winter of 1984, at the height of the Cold War. I deeply loved my country and wanted to serve it the best way I could. Because of my wild past, I never entertained the idea I would be hired; thinking surely I would never make it through the CIA's stringent clearance process. A close friend of mine, whose identity I cannot reveal, talked me into applying to the agency. Upon doing so, I brushed it off, thinking I would never hear from them again. To my surprise, I received a call.

"Mr. Shipp, this is Mr. ████████████ with the Central Intelligence Agency."

"Yes, this is Mr. Shipp"

"Mr. Shipp, you have placed an application for employment with the CIA. I am calling to find out if you are still interested in your application going forward."

"Yes, I am."

"Fine. We will continue your application processing. Thank you for your time."

"Thank you. Goodbye"

I hung up the phone and had no idea what "continue with your application processing" meant.

I heard nothing from the CIA for three months. I was convinced once they took a look at my college life that would be the end of it. I discounted the possibility of them ever hiring me. After three months, the phone rang again.

"Mr. Shipp, this is Mr. ████████████ with the Central Intelligence Agency."

"Yes, this is Mr. Shipp."

"Are you still interested in continuing with your application with the Agency?"

"Yes I am."

"Good. Would you be willing to attend an interview at CIA headquarters on ████████████ ?"

"Yes sir, I would."

The interview was arranged and I was to report to CIA headquarters in Langley, Virginia.

The day of the interview arrived. I drove to the main gate of CIA headquarters, was processed in and escorted to the old headquarters building. As I walked into the spacious lobby of headquarters, I took in the entire scene. To my right were the engraved stars on the wall, CIA officers killed in the line of duty; many with no names listed because they were under cover at the time of their death. To the left, in huge letters on the marble wall was the verse from John 8:32, "You shall know the truth and the truth shall set you free." I found the verse inspiring. I was escorted down a back hallway, given a visitor badge and seated in the waiting area.

A woman dressed in business attire came out of the doorway.

"Mr. ████████████ will see you now. Please follow me"

"Yes Ma'am."

The woman walked me down a hallway with unmarked doors to a large office at the end.

"Mr. ████████████ this is Mr. Shipp."

The silver-haired man stood up from behind the large walnut desk.

"John ████████████ nice to meet you. Please have a seat."

I thanked him and took the seat in front of the desk.

"Kevin, you know you are in process for a job with the Agency," he said.

"Yes sir."

The man was smoking heavily, filling the room with cigarette smoke.

"Kevin, let me ask you a question. Have you ever broken the law?'

"Uh-oh. Here we go," I thought to myself.

This is where my college days would rear their ugly head. Since I had cleaned up my act nine years ago, I decided I would just tell the truth; the colorful, ugly truth.

"Yes sir, I have."

"Why don't you tell me about it?"

I went into a long litany of drinking, carousing, climbing to the top of the WMOD radio tower and touching the blinking light at the pinnacle, etc., etc. When I was finished, I thought to myself,

"We'll that's it. That's the end of this interview. At least I told the truth."

The man sat back and took a long drag off his cigarette, blowing the smoke out his nose. I waited and said nothing. It seemed like there were five minutes of silence.

Then, he sat up in his chair.

"I have no problem with that. We'll continue with your processing. Thanks for coming in."

"Thank you Sir." I felt a mixed feeling of relief and joy.

I was escorted out of CIA headquarters to my car. I drove home, now thinking there was some hope I would be hired. But, they still had to look into my background. I kept my reservations about the idea.

Three more months went by. I received another call.

"Mr. Shipp?" A lady was on the other end of the phone.

"We have you scheduled to take your polygraph test for employment with the CIA. You will need to report to ██████████ on ██████████ to take the test."

"Thank you. I will be there," I said.

We bid each other goodbye.

The day of the polygraph test arrived. I was nervous about the procedure. Giving the test a good deal of thought, I decided to stick to my new set of ideals. I would just tell the whole truth; the good, the bad and the ugly. I arrived at the waiting room, full of new applicants. Everyone exchanged pleasantries as we sat, waiting for our test. Despite the fact that we were all strangers, there was a certain unspoken sense of camaraderie. It was like we were all waiting to be called back for surgery. Surgery was not far from the truth, although it was not the physical kind.

During the pre-test interview, the polygraph examiner asked,

"Is there anything you would like to discuss with me before the test?"

"Well, here we go again. Might as well just lay it all out," I thought to myself.

"Yes there is."

I went through the long litany of partying, drinking, use of Marijuana ten years earlier, the radio tower and all the other pranks I had pulled in my earlier years. Then the test began. A CIA polygraph is always an interesting experience, to say the least. It is like a dental exam, with an occasional tooth pulling. I sailed through the test. We were finished in two hours. Later, I learned that was a good sign. After I spilled my guts to the examiner, it was easy to answer the questions after being connected to all the wires. Apparently, that was a good procedure to follow. The rest was simply answering a set of very specific questions.

I began to get calls from my neighbors and friends telling me some man in a dark suit "from the FBI" had visited them and was asking questions about my background. Of course, the FBI does not do investigations for Intelligence Community employment applications, but that is the conclusion every one reached. Once again, I thought to myself, "We'll see what they say when they talk to my old drinking and smoking buddies."

Another month passed. I received a call from the CIA stating my background investigation was in process. The caller advised the Agency had a new program, hiring prospective employees before their investigation was complete to retain them and keep them from applying elsewhere. I was processed into the agency and placed in a room behind a combination locked door, eight hours a day. I sat in that room, waiting, for seven weeks. Then, an Agency official visited the room, took me aside and told me I had been accepted for employment with the CIA. It was a tremendous relief. For the last seven weeks, I sat in the room and watched as applicants were given the news, one by one, they had not passed the clearance process and were walked out the door. I met one of my life-long friends in that room, Dan. Dan and I would follow each other in our careers over the next seventeen years, eventually winding up as protective agents for the Director of the CIA.

Next, I was to report to my Enter on Duty (EOD) briefing, located in an auditorium deep in the headquarters building. All of us sat there for three eye-opening days as the CIA briefed us on much of what really goes on inside the organization; a very sobering experience. It was ironic. Over the next seventeen years, I would occupy assignments as an investigator, polygraph examiner and the senior EOD briefer in this same auditorium for new employees. I would see the process from both sides. Having this perspective gives one a broader view of the big picture. You have more of a sense of mercy for those you are investigating; having been one yourself.

Chapter 3

In Training

After I joined the CIA, I underwent testing for the Security Officer Recruiting and Training (SORT) program. To qualify for the program, I took the CIA's equivalent of the Graduate Records Exam. Candidates had to score a 3.0 or higher on the test. The test also included extensive IQ and psychological test questions (a full eight hours). Testing covered extensive questions on world geography and political history. I passed and was admitted into the CIA Office of Security, staff security officer generalist program, where I underwent the intensive security officer training program.

In the CIA, generalist security officers are responsible for internal and external security and counterintelligence investigations, applicant background screening and clearances, staff periodic reinvestigations, personal protection of the Director of the CIA (DCI), Deputy Director of the CIA (DDCI), Chiefs of Station (COS) overseas and the protection of defectors handled by the CIA. Security officers are also responsible for operational security during Directorate of Operations (DO) operational missions.

My introduction began with an intensive training program at the CIA's training facility affectionately known as "The Farm." The farm is a beautiful tract of land, equipped with all the latest agency training props and role players. There is a quiet air of mystery hanging over the farm. At night, you can hear a pin drop, except for the occasional burst of automatic weapon fire. The program consisted of training in performing internal CIA investigations, interviewing and interrogation. My later counterintelligence and polygraph training would amplify the instruction I received there. During my time at The Farm, I also underwent training in counter surveillance and surveillance detection. This would become the cornerstone of my operational skills in the Counter Terrorism Center. Our team went through extensive firearms training, operational driving training and we received our indoctrination to technical security countermeasures, or "bug" prevention and detection. Our final training involved intensive, scenario driven training on operational VIP protection. Those of us who successfully completed the course left exhausted, relieved and excited about the assignments that lay ahead.

I was assigned to the detail of security officers dedicated to protect the DCI and DDCI. We were put through more extensive training in protective operations. This training consisted of Secret Service grade VIP protection techniques, coupled with CIA specific operational protective intelligence. We were drilled in the use of several advanced weapons systems.

Training for Counter Terrorism Center assignments consisted of counter terrorism driving, advanced tactical firearms, surveillance and counter surveillance and other training I cannot discuss. The greatest training we received came during actual operations in the field. There is simply no substitute for the experience you gain on an actual assignment. Some of the experience is fulfilling and some is very humbling. It is amazing how your head shrinks when there is actually a possibility you may be killed on an assignment.

Chapter 4
The End of an Era

The Director of the CIA lay dying in a Washington, D.C., hospital. The Iran Contra Scandal had become white hot and the Agency was under intense pressure to release documents related to the affair. Internally, Agency lawyers were scrambling to produce information demanded by Congress regarding the alleged "Arms for Hostages" deal.

Rumors were circulating that William Casey's illness was simply a ruse to protect him from accountability for the scandal. Calls for his testimony in front of the House of Representatives and the Senate were growing. There was a firestorm of media demands for interviews with Casey and for information related to the scandal. The President of the United States was being asked for an explanation. The Agency was in trouble.

I was assigned to CIA Director William Casey's staff as a Protective Agent. During these events, all of us were working long hours, seven days a week, to provide for his continued protection and to look after his wife, Sophia and daughter, Bernadette. Their world had been turned upside down. Sophia Casey was a woman of true grace and elegance. She was handling these traumatic events with poise and patience. All of the agents on the detail had grown to deeply respect her. We observed her quietly sitting in her sun room praying. It was clear her personal faith kept her going.

A month after surgery for a large tumor in his brain William Casey took a remarkable turn for the better, and his health seemed to be returning rapidly. He regained his weight and mental acuity. Late one sunny afternoon, as I occupied the "hot seat" outside his hospital room, Casey asked me to come in to his room to talk. It was a moving moment (discussed in more detail in Chapter 6).

Bill Casey went through a dramatic and inspiring change at the end of his life. Sadly, a few months later, the cancerous tumor reared its ugly head again and his health began to decline at an alarming rate. He entered into a semi-conscious state, unable to talk or move on his own. The cancer eventually took his life.

Part of the momentum behind the Iran Contra Scandal was Casey's intense friendship with Lebanon Station Chief William Buckley and their loyalty to each other. Buckley had been kidnapped by Iranian terrorists and was being tortured– daily. The amount of CIA information being extracted from Buckley as he was tortured to death by Hezbollah was of grave concern to the CIA. Casey felt personally responsible for Buckley's plight. Motivated by his own long-held loyalty to his country and his independent, maverick-like personality, Casey sought the most rapid means possible to ensure Buckley and the other hostages were rescued. It backfired. It was the first lesson in a long line of failures, demonstrating you cannot negotiate with terrorists. Radical religious fundamentalism has no heart and no soul. It has only one goal; a global theocracy established through "Jihad" (Arabic word meaning struggle). I discuss this dark, menacing threat in chapters sixteen through twenty-two.

There was a part of William Casey's past known by only a few people. I learned about it after his death, during the wake in his Roslyn Harbor, New York home. One of his former Office of Strategic Services (OSS) associates shared with me a book, now out of print, called Piercing the Reich. The book describes William Casey and other OSS members' roles in penetrating the Third Reich during a courageous and bold attempt to gain intelligence. It was truly heroic.

Although he was gruff, somewhat of a mumbler, and had a strong dislike for most members of the news media, Casey was one of the last real dedicated servants of democracy, who continued to take personal risks rare among officials at his level. It is my opinion he knew his health was deteriorating and his time was limited. He had been battling prostate cancer, which apparently had spread to other parts of his body. I watched as he began to stumble and, bit by bit, lose slight amounts of his motor skills.

As Casey lay dying in the hospital, death threats from radicals and bizarre individuals, convinced he was controlling the globe, continued to come into the CIA. As agents assigned to assess the threat against the Director, we continually received, analyzed, and if warranted, followed up on these threats. During his tenure as Director of Central Intelligence (DCI), his time terminally ill in the hospital, and even after his death

- death threats continued to arrive by mail and via the telephone (to Agency operators). Several letters claimed Casey should die for his involvement in the Iran Contra scandal, and others came from unstable or mentally ill people who thought either they were super-intelligent and ruled the universe, or the CIA was controlling their brain. Most disturbing was the fact that Ayatollah Khomeini had placed a significant price on Casey's head.

Following Casey's death, a pall hung over the Agency. The organization had suffered the loss of one of the last staunch, historical defenders of democracy. The CIA was under intense investigation and its future was uncertain. There was a tempest brewing inside and outside the organization.

Shortly after he passed away, the event Bill Casey dreamed of occurred. The Berlin wall was destroyed – by the people; East Germany and West Germany were united. The Soviet Union, the Great Bear, had fallen. This was one of the most remarkable miracles of the Twentieth Century. Although many believed it was the CIA that was at the heart of the fall of Soviet Communism, this could not have been further from the truth. As a senior lecturer to employees and liaison officials entering the Agency, I did a lot of study on the events surrounding this period. What I found was remarkable. Communism in the East did not fall because of the power and intelligence of the CIA. All we did was hold it back for years. In reality, the fall of Communism was the result of a huge undercurrent; a longing for civil and religious freedom among the people which could no longer be restrained.

One of the catalysts of what became a revival of religious and political freedom in Russia was the 1984 and 1988 crusades held by Billy Graham; for the first time in Moscow. Soviet officials tolerated the event, thinking it would be insignificant, give the appearance of tolerance, and fade away. Instead, it created an explosive undercurrent throughout the Soviet Union and the East. This undercurrent grew at a remarkable pace, involving huge numbers of people tired of religious oppression and the robbery of individual freedom. In the Soviet Union, the movement spread like wildfire. People rebelled against their oppressive governments, tore down the statue of Vladimir Lenin and poured out into the streets. I observed these events from inside the CIA, witnessing the remarkable events that unfolded. When Communism fell in the East, the people did not pour into the streets waving American flags, or praising the CIA for its power and prowess. They broke out into the streets in droves and celebrated communion. Churches barely tolerated during the Cold War which had not been closed down by the government were swamped. The Soviet Duma began having daily Bible studies during its sessions. The sad part was, while the former Soviet Union was introducing the Bible in its government sessions and placing it as a part of student curricula in its schools, America had kicked the Bible out of education and almost every part of open public life. I watched the beginning of one inspiring revival of religious freedom in the East, and the slow elimination of another in America, occurring despite the warnings of the framers of the Constitution. It was as if we had become so fat and happy we had forgotten the fundamental truths which gave us our freedom and liberty.

As the Berlin Wall crumbled, high value intelligence files were eagerly collected by Western intelligence as they were cast out onto the street during the ransacking of intelligence offices. East German intelligence and even the KGB opened their secret files for review by US intelligence officers. The Soviets revealed they had frozen the brains of great former Soviet leaders and were studying them to learn what made them stand out from other people. They gave members of the US media tours of their secret gulags where thousands of political prisoners had been held. Former arch-enemies were now strong political allies. It was truly amazing.

After the fall of communism, I spent a period of time with a former Communist intelligence officer. I cannot reveal his name or his country, but I will never forget our time together. When we first met, we glared at each other across a large walnut conference room table with a sense of distrust; former opponents - now allies. It was a curious and awkward feeling. Neither of us believed the other's intentions were honorable. He was the typical blond, now graying, blue-eyed East block intelligence agent, and I was his counterpart in the free world. He and I spent weeks working together and, over time, became good friends. Unfortunately, when you are an Agency officer, you have to leave your foreign friends behind when you depart.

One bright and beautiful afternoon, my friend took me on a walking tour of a small town in his country. We talked about the remarkable fall of communism in his country and the people's new found freedom. As we walked, he turned to me and made a startling statement, a statement once common in America.

"You know, Kevin, our country has left communism and is now a democracy."

"Yes, I know, that is wonderful."

"But, there is one thing we have learned."

"What is that?"

"We have learned a free society cannot function without a belief in the Bible."

Amazed, I responded, "You know, you are right!"

I will never forget that moment and how ironic it was the opposite seemed to be happening in America—the country which had communicated this truth to the world for so many decades. Communism had fallen because of human being's innate thirst for true religion, freedom and meaning in life. It also fell because people never forget the imprisoning, persecution and execution of their friends and family.

The CIA in Decline

After Casey's death, following the tenure of DCI William Webster, Robert Gates was nominated to become the new Director of the CIA. I served as an agent on Gates' protective detail when he was Deputy Director and while he was Acting Director after Bill Casey's death. After shocking resistance from Agency officers, who protested at his confirmation hearings, he was sworn in as DCI. Robert Gates was a man of tremendous integrity, discipline and devotion to his country. He also had a tremendous sense of humor. His intellect and professional humility were remarkable. Indeed, Robert Gates ran the CIA following Casey's death and largely during the tenure of William Webster.

I found Gate's 2007 appointment as Secretary of Defense to be an excellent choice for a position demanding his basic trait of objectivity. It was a remarkable irony to watch the meeting in Russia between Gates, former Director of the CIA and now Secretary of Defense, and Vladimir Putin, former officer in the aggressive Foreign Intelligence, First Chief Directorate and Lieutenant Colonel in the KGB, now President of Russia. Two former gut-level enemies were now meeting together as (shaky) allies in non-intelligence positions. I can imagine what they both must have been thinking.

Unfortunately, following the election of President Bill Clinton, and Gates' pre-briefing to him, Gates summarily resigned—I believe seeing what was coming on the horizon for US Intelligence. During Robert Gates' going-away ceremony at CIA headquarters, I met Sophia Casey again with her daughter, Bernadette. We gave each other a warm hug.

We had spent a substantial amount of time together and I had watched her endure painful, personal agony.

"Kevin, what the heck is going on around here?" Mrs. Casey asked, referring to the rapid decline of the Agency and Gates' resignation after the election.

"Ma'am, I don't know, but I think it is bad."

She looked at me seriously and said, "Well, why don't you do something about it?"

The Author in front of armored limousines at DCI Casey's residence. *(Photo courtesy of the Author)*

"Ma'am, maybe I will," I replied politely.

Although I am by no means a hero or a crusader, I had no idea of the level of internal corruption I was to face later as the Agency imploded.

My last assignment as a CIA DCI Protection Agent was to participate in the turnover of the position of DCI to John Deutch, the appointment of the new DDCI, George Tenet, and the assignment of their first Executive Officer, Nora Slatkin. This was the new CIA Executive Management team.

Although we had lived through the death of the DCI we had served and respected for so long and witnessed the resignation of the new DCI (Robert Gates), whom we all admired, we still remained hopeful a new day for the CIA had begun. We were sorely disappointed.

Tenet eventually made it to the position of DCI. He worked hard and was able to raise the extremely low morale existing in the Agency for a time. Unfortunately, he became the first DCI to repeatedly use the "States Secrets Privilege" to shut down suits against the Agency by employees and their families, denying them their basic Constitutional rights. Under his tenure, as intelligence became more arrogant, it also became more inaccurate. Never was this more evident than in the invasion of Iraq.

The Author on assignment overseas as a DCI protective agent. *(Photo courtesy of the Author)*

Following Gates' resignation, the new DCI, John Deutch, came to visit the CIA Counterintelligence Center (CIC) to congratulate us on our work on internal espionage investigations. He spoke in such a low voice we could barely hear what he was saying. He was usually somewhat disheveled in appearance. Deutch's Executive Officer Nora Slatkin became known among the Agency population as the "Dragon Lady." She built a reputation for displaying angry outbursts in public against Agency officers, which bore no reasonable explanation.

As I reported for duty one day, CIA headquarters was abuzz with reports a CIA Security Protective Officer, or SPO, had stopped Slatkin (not knowing who she was) for not wearing a CIA badge. As the SPO remained calm and asserted the CIA's policy for displaying a badge while inside CIA headquarters, Slatkin publicly berated the officer. This was part of a long litany of Slatkin's outbursts directed towards junior and senior CIA officers alike.

The Author with then DDCI Robert Gates during an appreciation ceremony for DCI protective agents. *(Photo courtesy of the Author)*

In December 1996, Deutch was confronted with allegations he removed his CIA laptop, which contained Top Secret information, from his CIA office, taken it to his home and used it to connect to unsecured sites on the internet. Investigation revealed the allegations were true. On April 14, 1999, following an investigation by the Department of Justice (DOJ) confirming the allegations, Attorney General Janet Reno sent a letter to DCI Tenet declining to prosecute Duetch for compromising national security information. This was just another example of the CIA, and sometimes the DOJ, severely punishing lower level CIA employees who made mistakes, while looking the other way when senior officers did the same; a fact well known among the agency populace. In many cases, senior officers were actually promoted after this kind of blunder.

Sarajevo Tragedy

Later in my career I was assigned as an officer to the CIA's Counterterrorism Center, the CTC. Slobodan Milosevic and the Serbian army had just unloaded their fury on the city of Sarajevo, Bosnia. I led the first team of our division into the ███████████ Sarajevo had become a model of the world's different religious and ethnic groups living together and actually getting along. Muslims, Christians, Jews and Secularists were living along side each other in apparent harmony. This was Sarajevo's exciting message to the world.

One day, the music stopped. Milosevic and the Serbian forces decided they had enough of Bosnia's freedom and ethnic underpinnings. Slowly and methodically the Serbian military surrounded the city. Centuries of hatred were unleashed on the people in shocking, murderous fury.

The residents of Sarajevo, especially the young educated population, simply could not believe the Serbs did not understand the message of acceptance they held. Led by a young Bosnian student, a crowd marched down the streets of Sarajevo and out into the open, in an attempt to convey to the Serbian Army they were not a threat and wanted peace. Upon orders, a Serbian sniper's shot rang out, and the young visionary fell to the ground, her life snuffed out - and the hopes of Sarajevo gone. In two horrifying hours, the Serbian army shelled several tons of artillery onto the unsuspecting population, killing scores of innocent men, women and children. Serbian forces moved into the city, going door to door and summarily executing families using AK 47s, as they pled for mercy. To finish the job, the Serbs mined the neighborhoods as they moved on to the next human targets, who were unaware of the impending danger as they slept. Houses and apartment complexes were so riddled with bullets and artillery fragments the holes touched each other. ██████████████████████ had several AK 47 bullet holes in the curtains. ████████████████████████. The Serbs dumped the bodies of the murdered Bosnians into huge mass graves. This was ethnic cleansing.

Slobodan Milosevic was the closest thing to a modern-day Hitler. We all thought the world was too "evolved" for a holocaust style mass murder to ever occur again; but it did. Driven by ego and political ambition, Milosevic decided to personally purge Bosnia from the Muslim population whose ancestors had done damage to the Serbs in years past. Milosevic had no conscience. He had no soul. We must be reminded that even in our "modern world" this can happen again. If we ignore that possibility, it will. One of the most fulfilling assignments in my Agency career was having a part in his eventual downfall and arrest.

A disheartening fact for many CIA officers, who personally witnessed the carnage wrought by Milosevic, was the time it took for the CIA to realize what was going on. As early as 1995 the world press was reporting mass killings by the Serbs. US reconnaissance satellites were sending back pictures of large groups of prisoners guarded by armed Serbian troops. The CIA overlooked the aerial photographs and the press reports for three deadly weeks. ██████████████████████ . The Agency simply did not have the resources. █████████████████████ .

This would be one of the largest mass killings of men, women and children since the death camps of Adolf Hitler. No one thought it could happen again. It was a gross underestimation.

While I was in Bosnia, I became friends with some of the Bosnian Muslim ████████████████. They were not the Muslims we typically think of in the West. There were pockets of radical Muslims there, but these people were largely progressive, modern folks who dressed like many other Europeans. Their form of Islam was peaceful.

I listened to one heart breaking story after another as they told how their children, mothers and fathers were killed by the Serbian onslaught. I became able to recognize those who had experienced this agony by looking in their eyes. There was a kind of sad, hopeless emptiness in their gaze.

One afternoon, leading me through a field of land mines, telling me to step exactly where they stepped, my friends showed me the tunnel the Bosnians had created when they were under siege. This tunnel was

Photograph showing the devastation and carnage of a modern Bosnian apartment complex. Following the massacre of men, women and children during the night, the Serbs mined the area as they moved to the next site of "ethnic cleansing." *(Photo courtesy of the Author)*

Tunnel used to smuggle members of the Bosnian government in and out of the city during the Serbian attack. The Author was led through a mine field to the site. *(Rare photo courtesy of the Author)*

dug by the Bosnian people and used to smuggle food, supplies and ammunition into the city. It was also used to move members of the Bosnian government in and out of the city. It was an astonishing act of survival.

My Bosnian friend, a former police officer (most of the Bosnian resistance was made up of police officers) related to me that the worst part of the war for him was to be up in the hills fighting, while his wife and children were hiding in their house, being shelled by the Serbian Army. They suffered in terror as tons of artillery was unleashed in a matter of just a few hours. I had dinner one evening with my friend and his wife, who was a beautiful and gracious woman. She had that look in her eyes. I learned to recognize it in the Bosnian people I met. It was a look of sadness, with a kind of "please help us" despair. Years later, I recognized this look in a pizza delivery man's eyes in Des Moines, Iowa, while I was on a protective detail there, and another time in a young man's eyes and facial expression at a shopping mall in Herndon, Virginia.

"You are Bosnian, aren't you?" I asked the young man in Herndon.

Surprised, he replied, "Yes, I am."

He had been there during the war. I welcomed him to America and bought him lunch. This happened again and again after my return to the States. I will never forget the pain and sadness I saw in their eyes.

During my tour in the Counterterrorism Center, I was assigned as a Counterterrorism Tactics, Protective Operations and Advanced Firearms Instructor. I traveled around the world training the protective details of foreign presidents and prime ministers. I was gone from home for the better part of two years. I met many fine protective agents in multiple countries and it was the most fulfilling assignment of my career. But, it took a toll on my marriage and family.

On one such protective operations training assignment, I led a team into Bosnia. During the training, a moving and memorable event occurred. Because of a shortage of translators, the host of the training assigned a young Bosnian police woman to translate for my team and me during the training. "Aida" had become a police woman to provide for her brothers and sisters because her mother and father had been gunned down by the Serbs.

During the protective operations course, the young woman accompanied me and the other instructors through each part of the training. Every now and then, I asked Aida if she would like to take part, act as a role player and try her hand at firearms. She excitedly joined in the training. I noticed she not only had an outstanding attitude, but a talent for this sort of work.

Several weeks went by, and we were informed the government had finally located a translator. They ordered Aida back to work on the street. Because of her attitude and talent, I asked the Bosnian government to let her stay on and continue as a student for the rest of the course. They agreed to do so. Aida was thrilled. Over the next several weeks of the course, she shined in each part of the training; eager to learn everything she was being taught.

When course graduation day came, Aida graduated at the top of the class. I wrote a recommendation for her to the Bosnian government. After graduation, I was invited to a final celebration dinner with local authorities. Aida and the other students, many of whom were also outstanding, were whisked away for their own student graduation ceremony.

As I was leaving the official dinner, one of the lead students ran up to me and jubilantly relayed that Aida had just been told she was awarded an assignment on the Prime Minister's protective detail. As she left the ceremony, she was in tears of joy; her life had changed; now there was a new hope. Aida had earned it.

I never got to see Aida again. But, I will always remember her story, her tenacity for learning, and the good ending to the tragedy she had been through.

A New World War

During my tours as a CIA officer, I traveled around the world, working with people from several different countries, including those in the Middle East. I learned most people, regardless of nationality, are all the same at heart. They respond to love and respect. Regrettably, there was an exception to the peaceful kind of Islam I saw in ██████████, the emerging form of radical Islam. Some of these people I came in contact with were, essentially, sociopaths—taught from birth to hate the West and live for Jihad; through murder.

In 1998, after the US embassy bombings in Africa, and upon seeing the intelligence coming in, I reached the conclusion we were entering into a new world war. This war is not like the one we predicted could eventually happen. It is a total global conflict, including within our own country. The extent of radical Islam's goal of establishing a global caliphate

(Islamic government) through death and destruction is chilling. It is the same evil force which drove Milosevic to commit mass murder—just a in a different form.

As a ████████████..████████████ Assistant Team Leader and Protective Operations Training Team leader, several of the missions I was sent on by the CIA were potentially one-way assignments. There was a real chance we could be killed in a fire-fight or, even worse if we were caught, be tortured to death and not return. Some officers, not willing to make the sacrifice, dropped out. The qualification process and psychological testing were tough. After completing one of these assignments our team received a Meritorious Unit Citation. We had stopped the terrorists from their murderous goal.

During long missions, I could not tell my wife where I was and could not provide her contact information. I was able only to contact her from discreet locations occasionally. This put a great deal of strain on my marriage, and at one point almost ended it. The life of the spouse of a CIA officer can be very difficult, and these wives receive very little or no recognition for their sacrifice. The divorce rate in the CIA is high. Officers are aware the mission must come first, above everything. Some eventually learn, when you leave the CIA, you simply become a file locked in a secure vault, with people lining up to take your place. Many of your awards for classified assignments are locked in a safe, where they remain permanently hidden. Your wife and children are all you really have left in the long run. You eventually realize this, or lose them and join the ranks of many CIA officers, who, after retirement, return to the CIA, divorced and with no life other than the organization. It is a sad existence.

Just prior to deployment on one of these missions, after qualifying on multiple advanced weapons systems, I went through the final battery of medical and psychological testing, all of which I passed. After the final psychological test, I was called into the CIA's Office of Medical Services, the OMS, for some kind of "interview." I could not deploy until I met with the OMS psychiatrist. Let me say here I met many fine CIA "shrinks" while I was there; I think this fellow was, perhaps, an anomaly.

I sat in the OMS interview room and the CIA psychiatrist entered with my file in his hand. He sat down, and informed me,

"Mr. Shipp, we have a problem with your psychological test."

"And where would that problem be?" I replied, somewhat miffed.

He opened my file, and I could see the test had been torn apart, re-taped and added to the file.

"We have a problem with your answer to question number (X)," he said.

"The question is: 'Sometimes, I tell a lie.' You answered no to the question." Respectfully, I responded that, although I do not expect others to adhere to my moral beliefs, and I am by no means perfect, I try my best not to lie. He, in a poor attempt to use body language and behavioral interview techniques, feigned an incredulous look and described a scenario of a retarded man asking me if I liked his ugly tie. He asked if I would tell him the truth, the tie was ugly, and hurt his feelings. I responded I would simply say, "Wow that is really something." He got even more frustrated.

Finally, I said, "Listen, I am under cover. My job title and organization are simply not true. However, my cover on these assignments is used to protect the lives of my team and people connected to our mission. That title, of course, is not my real job, but it is official, legal and not from some dark motive of my own. It is in the service of my country. I have no problem with that."

He seemed pleased with my answer, but said, "If you do not answer yes to this question, you will not go on the assignment."

He ended the interview.

I took the test again, reached the question and after several minutes of agonizing over it, answered "yes," the mission was too important. I passed the test, but I felt I had compromised my own personal ethics. I just put the incident behind me.

When I joined the CIA, the first thing which impressed me was the inscription engraved in the marble wall in the lobby of CIA headquarters: "You shall know the truth, and the truth shall make you free." John 8:32, the Bible. The verse was chosen and placed there by Allen Dulles, the son of a Presbyterian minister, as a noble and patriotic reminder of the mission of US intelligence. Over the years, I began to realize, this foundational belief had changed. The noble mission the CIA once had was perverted. Deception and lying had become a way of life, not just a part of tradecraft, even against some of our other government agencies and Congress itself. This was happening both in classified and unclassified venues at the Agency. Frankly, lying had become a badge of honor. The verse, as powerful as it is, was now being subverted as a normal way of doing business; many times not to protect national security, but to protect the Agency's wrongdoing, civil and constitutional violations. Essentially, the verse on the wall had been reinterpreted to convey "the ends justify the means."

A Cherished and Fulfilling Career

By my fifteenth year in the CIA I received a meritorious unit citation for a life threatening mission against a deadly terrorist organization, an exceptional performance award for uncovering a global vulnerability which threatened the lives of our agents abroad, a second meritorious unit citation for an international operation conducted with some of our closest allies, two more exceptional performance awards and two awards for my work as a liaison officer with foreign officials. I was in the top career performance category. The CIA was my career. I loved it and was dedicated to the mission I was assigned to, even to the point of giving my life.

Chapter 5

Hamstrung

Following the fall of the Soviet Union, the CIA began to implode. The Soviet bear was gone. The Agency, a huge organizational monolith created to defend against Russia's global presence, no longer had its arch enemy or the mission it was embroiled in for so many years. Entire divisions within the Agency were eliminated, jobs were cut and careers were in danger. In the words of a former CIA Deputy Director I spoke with during these events, [as career CIA officers] "You are in deep #$@!" Agents were resigning in droves and going into private industry.

Under the Clinton administration, the CIA began to turn on itself. Career infighting became rampant within the organization. Agents took assignments in the field just to get away from the underhanded practices occurring at headquarters. Promotions were slowed down and a freeze was put on "Exceptional Performance Awards." In the midst of this, the new seventh-floor management directed a huge demographical shift among the employee population. The Agency became divided into competing, opposing and sometimes hostile racial and cultural employee groups. Instead of the once family-like unity, which existed because of the belief we were all Americans fighting a real enemy; the organization was split along racial and ethnic lines. Robert Baer described this period in his book *See No Evil*, commenting that the Agency would spend more money on changing the population's demographics and funding sexual harassment training than on important operations, such as those countering terrorism. Baer was right. I was a manager at Langley at the time and, to my chagrin, saw this new trend in CIA administrative restructuring occur.

Instead of the good and healthy brand of Equal Employment Opportunity and acceptance of diversity, which are America's past and future keys to greatness, a false version of diversity arose, which split the organization into fragments. CIA positions which once required passing the equivalent of the Graduate Records Exam with a 3.0 or better grade point average, were now adjusted and those requirements eliminated to comply with the new demographic mandate. The organization was being dumbed-down. Instead of promotions though employee equality and meritocracy, heavier weight was placed on racial and ethnic demography than on experience and performance.

As a manager, I witnessed several employees who had earned promotions; lose those promotions simply because they did not fit the proper demographical group. We were losing our competitiveness, talent and street smarts. Senior managers with years of real world experience resigned in large numbers. They were replaced by younger, less experience officers. Morale, once again, was at an all-time low.

During the same period, under the Clinton administration, an action was taken which virtually hamstrung the CIA's ability to collect intelligence, especially against terrorist targets. Senator Robert Torricelli (D-NY), by trumpeting a number of unsubstantiated conclusions regarding the CIA's role in the deaths of an American hotel owner, Michael DeVine, and a Guatemalan guerilla named Efrain Bamaca Velazquez (during which Torricelli allegedly leaked classified information), coerced the Clinton administration into issuing an order dictating no CIA officer could have any contact, for recruitment or other purposes, with a foreign national who had any human rights violations, including potential high value terrorist cell targets. Agency officers would be reprimanded and possibly terminated if they did so - and some were.

I was in the CIA's auditorium, referred to as "The Bubble," when DCI John Deutch gave his speech, conveying this order from the President. I have never seen anything like the events of that day. Seasoned station chiefs and case officers laughed and booed during Deutch's attempt to convey the President's directive and the incredible incompetency of its context. Several stood up, publicly decrying the decision and protesting they could no longer do their job. Really, the directive is akin to telling a drug enforcement agent he or she can have nothing to do with an informant who uses cocaine or has broken US drug laws.

As a Counter Terrorism Center (CTC) officer, I experienced the stinging reality of this personally. Out in the field, I identified a Middle Eastern individual who was clearly connected to terrorism, and occupied a high level position. I sent an intelligence report back to headquarters documenting the information I had elicited over several meetings. Summarily, I was verbally reprimanded and told, "What would the President of the United States think if he knew you had associated with a terrorist with human rights violations!"

I strongly reminded this headquarters official it was because of my report this man was identified, when, based on headquarters' intelligence blunder, the man had gotten close to US embassy personnel without their knowledge. In addition, based on his skills, he could have killed me at any moment, but, instead, seemed open to more discussion and a continued relationship. There was a possibility we could have turned him. Now we will never know.

Without my report, the Agency would not have known this individual had gotten close to embassy staff. After I reminded them of their oversight, they left me alone, but proceeded to reprimand the case officer working with me on the operation. He was, without question, an outstanding officer with a flawless reputation and one of the best operators I worked with. He was putting his life on the line daily for his country. But he was in the wrong place at the wrong time. Politics trumps patriotism.

Because of the Clinton/Torricelli order, chiefs of stations began to hide in their offices and generate shallow intelligence on terrorist targets, with no actual penetrations or access. They could not take the career or legal risk of getting close to a possible terrorist cell asset who had human rights violations. Because of this, the CIA was seriously under-informed regarding the coming Jihad which would take place on American soil and in the countries of our allies. When the 9/11 attacks occurred, the CIA was deaf, dumb and blind. Intelligence gathering on the terrorism target had degraded to analysts sitting at their terminals in headquarters, surfing the internet for information and writing reports from largely open source information. We had reached the point that, many times, the news network CNN had overseas intelligence information before we did. Ironically, as a young officer, during my first operational training class, we were taught the news media was the enemy of the CIA, continually trying to steal our information. We were shown an interview with journalist Brit Hume (in 1972 Hume, his wife and children had been placed under surveillance by the CIA under the Nixon administration while working for journalist Jack Anderson, who published classified documents to expose administration wrong doing and misrepresentations to the public). The interviewer asked Hume if he would publish information he obtained even if it involved US intelligence. Hume responded, essentially, as a journalist he was obligated to do so. The instructor of the course was aghast and attempted to portray the press as essentially against our mission. Ironically, it turned out the CIA eventually came to rely somewhat on journalists (e.g., CNN) for immediate information on overseas crises and Hume is now respected, both within and without the government, as one of the finest and most objective journalists in the country.

In reality, the American news media is one of the most important protectors of US national security, as long as they are not afraid to occupy this role. This includes protecting the security of journalists exposing the government when it gets out of control. Personally, I found the July 7, 2005 arrest of Pulitzer Prize winning journalist Judith Miller, during the Valerie Plame case, threats of possible arrest and subpoenas issued to other credible journalists, chilling. What concerns me most is many journalists are now afraid to expose CIA and other government corruption, using information given to them by credible sources, and are reluctant to challenge an organization that has spent years developing a system to quietly silence citizens and the press with threats of, and actual criminal prosecution. Some journalists cooperate with the CIA and withhold information from the public so they don't lose their CIA contacts, who know this and selectively feed them information. If we have reached this point in our country, our democracy has been subverted.

During this time, the CIA placed an over-reliance on information provided by defectors, simply because it had no penetration agents in place. Iraq was a perfect example. Large sums of (taxpayer) money were paid to Iraqi officers, in some cases ███████████ each, who, it was later determined, provided false or inflated information to the CIA, just to get the cash or obtain revenge against Saddam Hussein. My experience in this arena showed me any defector doing it primarily for money is automatically suspect. Defectors who turned themselves over to the US for ideological reasons, or to flee from religious persecution, were generally the most reliable, because their motives came from conviction rather than greed.

A 'Mole' and Disaster

In 1994, after the CIA had just gone through a far-reaching and painful reorganization, the unthinkable—and what the organization feared most—happened; a "mole" was discovered inside the CIA. Aldrich Ames, a career CIA supervisor and case officer, assigned to work against the Soviet target, was arrested for espionage.

For years, Ames had been secretly selling damaging secrets to the Soviet KGB. The destruction to US intelligence was immense. The Congress was irate. A security commission was formed and the order was given for the FBI to take over management of the CIA's Counterintelligence Center (CIC) and co-locate with Agency counterintelligence officers at Langley.

I was one of those officers. Our job was to ferret out other "moles," or vulnerable employees who could be the subject of foreign intelligence attempts at recruitment. A huge push was on to investigate all employees who gave any appearance of unauthorized activity in the area of security and counterintelligence. Although this was of critical importance, a paradigm shift occurred in the CIA. The Agency began to eat its own.

As counterintelligence investigations were opened on employees, hundreds of careers and, in some cases, lives were ruined. Agency employees, many of whom had made low-level mistakes—for example, had affairs with foreign nationals—and were innocent of espionage and treason, had to endure the torment of investigations lasting a year or more.

I worked closely with FBI agents assigned to the CIC, found them to be very professional and we had a good working relationship. At the FBI supervisory level, however, the FBI was accusing the CIA of being unable to run a counterintelligence operation and continually boasted the FBI had never had a major intelligence penetration. Tragically, a short time later the Robert Hanssen espionage case occurred. It was the quintessential "egg in the face" for the Bureau. The damage Hanssen, who had access to FBI and CIA counterintelligence files, caused was massive. His actions made "Rick" Ames look like a school boy. The FBI learned the same lesson the Agency had just suffered. As soon as you become self-absorbed and arrogant, you are heading for trouble. It's a kind of blindness, and one to be shunned, in the Intelligence Community because of the level of vulnerability it can create in the security of our country.

The FBI and the CIA conducted extensive studies, trying to determine what would make someone spy. Those of us who were counterintelligence officers went through briefing after briefing, training class after training class. First, the theory was committing treason was tied to alcohol abuse, serious financial debt, family problems, or dangerous ideological views. None of these theories, either individually or collectively, could wholly explain why people commit espionage and treason against their country. There was a plethora of CIA and other Intelligence Community employees who had some or all of these problems, but remained loyal to their Agency and to their country, despite significant life stresses.

After working the cases I was assigned, going to briefing after briefing covering every case which had occurred and studying all the reports we were given on US internal espionage—including, of course, Aldrich Ames, Harold Nicholson and Robert Hanssen—I reached a different conclusion. The majority of these people were narcissists. It had very little to do with their life stress. Primarily, it was not about the money, or their drinking and gambling habits. It was about their over-inflated view of themselves, belief they were smarter than most of their counterparts and the drive for ego gratification. In the majority of espionage cases I reviewed, the act began with an overinflated ego, disdain for the organization's purpose and the circumvention of internal rules and regulations.

In the CIA, the polygraph test was one of the primary tools used during the post-Ames counterintelligence explosion. Officers who failed their polygraph test on counterintelligence issues were turned over to the FBI for investigation; based on this event alone. The CIA Office of Security did attempt to make an effort to balance the emphasis on information derived from the polygraph, but to no avail. The Agency just could not ignore employees who failed the polygraph on counterintelligence questions.

The careers, and mental health, of multiple employees were damaged. Although I performed well at the job, I was disgusted to see some of my fellow counterintelligence investigators more interested in busting the next Subject, so they could become famous or gain recognition to support their next promotion, than having a concern for finding the real truth and justice for the people whose lives they were tearing apart (Chapters 12 and 24 discuss the polygraph and CIA Counterintelligence in greater detail).

Because of the CIA's reputation and the fashion in which it has treated its employees, contractors, applicants and counterparts in foreign countries, it has developed a significant level of domestic and international mistrust. This has only served to hurt its mission.

Chapter 6

Providence

After his brain surgery, performed at Georgetown University Hospital on December 18, 1986, CIA Director William Casey appeared shockingly ill. He was due to appear before the House Permanent Select Committee on Intelligence (HPSCI) on December 16, but was rushed to the hospital after a seizure the day before. Casey had lost a significant amount of weight and the prognosis was grim. I was one of the agents assigned to the "hot seat" at the entrance to his hospital room. Late one evening, the nurse requested I and another agent help move him in his bed. As we did, I held his feet and prayed for him.

Over the next month, William Casey began to take a turn for the better. He regained his weight, his hair grew back and he became mentally alert. However, because of the damage done by the tumor in his brain, he could not speak.

Bob Woodward's Alleged Visit with the Director of the CIA

In the book *Veil the Secret Wars of the CIA* (page 587, paragraph 7), Bob Woodward writes he was able to enter Casey's hospital room and have an important conversation with him (late January – early February 1987, although he does not give an exact date). I consider Mr. Woodward a fine journalist and a very nice person. However, I must disagree with this account. Indeed, Mr. Woodward did try to enter the hospital room, but was interdicted by the agent in the hot seat and gracefully shown to the exit. In addition, during the time frame Mr. Woodward claims to have gotten into the room, Casey could not speak due to the effects of the tumor on his brain (I witnessed this personally). None of the agents allowed Mr. Woodward into the room. We were there twenty-four hours a day, seven days a week. All of us were under orders not to let anyone into the room. Frankly, we all were frustrated by this fabricated account when it was published, because it never happened. One reporter has alleged Woodward told him he had help from someone else to get into the room (perhaps dressed as a doctor - or nurse (kidding about the nurse)). Even if this were true, the account still lacks credibility; Casey was unable to talk, and could only make grunting noises because the tumor had attacked the language part of his brain. We were with him daily, took him for his medical tests, etc., saw the damage to his brain and heard his attempts at speaking.

The lack of detail in Woodward's account just reinforces this incident never happened. Regarding Robert Gates' later statement that Casey could still form words during his discussion - the time frame of Woodard's "visit" occurs after Gates' visits with Casey and the blocking of Woodward's first attempt to enter the room by the agents. By then, Casey's condition had deteriorated even worse and he eventually lapsed into a coma.

Just after publication of his book Veil. The Secret Wars of the CIA, Gates paid a visit to Woodward's residence to get a copy of the book the CIA did not have. Woodward claims during the visit Gates stated "I guess your security is better than ours," commenting on Woodward's alleged penetration of Casey's hospital room. Gates was always a humble, humorous and congenial man, and fiercely loyal to the CIA. I am certain this was simply a graceful attempt to get a copy of the book and perform an intensive personal analysis. At his career core, Gate's was an analyst. The agents were with Casey day and night, twenty-four hours a day, seven days a week; many times more than Gates' occasional visits with the Director. Gates was busy running the CIA and holding back the firestorm of legislative and press demands.

On September 29, 2010 Woodward was interviewed on Larry King Live to discuss his new book, *Obama Wars*. My previous book *In From the Cold. CIA Secrecy and Operations*, which brought to light the above information, had been published, and was the subject of a Washington Post article. Woodward was forced to respond to the article and stated he could not remember details of the incident. In discussions with the Post reporter, I was called a "peon," far below any need for Woodward to take the time to respond to my assertions.

However, during the King interview, Woodward completely digressed from the subject of the interview (his book *Obama Wars*) and made the statement:

"And there's a fascinating story about Gates' view of the world and sense of humor. In 1987 when I was coming out with the book "Veil" about the secret wars of the CIA during the Reagan era, it was about to come out and the CIA couldn't get a copy.

And Gates called me up. And he said, can we get a copy? We won't leak it to The New York Times. And I said, fine, send somebody by to get it, come by my house. And he said, I'll come myself. And so he came. Walked up on the doorstep. I gave him two or three copies. And he looked at me. And he said, sometime we have to have a talk about security. Because obviously yours is better than ours."

If the account I wrote did not bother him, why did Woodward feel the need to depart from the subject of the interview and justify his old allegations? I'll let you be the judge.

The Agency conducted an extensive investigation of the incident, interviewing all the agents involved, and reached the conclusion it simply could not have occurred.

It was clear, however, before his illness Casey met with Woodward on several occasions. Casey, who usually had nothing but chagrin for the news media, liked Woodward and granted him several interviews during his tenure as DCI. I'm convinced that it was during those interviews that much of the information in Woodward's book, which in my view is accurate, was provided to Woodward by Casey himself, on purpose.

The William Casey I knew, and spent more time with than my own family, was an unstoppable patriot with an unbendable love for democracy, America and the CIA. I am convinced Casey knew he was dying and intentionally gave Woodward information he wanted the American public to know before he died. The CIA, of course, energized by its obsession to guard its own power, was outraged by this and hunted for those responsible for providing the information in Woodward's book. My observations convinced me it came from the CIA Director himself.

On a sunny afternoon, as I took my shift in the "hot seat" outside the DCI's hospital room, the nurse entered the room and asked Casey if he needed anything. I could hear him trying to put his thoughts into words, which he was unable to do. I heard him making undistinguishable groaning sounds as he tried to express to the nurse what he wanted. She could tell he wanted her to bring someone into his room.

"Sir, do you want me to bring your wife into the room?"

He spoke unintelligibly and motioned to the nurse "No."

"Would you like me to bring your daughter to your room?"

He loudly made attempts at forming words and again motioned "No."

"Do you want your son-in-law, Owen?" He again motioned "No."

"Do you want an agent to come into your room?" He loudly made attempts to speak and gestured, "Yes."

The nurse came out to me and said, "I think he wants you to come into his room."

I walked into the hospital room and Casey sat straight up in the bed and stuck his hand out to shake mine.

I grasped his hand and said, "Hello, Sir, how are you doing?"

Casey looked me directly in the eye and squeezed my hand as hard as he could. He could not speak.

It appeared to me he was saying, "See, I am getting strong, I am coming back."

He motioned for me to sit down in the chair next to his bed.

I sat in the chair and he motioned to me with his hands, giving a facial expression conveying, "Tell me what is going on out there."

"Sir," I replied, "I saw the President interviewed on the news yesterday and they asked him if, in the light of Iran Contra, you still have his support. The President responded he is pleased with the job you are doing and you have his full support. Also, last night I saw Jean Kirkpatrick (a close personal friend of Casey's) on the news as well and they asked her the same question. She responded she considered you a great Director and one of her closest personal friends."

Casey broke down and began to weep, tears streaming down his face. Before I could say anything more, the nurse came into the room. It was time for another CAT scan. These were always solemn moments. The results were not good.

After this meeting, a fascinating event occurred. Chuck Colson, former White House Counsel and Watergate figure, now an evangelist and head of Prison Fellowship Ministries, was checked into the same hospital and had undergone major surgery for stomach cancer. As a nurse attended to Colson, she mentioned William Casey was in the same hospital and terminally ill. She asked Colson if he would like her to find out if Casey wanted prayer. Colson told the nurse he would. This nurse conveyed Colson's message to Casey, asking if he would like Colson to pray with him. Casey responded he did. Shortly thereafter, Colson visited Casey in his hospital room and the two prayed together. At the end of his life, William Casey became a Christian. It was an inspiring event. I am sure it was the subject of Sophia Casey's prayers as she sat alone in the sunlit sitting room in their home. Those of you who are secularists will have to bear with me during this account. I hope I am not offending anyone. I have to accurately describe these events exactly as they happened.

After Colson's visit, Bill Casey became a changed man. Formerly a gruff man who did not suffer fools lightly and regularly reprimanded the agents, or anyone else for that matter, for even small mistakes, he became a kind, gentle man. During his last days in the hospital, although he could not speak, he went out of this way to attempt to communicate to the agents and nurses how much he appreciated them and what they were doing. Some of the agents were shocked at the change. An agent, and close friend of mine, who accompanied him as he was transported back to his home in New York relayed to me Casey spent his last days requesting by gestures his nurse come into his room and read the Gospels to him as he lay in bed. On May 6, 1987 William Joseph Casey passed away in peace, leaving the legacy of a true American patriot.

William J. Casey,
Director of the CIA

Reporter Bob Woodward

Senator Robert Torricelli (D-NJ)

DCI George Tenet

Chapter 7

Defectors

The Central Intelligence Agency Act (CIA Act of 1949, Publication L. 81-110), or Public Law 110, gave the CIA the authority to keep its budget, fiscal operations and administrative procedures confidential and exempt from public disclosure. The act is codified in 50 USC., 403a. This exempted the CIA from legal limitations on the use of federal funds. Section 6 of the 1949 act exempted the Agency from revealing its "organization, functions, officials, titles, salaries, or numbers of personnel deployed." Section 6 was created to protect the CIA from hostile foreign intelligence services, which could exploit this information to determine CIA structural and operational planning.

The CIA Act of 1949 created the program titled "PL-110." PL-110 gave the Agency the responsibility of handling defectors and "essential aliens" using classified techniques outside federal immigration procedures. The program also provided these persons with official cover stories, similar to a witness protection program, as well as financial support, housing and US citizenship.

Defector Protection

CIA regulation assigns the task of protecting defectors to the Office of Security. Trained security officers are responsible for protecting defectors from assassination, or any other threat to their personal safety, while they are being debriefed by their Agency handlers. In the past, defectors were assigned only security officers for their protection. ██████████████████ ████████ ████████ ██████████████████████████

██I was assigned as the team leader for security officers assigned to protect defectors just after the re-defection of Vitaly Yurchenko.

Public Law 110 does not give the CIA authority to keep these aliens, or defectors, as prisoners in the US. They are free to leave if they elect to do so. This provision is important because, without it, not many foreigners would defect to the US.

KGB Defector Yuri Nosenko

The CIA has misused the privilege of the P.L. 110 in the past, most notably in the case of KGB agent Yuri Nosenko. It has since learned from this mistake, but is still adjusting to the nuances of this risky type of operation. Nosenko was one of the most controversial defectors of Cold War espionage. A debate still rages over whether Yuri was a credible high-value KGB defector, or a plant sent by the KGB to counter the information provided by an earlier Soviet defector, who had implied Moscow was involved in the assassination of President John F. Kennedy.

The CIA was deeply divided over Nosenko's bona fides. This dispute was never fully resolved, even leading up to Nosenko's death. Nosenko was a KGB officer assigned to the American desk, an operative in the KGB Seventh Department and was assigned to recruit Western tourists to spy for the Soviet Union. In 1959 former US Marine Lee Harvey Oswald approached the KGB, offering to betray his country. Nosenko was one of Oswald's case officers. Oswald lived in the Soviet Union for three years. When Nosenko contacted the CIA in 1962 to defect to the US, his connections with Oswald purported to cause a significant rift in Soviet-American relations. During his debriefings by the CIA, Nosenko told his handlers Oswald was not a Soviet agent. According to Nosenko, Oswald was considered too unstable to be recruited. He also claimed Moscow was in an uproar, concerned it would be held responsible for Kennedy's assassination and drawn into military conflict.

Nosenko's first CIA handlers were immediately suspicious of his claims. He had requested a mere two hundred dollars for betraying his country, to settle his drinking debt. Other parts of his story just did not add up.

KGB Defector Anatoly Golitsyn

Nosenko's story was further weakened by KGB defector Anatoly Golitsyn. Golitsyn had defected three years earlier. Golitsyn was the real thing. A KGB Major, he had revealed the identities of several high-level spies who had penetrated NATO. Golitsyn provided information indicating Moscow was implementing a vast operation to gain global dominance. He also provided information indicating Western intelligence services were infested with "moles" at high levels and Soviet defectors were now KGB double agents.

CIA Counterintelligence Chief, James Jesus Angleton considered Golitsyn the most important defector the West had ever entertained. Angleton's sensitivities to Soviet penetrations were heightened by the defection of his close friend Kim Philby. Harold Adrian Russel "Kim" Philby was a counterpart of Angleton and a high ranking member of British Intelligence. In 1963, in one of the most damaging espionage cases in British history, Philby was exposed as a member of the "Cambridge Five" spy ring, which included four other British officials. Philby had been providing Moscow with secret British intelligence and eventually defected to the Soviet Union. Philby was a KGB operative.

Angleton was faced with a dilemma; trust Golitsyn and Nosenko was a plant. Trust Nosenko and Golitsyn could be a plant. Angleton chose to believe Golitsyn. Golitsyn convinced Angleton Nosenko was sent to discredit his information and claim his story about the Kennedy assassination was a fabrication.

Nosenko's CIA debriefings turned into hostile interrogations. He was imprisoned by the CIA for three years in solitary confinement in a small cell, with disgusting food to eat and continual humiliation bordering on torture.

Nosenko never broke, and did not change his story. He passed several polygraph tests. Defectors who followed Nosenko confirmed his story that Moscow had nothing to do with the Kennedy assassination. He was eventually released, given a new identity, provided a life-long salary and resettled in the US. He never lost his dedication to America and did not regret his defection. Nosenko died in 2008.

Angleton was forced to resign from the CIA in 1975. He was never able to successfully identify a Soviet mole. Nosenko's credibility remained and Golitsyn, also resettled in the US, became a forgotten artifact of the Cold War.

In his memoir, Nosenko's original CIA handler, Tennent H. "Pete" Bagley, continued to maintain Nosenko was a KGB plant.

A Classic KGB Defector

Stanislav Alexandrovich Levchenko, a Russian KGB Major, defected to the US in 1979. Levchenko was one of the most important Soviet defectors in the CIA's history. In 1964 Levchenko graduated from the Moscow State University Institute of Asia and Africa with a degree in Japanese language, literature and history. He did his post graduate studies at the Institute of Oriental Studies of the USSR Academy of Sciences, where he majored in modern history of Japan. Levchenko joined the KGB in 1968 and was eventually promoted to KGB staff operations officer in the Foreign Intelligence Service. In 1975, the KGB assigned Levchenko to Japan using the cover of bureau chief of the Russian magazine Novoye Vrema (New Times) in Tokyo, Japan. Based out of Tokyo, Levchenko collected political intelligence and conducted far reaching Russian covert operations in Japan and the Far East. He was promoted to the rank of Major in the KGB in 1979, where he became the chief of the KGB Covert Action Group in Tokyo. In October of 1979, he approached US officials and requested political asylum.

A Soviet court condemned Levchenko to death in 1981 and Soviet KGB officers tried to hunt him down in the US to assassinate him. The assassination plot was foiled when KGB access agents Svetlana and Nicolai Orgorodnikov were discovered and arrested during the espionage investigation of FBI Agent turned traitor Richard Miller.

Levchenko exposed the entire Soviet spy network in Japan and the Far East. He provided the names of two hundred Japanese agents working for the KGB. This included the former Labor Minister for the Liberal Democratic Party and the leader of the Japanese Socialist Party.

Stanislav Levchenko was a classic defector; a high ranking Soviet intelligence officer who defected to the US for ideological reasons rather than greed or revenge. Levchenko defected to America because of his disdain for the atheistic Soviet system and his fundamental, secretly held, belief in democracy, freedom of speech and freedom of religion. While in the Soviet Union, he had secretly converted to Christianity. Stanislav, or "Stan" as his friends call him, was, and is, an intellectual; a man of insight and a gentleman. He exposed in great detail the inner workings of the Russian KGB. He will go down in history as one of the most valuable, successful and distinguished defectors the CIA has hosted in its sixty-one year history.

A Defection Gone Wrong

This brings us to the dramatic story of a KGB defection gone terribly wrong. As in the Nosenko and Golitsyn cases, it provides another painful example of the complexity and risk involved in handling defectors. During my days at the CIA, I was assigned as a counterintelligence investigator, collocated with the FBI and tasked with hunting for moles in the CIA. After handling multiple internal espionage cases, I reached a conclusion about counterintelligence and espionage cases, including handling defectors. I summed it up in a sign I posted at my desk: "The only thing predictable about counterintelligence cases is that they are unpredictable." This could not be more true than in the case of handling defectors.

Vitaly Yurchenko

Vitaly Yurchenko was a high ranking KGB officer. In 1972 he was appointed as the Deputy Chief of the KGB's Third Department, Third Chief Directorate. He was tasked with running foreign agents spying for the Soviet Union. Yurchenko was assigned to Washington, DC in 1975, in charge of Soviet embassy security in the prestigious Soviet embassy located on Mount Alto, Washington, DC. The new Soviet Embassy on Mount Alto amounted to a classic example of bad judgment on the part of the US Department of State. The Soviets could not have chosen a better location themselves. In 1973 the US government gave approval for the Soviet Union to build the new embassy building on Mount Alto, at an altitude of three hundred and fifty feet, the third highest point in Washington, DC. The embassy had direct visual line of sight to the US Capitol, the White House, the Pentagon and the State Department. From this location, the Soviets would be capable of electronic surveillance of all communications dealing with national security unless they were encrypted. It also allowed the Russians to intercept business and personal conversations and the "chatter" of US government employees. Thus, the Soviets conducted highly sophisticated electronic surveillance from this prime location. From this platform, the Soviets conducted espionage activities which included the stealth of US technology secrets. No doubt, Yurchenko was part of this program. He returned to Moscow in 1980 and became the KGB section chief in charge of ferreting moles out of Soviet intelligence. Yurchenko was then assigned as deputy chief of KGB intelligence operations in the US and Canada. This high-level position potentially gave him access to the identities of all Soviet agents in North America.

In 1985, after twenty-five successful years in the KGB, Yurchenko was driven by his guards to Villa Abamelek, a Soviet embassy outside of Rome. On the morning of July 28, he told his companions he wanted to visit the Vatican museums alone. He departed for the museums and never returned. On August first, he walked into the US Embassy in Rome and defected to the CIA. The US State Department issued a statement explaining Yurchenko approached US officials and requested political asylum. He was transported by the CIA to a classified location in the Suburbs of Virginia. He was debriefed by CIA officers over the next three months. He passed his CIA polygraph examinations.

During covert meetings with the CIA he was debriefed by Aldrich Ames, who had begun spying for the Soviet Union just a few months before. It is apparent Yurchenko did not know Ames was a Soviet mole, but may have reached this conclusion during his debriefings with Ames. This could have been part of the impetus for his re-defection back to Russia. During debriefings, Yurchenko fingered Edward Lee Howard, a CIA trainee who was fired in 1983 and turned over information to the KGB and Ronald Pelton, an NSA employee who sold information to the KGB. Pelton was convicted and sentenced, but Howard eluded his FBI surveillance team and defected to the Soviet Union before he could be questioned. Although Yurchenko probably knew the identities of scores of Soviet agents in North America, he did not provide this information to the CIA. It has been theorized that he chose to reveal the information he knew selectively for his own benefit, or he was indeed a KGB double agent.

CIA Director William Casey personally acted as Yurchenko's Chief debriefer. During debriefings, Yurchenko also provided information about the "Spy Dust" the Soviet Secret Police employed against Americans in Moscow to track their movements. He also revealed that Soviet Defector Nicholas Shadrin, who had disappeared without a trace in Vienna in 1957, had been kidnapped and assassinated by KGB agents.

Yurchenko revealed he was having a romantic affair with the wife of a Soviet diplomat assigned to Canada, whom he had met during his tour in Washington, DC. The CIA arranged for him to meet the woman in Ottawa. He was rejected by the woman, possibly because she spurned him as a defector. After he was rejected by what he thought was his true love, Yurchenko became dark, depressed and suffered from insomnia. He was a hypochondriac, afraid to drink water that was not boiled and was disgruntled by the fact that the information he disclosed to the CIA about Edward Howard and Nicholas Shadrin had been made public. There were also indications his CIA handlers did not take his mental state seriously and he was roughly treated during interviews.

On a Saturday night in November 1985 Yurchenko was accompanied by his CIA security officer to the Georgetown bistro Au Pied de Cochon. As the security officer was paying the check, Yurchenko surprised him with the question,

"What would you do if I got up and walked out? Would you shoot me?"

"No, we don't treat defectors that way."

"I'll be back in fifteen or twenty minutes….if I'm not, it will not be your fault."

It was not the security officer's fault. He was placed in the position of protecting Yurchenko from assassination by the KGB, but he had no authority to protect Yurchenko from himself. Yurchenko was free to go of his own volition, a fact unknown by most of the public. The security officer was placed in a catch 22 situation. In essence, he was given no training or tools to handle this kind of event. He was also not a trained psychiatrist. Yurchenko was in a morose state of mind, deeply depressed and in a state of self destruction. The CIA should have recognized this, provided him with the appropriate treatment, not left him alone on weekends, and had a trained officer with Yurchenko and the security officer at all times. ███████████████████████████ ████████████████ ████████████████████████In the case of Yurchenko, this change came too late.

Yurchenko was not heard from until the following Monday at four o'clock p.m. Soviet Embassy Press Counselor Boris Malakhov called the State Department correspondent of the *Associated Press* and advised the Embassy would hold a press conference in ninety minutes.

"We'll have Vitaly Yurchenko." He said.

Ninety minutes later, fifty journalists were gathered at the Soviet compound on Mount Alto. Vitaly Yurchenko appeared with a statement for the press. Yurchenko claimed he had never defected. He related the tale of being "forcibly abducted" in Rome, drugged by the CIA and flown to the US. He revealed he had been held at a safe house in Fredericksburg, Virginia. He claimed on November second, his CIA "torturers" let down their guard and he was able to escape. He denied providing any KGB secrets to the CIA. He claimed he did not know what he had said while he was drugged.

"Please ask CIA officials what kind of secret information I gave them," he said.

"It would be very interesting for me to know too, because I don't know."

"I am not going to make any comments about spying business," he responded to questions about his connections to the KGB. His answers were contradictory and suspicious. It was apparent to most he was lying. The question was; why?

The State Department demanded to interview Yurchenko to make sure his departure was voluntary. He was interviewed by senior State Department officials and a government psychiatrist. The conclusion was reached his decision to go back to the Soviet Union was voluntary.

Yurchenko boarded an Aeroflot plane and was flown back to the Soviet Union. Soviet officials reported he was awarded the Russian Order of the Red Star upon his return. Skeptical CIA officials predicted after Moscow's public display, Yurchenko would be executed.

Most intelligence officers, including this humble author, are convinced Yurchenko was a legitimate defector, who was holding back information to ensure his security. Documented reports of his deep depression and physical symptoms were indicative of a man in severe emotional and mental dissonance. These symptoms appeared to be very real. The intelligence he did turn over was legitimate. It is unlikely the KGB would jeopardize one of its highest ranking officers, possessing his knowledge of Soviet operations in North America, for such a risky operation. Although the truth will never be fully known, it appears Yurchenko was simply love sick, clinically depressed and homesick.

Iranian nuclear scientist Shahram Amiri

During a pilgrimage to Mecca, Saudi Arabia from May to June 2009, Iranian Nuclear Scientist Shahram Amiri disappeared. Iran accused the US of kidnapping Amiri. *ABC News* reported Amiri "wanted to seek asylum abroad." The US government confirmed he had traveled to reside in the United States with the assistance of the CIA.

Iranian reports said Amiri was an employee of Iran's Atomic Energy Organization. The Iranian government would not confirm he was a nuclear scientist. Amiri's disappearance came three months before the news media revelation that Iran had a second uranium enrichment facility near the city of Qom. He was suspected of giving the West information on Iran's nuclear program.

The New York Times reported Washington "sources" confirmed Amiri was a US spy working in Iran for years. He traveled to Saudi Arabia and was transported out of the country by the CIA. According to the *Associated Press*, Amiri was paid the sum of five million dollars for providing significant information to the CIA.

On July 13, 2010, Amiri unexpectedly arrived at the Iranian Interests Section of the Pakistani Embassy in Washington, DC and requested to be returned to Iran. US officials commented on the likelihood the Iranian government was threatening to hurt his family in Iran if he did not return. A source told *The Wall Street Journal* the Iranian government had threatened Amiri's family and threatened to kill his son.

Amiri returned to Iran on July 15, 2010. At an Iranian press conference, he claimed he had been psychologically mistreated by "the US intelligence Agency" after his kidnapping. He stated he had been kidnapped by armed men in Medina, drugged and interrogated by the CIA and Israel. "Americans wanted me to say that I defected to America of my own will, to use me for revealing some false information about Iran's nuclear work," he said upon his arrival back in Tehran. "I have some documents proving that I've not been free in the United States and have always been under the control of armed agents of US intelligence services." Iran claimed he was an Iranian intelligence officer secretly working against the US

It was clear Amiri had defected to the US and had been cooperating with the CIA. His decision to return to Tehran, probably in an effort to save his family, placed him at great personal risk of retribution. US officials confirmed the CIA paid him over five million dollars in exchange for information on Iran's nuclear program. *The Washington Post* reported CIA officials were "stunned" by his request to return to Tehran and he had been working with the CIA for a year.

Following Tehran's public display of Amiri's triumphant return to his homeland, his fate is uncertain. It is the opinion of this author that, when the propaganda is over, the interrogation will begin. Under Iran's Ja'fari school of Sharia law, Amiri's punishment for defection could be a violent but secret death by stoning.

Over Reliance on Defector Information

Historically, defectors have been one of the most important sources of human intelligence (HUMINT) collected by the CIA. HUMINT was the cornerstone of CIA intelligence collection until the mid 1970s. Its importance and use were significantly hampered beginning in the late 1970s and culminating in 1996. This reduction in the CIA's HUMINT operations left the CIA, and the US, vulnerable; especially to domestic terrorist attacks. The CIA's intelligence senses had been blinded and deafened. This led the CIA to place an over reliance on information provided by defectors. The reduction of capability in one area, HUMINT from recruited agents, led to an over reliance in another; defectors. Two significant events led the CIA to this over reliance on defector provided information.

In 1979, CIA Director Admiral Stansfield Turner eliminated eight hundred and twenty operational human intelligence positions from the CIA. Turner's view was HUMINT was no longer necessary and could be replaced with Technical Intelligence (TECHINT), Imagery Intelligence (IMINT) and Signal Intelligence (SIGINT). Letters were sent to case officers simply stating "your services are no longer needed." This action set back CIA HUMINT collection efforts to such an extent the CIA still has not fully recovered.

As discussed in Chapter five, in 1996 the Clinton Administration enacted the policy known as the "Torricelli Principle," proposed by Senator Robert Torricelli (D-N.J). Releasing the classified name of a Guatemalan Army Colonel, Torricelli accused the CIA of illegal funding and the Colonel's role in the killing of an American. Investigation revealed the Guatemalan Colonel had not killed the American and allegations the CIA was engaging in back-channel funding were proven false. The Torricelli Principle banned CIA officers from recruiting any sources who had done anything illegal. Subsequently, CIA Director John Deutch and his Executive Assistant Nora Slatkin implemented a "human rights scrub" policy, which forbad CIA officers from recruiting any asset with human rights violations. This is akin to telling a DEA agent he cannot have any contact with an individual who uses drugs. By definition, most notorious terrorists are culturally human rights violators and engaged in criminal activity. This principle tied the hands of the CIA and prevented the Agency from recruiting any valuable terrorist sources leading up to 9-11. Before a Senate panel on bio-terrorism, CIA Director James Woolsey decried the restriction.

"These rules make absolutely no sense with respect to terrorist groups because the only people who are in terrorist groups are people who want to be terrorists," Woolsey testified. "That means they have a background in violence and human rights violations."

"If you make it difficult for a CIA case officer in, say, Beirut, to recruit spies with this sort of background, he'll be able to do a dandy job for you, telling you what's going on inside, for example, the churches and the chambers of commerce of Beirut, but we don't really care what's going on there. He'll have no idea, however, what's going on inside Hezbollah." Woolsey went on to say the US was now the only country that engages in "politically correct spying."

As the CIA attempted to recover from the reduction in human intelligence capability in the Directorate of Operations (DO), the Torricelli Principle and the policy of Deutch and Slatkin, defectors became a priority source of intelligence and counterintelligence information on the inner workings, planning and intentions of hostile intelligence services. Now, the CIA had virtually no substantial penetrations of target terrorist organizations. Prior to the invasion of Iraq, the CIA turned to defectors as a primary source of pre-war intelligence. Iraqi generals, who defected to the US, were paid millions of dollars for information on Iraq's Weapons of Mass Destruction program. It turned out the information was erroneous. This colossal failure of intelligence led to one of the largest military mistakes in US history. It was another stinging lesson demonstrating the consequences of placing too much emphasis on information provided by high-level defectors.

A Defector's State of Mind

I write about the above defector cases to illustrate the risk and complexity the CIA faces when handling defectors. I have seen the mental and emotional state defectors are in after they have been transported to the US Many have just committed what amounts to an act of suicide. Others are attempting to out-fox the CIA to gain large sums of money. Still, others have defected because they were passed over for a promotion or did not receive the recognition they thought they deserved. Finally, some defect because of ideological or religious reasons and are the most valuable, stable sources.

When a defector arrives in the United States, he or she has just committed treason against their country. More often than not, their government has activated its intelligence service through its Washington, DC embassy to find a way to exterminate him or her, before they provide the CIA with information. Back home, his family now knows he has betrayed them and their country. Some of their family members may likely be at risk of torture and even death.

The defector leaves what is usually a communist, socialist or Muslim culture, where life is quite a bit simpler and he is not responsible for every small detail of his life, finances, health and future. Many, already suffering from trauma and depression, are faced with significant culture shock. The American lifestyle is intense and complex compared to the lifestyle they knew. First, they are shown to "Disneyland," which is what they think America is. They are taken to the finest restaurants, stay in the finest hotels, are taken shopping at the finest clothing stores, and provided a stipend to spend on whatever they wish. They are promised nice homes and a good income for the rest of their life. This lifestyle must be earned through a long series of debriefings. These are not pleasant, even when conducted by the most adroit interviewer. Soon, "Disneyland" begins to fade and they are confronted with the thing they have never faced before; balancing a checkbook, managing the vast array of bills they now have to pay in America, and a complete change in their way of life.

Since many defectors are already traumatized and depressed, the experience of debriefings and the shock of a new culture amplify the dramatic emotional and mental upheavals they are experiencing. Some, like Yurchenko, cannot handle it and run back to the only thing they know, in a state of denial about what their own government will do to them when they return. They convince themselves a story about CIA cruelty will be believed by everyone. Surely, their government will understand and believe them. They even convince themselves the CIA has "tortured" them. Denial is their only way of escape. The pattern of self destruction they engaged in when they defected continues as they make the move to return to the country they betrayed. After the public show by their country, reality sets in as real interrogation begins by agents of their own government.

Other defectors are professional men and women who have made an intellectual or philosophical decision to leave what they are convinced is an oppressive system and transition to the democratic way of life. Although they face pressure similar to other defectors, because their motivations are more grounded, they are able to assimilate into American society and become life-long assets of the CIA and the US government, and even close friends with their handlers and other CIA officers.

The primary lesson here, learned the hard way by the CIA, is defectors desperately need mental and emotional support constantly throughout the entire time they are being processed. This has to be balanced with constant investigation into their credibility and continued diligence regarding their intentions. If either of these components is missing, the results can be catastrophic.

Defectors remain one of the most valuable sources of credible intelligence the CIA receives. Over the years, the CIA has instituted new procedures to treat them fairly, support them during their transition, treat them with dignity, help to protect their families by bringing them out of the country with them, and resettle them in the US with a stable new life. The CIA and the Intelligence Community continue to refine this process, for the sake of US policy information and the defectors themselves.

Chapter 8

Protective Operations

A frenzied crowd, numbering in the hundreds, began to gather around the line of crime scene tape marking the perimeter of the open grave. Only minutes before, members of the news media and curiosity seekers lingered among the headstones in the huge Holy Rood Cemetery in Westbury, New York. No one knew exactly where the burial was to take place. No one that is, except us. The colorful Director of the CIA, William Casey, had died of a brain tumor in the midst of the "Iran Contra Scandal." The timing of his death caused great controversy. He was due to testify before the House Permanent Select Committee on Intelligence and the Senate on December 16, 1986 for his role in the so-called "Arms for hostages deal." Before he was able to testify, on December 15, he was rushed to Georgetown University Hospital after experiencing a seizure at CIA headquarters in Langley, Virginia. He never made the hearings. On May 6, 1987 the cancerous tumor in his brain took his life. The timing was out of the ordinary. Casey's testimony was critical to the proceedings in the Iran Contra investigation. His death forever removed important information from the investigation. The scandal involved the President of the United States, Ronald Regan, members of the CIA, the NSA and the Department of Defense. The US had been secretly selling arms to Iran, which was under an arms embargo, in an effort to secure the release of American hostages held by Hezbollah. The plan included covertly funneling proceeds from the sale of arms to Iran, to support the anti-Sandinista rebels in Nicaragua, known as the "Contras." As a result of a congressional investigation and an investigation by the Tower Commission, appointed by the president, fourteen administration officials were indicted, including Colonel Oliver North, Secretary of Defense Casper Weinberger and National Security Advisor John Poindexter. North and Poindexter's convictions were overturned on appeal and Weinberger was pardoned by George W. Bush.

Some outside the CIA were making claims Casey was not dead, but was simply in hiding. Others claimed the CIA had organized the surgery to remove portions of his brain, so he could not remember the details of the scandal. These bizarre rumors were, of course, not the case. As I noted in chapter three of this book, reporter Bob Woodward claimed in his book *Veil the Secret Wars of the CIA* (page 587, paragraph 7) he had gotten into Casey's hospital room and the DCI had admitted to him in February 1987 he was aware of the diversion of funds to the Contras. I dispute Woodward's account of his meeting with Casey.

In preparation for Casey's burial at the cemetery in Westbury, I and two other agents were assigned to advance and secure the site for the funeral. Several cabinet level officials in the Reagan administration, current and former CIA directors, high ranking CIA officers, participants in the Iran Contra affair, celebrities and members of foreign delegations were due to attend the burial. A motorcade consisting of 80 limousines was expected. The President of the United States had departed for Washington following the memorial service held at St. Mary's Roman Catholic Church in Roslyn Harbor, Long Island.

A Rude Awakening

After twelve hour days and seven day weeks, the protective detail drove the armored limousines to Roslyn, New York to cover Casey's wake and funeral. We were tasked with protecting Casey's body and Agency officials who would be attending the ceremonies. We arrived in New York late in the evening and checked into the hotel. Over dinner we planned the operation. After planning was complete, we retired for the few hours of sleep we would get before the morning's movement. I checked into my room, rolled my luggage to the corner, climbed into bed and turned out the light. I slept like a rock. It seemed like only minutes had gone by when the alarm went off. I jumped out of bed and hurried to the bathroom to get ready. As I looked in the mirror, I was shocked. Smeared in my hair, all down the side of my face and on my T shirt was a brown, slimy substance. I had no idea what it was. Had I been the victim of a huge diarrhea "burst" in the middle of the night? Arrrggghhhh! Had I performed the first time ever feat of projectile number two? Slowly, I reached up and wiped the substance with my finger. I looked at it very carefully; I was very concerned. Upon inspection, I realized - it was chocolate; chocolate mint to be exact. All night, in a deep sleep, I had rolled in the chocolate mints the maid had left on the pillow, which had slipped into the crack where I could not see them. My shock turned to laughter. "What a Dufus" I said to myself. I was one relieved agent to find I had not experienced a catastrophic intestinal event.

The Burial

To perform the protective advance for the funeral we were given a map indicating where the grave would be located. Orders were given to secure the cemetery for the burial and the attendance of a large number of government officials from Washington. Our team proceeded to the location given to us on the map. There was an "X" where the grave site was supposed to be located. We arrived at the spot and, to our chagrin, there was no open grave. There were no preparations for a burial. There was no open grave even near the site. We were in the wrong place. In the huge cemetery, we had to perform a frantic search to locate the grave site before the huge crowd arrived. As we scoured the cemetery looking for the grave site, I noticed a couple who had arrived an hour early (thank God). I had met them at the wake the evening before. They were standing at a different location in the cemetery. I approached them with a greeting and began a pleasant conversation. During the conversation, the couple volunteered the open grave in front of them was the grave site for Casey's burial and did not bear the Casey name yet because Sophia wanted him buried next to relatives, whose name was on the headstone adjacent to the open grave.

Experiencing a *Les Miserable's* sort of relief and jubilation, I advised the other agents this was the correct burial site. How do you secure a large, open cemetery for a gathering of some of Washington's most high level and controversial figures? We did so using a very sophisticated process (tongue in cheek). The evening before, I devised a plan to secure the site using crime scene tape, and the team placed agents around the tape and through the cemetery investigating suspicious individuals. The idea worked. We bolted into action, ran the crime scene tape around the grave, with a loop opening for the limousines, maintained radio contact with the agents in the approaching motorcade and began questioning suspicious people lingering near the site; obviously not there to show reverence to loved ones.

I scanned the area around the burial site, before the news media and others lingering in the cemetery figured out the plan. I noticed two gentlemen standing across the street from the open grave under a small cherry tree. They had seen us cordon off the area. I approached the men, introduced myself and asked who they were. They responded in a Russian accent that they were "friends of the family." Obviously, the KGB had decided to attend the event. I cordially ended the conversation, went back to preparations and notified the other agents they were there.

Once the perimeter tape was up we took our positions, dressed in dark suites. The news media and curiosity seekers scurried to the site. Hundreds of people began to crowd around the perimeter, while the three of us held them back, waiting for the Nassau County police and the other agents to arrive. Reporters and cameramen began to force their way in and duck under the tape to get near the grave. We pushed them back, as politely as we could, ordering them to stay behind the line. During the wake the evening before, members of the news media had been very professional and gracious. In that case, I was the agent responsible for keeping people from entering the property, and was later posted at the door of the residence to screen people entering the wake. Reporters and their camera crew were courteous and cooperative. It made our job much easier. Because of the sheer intensity of events at the funeral and the significance of the story, the press was much more aggressive and difficult to control, but generally remained professional.

The night before the wake in Roslyn Harbor, we received information indicating certain groups were going to disrupt the event and throw cow's blood on the casket. Other CIA officials had been threatened with assassination. Cabinet level officials and personalities in the Iran Contra affair attending the ceremony were at risk as well. As the funeral proceeded, we created as much order as we could; out of sheer pandemonium. The motorcade was so long, it extended out of the established perimeter and down the cemetery street. Several high level officials had to walk some distance to the grave site, with their security and the agents we could spare accompanying them. The crowd pressed against the tape, stretching it to its limit. The remaining detail agents arrived with the motorcade, accompanied by the Nassau County police. The police posted outside the perimeter, controlling the crowd and traffic. The Nassau County police officers were outstanding throughout the entire event. We could not have done it without them. Our job was to face the crowd at the perimeter tape, scan them, watch people in the throng and keep an eye on those approaching from the cemetery. If there was ever a time an assassination attempt could take place, this was it.

I noticed a lady, dressed in a dark blue suit, coming from the back of the cemetery, her auburn hair pulled tightly back in a pony tail and wearing dark glasses. Aggressively, she pushed her way through the crowd, her right hand in the purse she held open in front of her. Her hand remained in the purse as she forcefully pushed her way through the crowd to the perimeter tape, next to the press and nearest the group of dignitaries attending the funeral. Her body language was rigid and her jaw was clenched.

"This could be it," I thought to myself.

My only recourse was to walk up to the edge of the tape, face the woman, block her and any shot she could take, using my body as a shield and be ready to take her down if necessary. This was my job. I stood face to face with her, staring directly into her sun glasses, conveying the message "Don't do it." We stared at each other for about five minutes. She turned around, pushed back through the crowd and disappeared in the multitude. I notified the other agents and the police, giving her description. We never saw her again.

Despite the size and complexity of the event, the entire operation went off without a hitch. When it was over, the agents went out to a small, private pub and had a cold beer. We had pulled it off. Robert Gates gave the agents a personal commendation for our performance. At the end of my assignment, I received a letter of commendation from the Chief of the DCI Security Staff for performance as an agent on the detail. It meant a great deal to me. Like so many other awards we received at the CIA, it was filed away in a classified safe, never to see the light of day.

My tenure as an agent on the protective staff of the DCI and DDCI was an intense, but personally satisfying time. I was part of the day-to-day successes, triumphs and failures that occurred at the top ranks of the CIA. My job was to give my life, if necessary, for the DCI, the DDCI and the CIA Station Chiefs we interacted with around the world. My fellow agents and I accepted this, were trained for it and fully intended to perform the duty if the need arose. I spent more time with the DCI and his family than I did with my own.

Chasing the Wind

One sunny morning, as I occupied the command post at a discreet location an alarming, but humorous, event occurred. Please forgive any vulgarity here, none is intended. Because of the long hours and the intense stress of the job, the agents developed humorous names for each other and running jokes we would jab at one another during long days. We had a daily contest to see which agent could "break wind" the most, do it the most often, and do it upon request. We called it "Boof on Command." One agent, whom I will not mention by name, had a particular gift for breaking wind upon request; anytime, anywhere, any place. It was some kind of gift.

This particular morning, the detail was preparing to drive the DCI to his office at CIA headquarters. The agents were posted in the armored motorcade vehicles, motors running, preparing for his departure. I occupied the command post with radios on to monitor the detail's movements. Unexpectedly, Casey burst into the command center and requested I activate the secure telephone so he could speak with a member of the President's cabinet. As the Director sat in the chair waiting for the answer on the other end of the phone, the agents in the motorcade began to engage in a wind-breaking contest over the radio; knowing we all would hear it. Unfortunately, there was an active radio right behind the Director's head as he waited for the secure connection. I had the radios turned up so I could hear the agents from wherever I was in the Command Post. The sound was relatively loud. The agents, one by one, began to break wind in their radios; loud "reports" coming out of the radio behind the Director. My adrenalin level skyrocketed. I could not go over, ask the Director to move and grab the radio. This would draw attention to what was happening. But, I could not let the radio "bursts" continue, potentially getting us in trouble. Fortunately, the Director's call went through and he became so focused on the conversation he did not hear what was emerging from behind him. Seeing my opening, I quickly ran out to the motorcade and, holding back the laughter, advised the agents to stop breaking wind in the microphones because the Director was in the Command Post. I have never heard so many radio-off clicks at one time. Fortunately for us all, the Director, focused on his duties, never heard the unique radio traffic. We laughed about it for months.

C05605759

SECRET
SECRET

PERFORMANCE APPRAISAL REPORT

Complete in Accordance with HR 20.55
See: Performance Appraisal Handbook for Supervisors

SECTION A			GENERAL INFORMATION		
1. SOCIAL SECURITY NUMBER	2. NAME (Last First Middle)				3. SO
	SHIPP, Kevin M.				
4. SCHEDULE	5. GRADE	6. AFFILIATION		7. OCCUPATIONAL TITLE	
GS	13	Staff Employee - Career			
8. OFFICE / DIVISION / BRANCH OF ASSIGNMENT			9. CURRENT STATION		10. HRS
DDO/CTC/			Washington		1
11. REPORTING PERIOD			12. DATE REPORT DUE IN HQS		13. TYPE OF REPORT
01 Jul 1998 - 22 May 1999			30 July 1999		

SECTION B	QUALIFICATIONS UPDATE
QUALIFICATIONS UPDATE (FORM 4640) IS ☐ IS NOT ☒ ATTACHED (Submit Only If There Are Changes)	☐

SECTION C — PERFORMANCE RATINGS

RATING NUMBER
1. Individual consistently fails to meet the work standard for the key job element performed. Performance is unsatisfactory.
2. Individual frequently fails to meet the work standard for the key job element performed. Performance is marginal.
3. Individual occasionally fails to meet the work standard for the key job element performed. Performance is acceptable.
4. Individual fully meets the work standard for the key job element performed.
5. Individual occasionally exceeds the work standard for the key job element performed. Performance is good.
6. Individual frequently exceeds the work standard for the key job element performed. Performance is excellent.
7. Individual invariably exceeds the work standard for the key job element performed. Performance is superior.

(b)(1)
(b)(3)
(b)(6)
(j)(1)
(k)(1)

KEY JOB ELEMENTS

Key Job Element No. 1 and Rating	
Perform as a team member and leader in the planning, administration, and presentation of	7

Key Job Element No. 2 and Rating	
	7

	6

Key Job Element No. 4 and Rating	

Key Job Element No. 5 and Rating	

SECTION D	OVERALL PERFORMANCE RATING	
Taking everything into account about the employee which influences his/her effectiveness on the job, I rate the employee's overall performance at this level	➡	7

Form 45 (EF)
$-98
PREVIOUS EDITIONS OBSOLETE

Classify as Appropriate

SECRET

SECRET

The author's Performance Appraisal Report from the Counter Terrorism Center.

C05605759

SECTION E (Continued)	NARRATIVE COMMENTS
SOCIAL SECURITY NUMBER	NAME
	SHIPP, Kevin M.

COMMENTS

On every ☐ that Kevin went on he acted as the team leader supervising staff officers and independent contractors. Mr. Shipp was universally viewed a☐ ☐ expert instructor, and as such, he was charged with indoctrinating new officers in how to provide ☐ course materials ☐ In the ☐ he coordinated, supervised and taught a ☐ Kevin mentored a new CTC officer through the course. ☐ Nothing would please ☐ management more than for each new officer to perform at Kevin's level.

The same new officer was treated to a second ☐ Kevin's mentoring of this officer proved to be outstanding, however, the new officer proved to be immature and a discipline problem. Mr. Shipp dealt with his less professional ward with maturity, tact, and discipline. During a difficult month, Mr. Shipp proved himself to be an effective manager and true leader. Comments from a former Deputy Director of the United States Secret Service praised Kevin for his handling of a sensitive and difficult situation.

☐ within ☐ are the backbone of any tour, but in between ☐ officers show their mettle. ☐ He manned the Agency's counterterrorist nerve center☐ Additionally, Mr. Shipp doggedly worked on improving course materials. He crafted ☐ In true team spirit, he shared the fruit of his labors with all of his coworkers. His slides became the office standard, and he unselfishly put all of the graphics on floppy disks to share. Kevin created course schedules that became the office standard, and his coworkers accepted the schedules faster than fraternity brothers grab an "A+" term paper from a historical resource file.

As testament to Mr. Shipp's outstanding performance in CTC/☐ he was awarded a $1500 Exceptional Performance Award. He was also offered the opportunity to Gateway to the Directorate of Operations, which carried the promise of attending the coveted ☐ Even without☐ Kevin was the highest intelligence producing SOPO in ☐ His production helped boost ☐ in the last year, and infinitely since he arrived in the branch. Mr. Shipp was universally viewed as the best officer in ☐ and his departure was a devastating blow. Mr. Shipp's performance in CTC proved that he is destined for future career ascension, and those of us who benefited from his expertise and hard work can only wish him the success he has earned.

Form 45 (EF)
9 88

PAGE 3

The author's Performance Appraisal Report from the Counter Terrorism Center.

C05605878

(b)(3)
(j)(1)

APPROVED FOR
RELEASED DATE:
02-May-2011

Central Intelligence Agency

Citation

OFFICE OF SECURITY

is hereby awarded the

MERITORIOUS UNIT CITATION

in recognition of their accomplishments in providing a safe environment for ⬚ personnel from January 1990 to May 1991. These officers performed their duties in a highly professional manner while working in a stressful and dangerous environment. It is a credit to the officers dedication to duty that during their tours of duty not one Agency official was harmed ⬚ All of the officers deployed ⬚ met the highest standards of the Central Intelligence Agency and for this reason are worthy of this commendation.

Meritorious Unit Citation presented to the Author for successful completion of a dangerous assignment.

C05605786

CAUTION: BLANK FORM REQUIRES
SECURE STORAGE IN FIELD

PERFORMANCE APPRAISAL REPORT

(NOT to be completed without
using Form 45) directions)

SECTION A		GENERAL INFORMATION				
1. SOC SEC NUMBER	2. NAME (Last, First, Middle) SHIPP, Kevin M.		3. DATE OF BIRTH	4. SD	5. SCHED GS	6. GRADE 07
7. AFFILIATION STAFF EMPLOYEE-CAREER			8. OCCUPATIONAL TITLE SECURITY PROTECTIVE OFF			
9. OFFICE/DIVISION/BRANCH OF ASSIGNMENT SEC			10. CURRENT STATION WASHINGTON, D.C.			11. HQS.
12. REPORTING PERIOD 861101 - 870617			13. DATE REPORT DUE IN OP ASAP		14. TYPE OF REPORT 2/R	

SECTION B	QUALIFICATIONS UPDATE

Qualifications Update (Form 444n) is _____ is not _____ attached. (Submit only if there are changes.)

SECTION C	PERFORMANCE RATINGS

Rating Number

1. Individual consistently fails to meet the work standard for the key job element performed. Performance is unsatisfactory.
2. Individual frequently fails to meet the work standard for the key job element performed. Performance is marginal.
3. Individual occasionally fails to meet the work standard for the key job element performed. Performance is acceptable.
4. Individual fully meets the work standard for the key job element performed.
5. Individual occasionally exceeds the work standard for the key job element performed. Performance is good.
6. Individual frequently exceeds the work standard for the key job element performed. Performance is excellent.
7. Individual invariably exceeds the work standard for the key job element performed. Performance is superior.

(b)(3)
(b)(6)
(j)(1)

APPROVED FOR
RELEASED DATE:
06-May-2011

KEY JOB ELEMENTS

KEY JOB ELEMENT NO. 1 AND RATING

Provides protection for the office suite of the Director and Deputy Director of Central Intelligence. Responsible for the processing and monitoring of all visitors to the suite.

6

KEY JOB ELEMENT NO. 2 AND RATING

Provides protection for [   ] the Director of Central Intelligence and has direct responsibility for [   ] Command Post.

6

KEY JOB ELEMENT NO. 3 AND RATING

Provides daily administrative and communications support for the DCI Security Staff.

6

KEY JOB ELEMENT NO. 4 AND RATING

During DCI/DDCI travel assists the DCI Security Staff in providing personal protection for the DCI and DDCI and is responsible for the protection of the classified material(s) that is in their possession. As such, is responsible for, among other matters, security with liaison, transportation, and communications.

6

KEY JOB ELEMENT NO. 5 AND RATING

SECTION D	OVERALL PERFORMANCE RATING LEVEL

Taking everything into account about the employee which influences his/her effectiveness on the job, I rate the employee's overall performance at this level.

6

FORM 45 USE PREVIOUS
10-83 EDITIONS

(4)

The author's Performance Appraisal Report
from the DCI Security Staff.

C05605786

~~CONFIDENTIAL~~
~~CONFIDENTIAL~~
(When Filled In)

SECTION E	NARRATIVE COMMENTS

1. By Supervisor

Mr. Shipp is recommended for continued employment.
Mr. Shipp was selected for a rotational assignment as a Protective Security Officer (PSO) with the DCI Security Staff and he served in that capacity from 16 June 1986 until his entry into the _____ Program in June 1987.

The undersigned supervised Mr. Shipp from December 1986 and he consistently demonstrated maturity and a genuine dedication to the mission of the DCI Security Staff. One of his most impressive attributes was his willingness to address issues that required considerable thought and research. For example, Mr. Shipp realized the need for Standard Operating Procedures for the PSO's in both the office and _____ Command Post environments. With a minimum of supervision, he pursued the development and implementation of this critical initiative. The final product has provided the DCI Security Staff with an important benchmark from which staff operations are conducted.

During Mr. Shipp's tenure, the DCI Security Staff maintained a 24-hour Command Post at the residence of the former Director of Central Intelligence, William J. Casey. His maturity and sound judgement attracted the Casey family and they relied heavily on him for guidance and support. During a time of personal crisis, the Casey's knew they could count on Mr. Shipp.

With regard to his office responsibilities, he developed a solid, professional rapport with the occupants of the DCI suite. He was always tactful, polite and eager to assist as required. He accepted his security responsibilities in a serious manner and his attention to detail reflected favorably on the entire DCI Security Staff.

In conclusion, Mr. Shipp's assignment to the DCI Security Staff was an unqualified success. He enhanced the stature of the rotational assignment to the DCI Security Staff by an outstanding performance of his assigned duties. He also will, in the opinion of the undersigned, be a success in the future for the Office of Security.

Months employee has been in this position 14	Months employee has been under my supervision 14	Interim discussion was X was not ___ held.	Reason for NOT showing employee the report is attached. Yes ___ No ___
DATE 8/14/87	TITLE DC/DCI/SS		

Employee Certification

I have reviewed my supervisor's comments and discussed my job performance ratings with him/her. My signature does not necessarily imply my agreement with either.	DATE	TYPED OR PRINTED NAME AND SIGNATURE Kevin M. Shipp *unavailable*

2. By Reviewing Official

I agree wholeheartedly with the above assessment of Mr. Shipp. He was an excellent addition to the staff and should do well as a staff agent. He will be invited back to the staff in the future.

DATE 8-26-87	TITLE C/DCI/SS	

3. By Employee

I have read my reviewing official's comments. My signature does not necessarily imply my agreement with them.	I have ___ have not ___ attached a statement containing my comments about this Performance Appraisal Report.
DATE	POSITION TITLE	TYPED OR PRINTED NAME AND SIGNATURE Kevin M. Shipp *unavailable*

~~CONFIDENTIAL~~
~~CONFIDENTIAL~~

The author's Performance Appraisal Report
from the DCI Security Staff.

C05605762

CONFIDENTIAL
CONFIDENTIAL

CAUTION: BLANK FORM REQUIRES
SECURE STORAGE IN FIELD

PERFORMANCE APPRAISAL REPORT

(NOT to be completed without using Form 45i directions)

SECTION A			GENERAL INFORMATION			
1. SSN REF NUMBER	2. NAME (Last, First, Middle) Shipp, Kevin M.		3. DATE OF BIRTH	4. SEX	5. SCHED GS-3	6. GRADE 13
7. AFFILIATION Staff Employee - Career			8. OCCUPATIONAL TITLE SECURITY RES OFFICER			
9. OFFICE/DIVISION/BRANCH OF ASSIGNMENT CIC			10. CURRENT STATION WASHINGTON, D.C.			11. HQS 1
12. REPORTING PERIOD 080196 - 021497			13. DATE REPORT DUE IN QP		14. TYPE OF REPORT	

(b)(1)
(b)(3)
(b)(6)
(j)(1)
(k)(1)

SECTION B	QUALIFICATIONS UPDATE

Qualifications Update (Form 444n) is _____ is not _____ attached. (Submit only if there are changes.)

SECTION C	PERFORMANCE RATINGS

Rating Number

1. Individual consistently fails to meet the work standard for the key job element performed. Performance is unsatisfactory.
2. Individual frequently fails to meet the work standard for the key job element performed. Performance is marginal.
3. Individual occasionally fails to meet the work standard for the key job element performed. Performance is acceptable.
4. Individual fully meets the work standard for the key job element performed.
5. Individual occasionally exceeds the work standard for the key job element performed. Performance is good.
6. Individual frequently exceeds the work standard for the key job element performed. Performance is excellent.
7. Individual invariably exceeds the work standard for the key job element performed. Performance is superior.

KEY JOB ELEMENTS

KEY JOB ELEMENT NO. 1 AND RATING Investigations/Analysis - Conducts special, sensitive investigations including research, analysis, and adjudications.

5

KEY JOB ELEMENT NO. 2 AND RATING Problems Solving - Provides coordination, support, and guidance for [ ] branches, CIC components, and appropriate OPS entities.

6

KEY JOB ELEMENT NO. 3 AND RATING Case Management/Organizational Skills - Management of the complete cycle of assigned cases.

6

KEY JOB ELEMENT NO. 4 AND RATING Communication Skills - Writing: Prepares reports, adjudicative memoranda, summaries, etc. Oral: Briefs senior Agency and non-Agency personnel on case specific information. May represent [ ] during informational briefings.

5

KEY JOB ELEMENT NO. 5 AND RATING Performs ad hoc duties in support of the CIC/ [ ] mission.

6

SECTION D	OVERALL PERFORMANCE RATING LEVEL

Taking everything into account about the employee which influences his/her effectiveness on the job, I rate the employee's overall performance at this level.

6

FORM 45 (EF) OBSOLETE PREVIOUS
12-82 EDITION

CONFIDENTIAL
CONFIDENTIAL

The author's Performance Appraisal Report
from the Counterintelligence Center.

C05605762

SECTION E	NARRATIVE COMMENTS

1. By Supervisor

Kevin M. Shipp has served in the [   ] of the Counterintelligence Center (CIC) and has been under my supervision for his entire tour in CIC which ended 14 February 1997.

. Mr. Shipps main responsibility was the handling of cases which were referred from OPS that had unresolved counterintelligence (CI) issues. [

[   ] Mr. Shipp expended a great deal of effort attempting to resolve the CI issues in a timely fashion. His efforts helped [   ] become a more efficient and effective counterintelligence resource for CIC and OPS.

During the rating period, Mr. Shipp showed flexibility and dedication in handling high profile cases. He frequently had to change priorities in a middle of a case to respond to senior management or change his plan and attack the problem from a different angle at the direction of management. CI cases change priority and direction rapidly. They are complex in nature, political, [   ] Mr. Shipps organizational skills enabled him to change priorities in mid-stream without hesitation or loss of focus. ·

[   ] officers are responsible for producing reports from both an OPS and DO perspective as well as communications to outside agencies. Mr. Shipp prepared memoranda for D/OPS, spot reports for the DDO, CIOLs to the FBI and other outside agencies. His reports were well structured and logical.

Months employee has been in this position. 23	Months employee has been under my supervision. 18	Interim discussion was __X__ was not _____ held.	Reason for NOT showing employee the report is attached. Yes_____ No _____
DATE 5/15/97	TITLE Team Leader, [ ]		

Employee Certification

I have reviewed my supervisor's comments and discussed my job performance rating with him/her. My signature does not necessarily imply agreement with either.	DATE 5/15/97	TYPED OR PRINTED NAME AND SIGNATURE [signature] Kevin M. Shipp

2. By Reviewing Official

I concur with the numerical scores and narrative comments prepared by [   ] Mr. Shipp joined [   ] at a time of fast braking events, both in terms of specific cases and the development of policies and procedures. Although Mr. Shipp lacked specific CI experience, his solid security background and outstanding enthusiasm enabled him to effectively meet the

DATE 15 May '97	TITLE C/[ ] CIC	

3. By E[   ]e

I have read my reviewing official's comments. My signature does not necessarily imply my agreement with them.	[ ] have not _____ attached a statement containing comments about this Performance Appraisal Report.
DATE 5/15/97	POSITION TITLE Security Res. Officer	TYPED OR PRINTED NAME AND SIGNATURE [signature] Kevin M. Shipp

FORM 45 (EF) OBSOLETE PREVIOUS 12-02 EDITION

The author's Performance Appraisal Report from the Counterintelligence Center.

Chapter 9

An Education on Professional Ethics

I left my assignment as a federal investigator to take a position with the Security Education Division (SED). In SED, I was assigned as the Chief of Training for the CIA federal police force. It was a demanding but rewarding job. I enjoyed supporting the men and women of the newly formed CIA federal police, the Security Protective Service (SPS). To my disappointment, during my first briefing with the incumbent, his advice was, "watch your back," referring to Frank Murdock, the Chief of SED.

"Oh boy," I thought to myself, "another snake to deal with."

Despite the warning given to me about Frank, I worked hard to make improvements and streamline the SPS program. I had four subordinates working for me in the Division. Two were senior members of the SPS. Frank decided he simply did not like one of my SPS subordinates and two of my co-workers. So, he proceeded to make their lives miserable, threatening to write nasty letters for their personnel files and ruin their careers. In the case of the two co-workers, he did exactly that.

Frank went after one of the SPS officers who worked for me, Pete Santori. Pete was a good SPS officer and a good employee. Everything I tasked Pete with he did; and did with all his might. I never had a problem with his performance. However, whatever creature inhabited Frank's mind decided one day he would go after Pete for sport. Frank was one of those CIA officers who was a little fish, until the agency took a risk and gave him some authority. Once he sat behind the big desk, he became a monster. I learned this sort of person is, basically, a coward, terrified someone is going to rise above him and take his promotion. People like this keep themselves from scrutiny by attacking everyone around them.

One morning, Frank took me into his office and told me he simply did not like Pete and wanted to get rid of him. His plan was to make

Pete's life miserable. When Pete became upset with the treatment, Frank would write his Performance Appraisal Report (PAR) with a low rating because of attitude and poor performance.

When it came time for Pete's performance evaluation, I gave him the rating he deserved; a good one. As soon as Frank saw it, he commanded his deputy, Larry Anderson, to pull me into his office for a meeting. During the meeting Larry, in a menacing tone, threatened,

"Frank is not happy with your rating of Pete on his PAR. He wants you to change it to poor."

"I can't do that."

"You what?"

"I can't do that. I rated Pete accurately and fairly based on his performance."

"I am ordering you to rate Pete down on his PAR!"

"I'm sorry, but I'm not going to do that."

"If you don't rate Pete down on his PAR, Frank is going to write a letter against you and put it in your personnel file."

"Well, then tell Frank to write the letter, because I am not going to do it. If Frank wants to write his comments in the review section he can do that. Pete's rating stays what it is."

"That will be all," said Larry with a low, threatening tone.

From that point on, I became Frank's target. When I went into the classified system, protected by passwords known only to me, I noticed someone in the office had broken into my files to access the PARs on my employees. And, sure enough, Frank began to write memos and make phone calls to destroy my career. I was not going to let him do it. I found out later there is a CIA regulation forbidding managers from ordering a subordinate manager to change the PAR of an employee. It was a serious infraction.

One afternoon, a fellow senior officer, who had been the brunt of Frank's retribution, came into my office and closed the door. She advised she had secretly gone to the CIA Inspector General (IG) and reported Frank and Larry's actions. The IG had opened an investigation and wanted to talk to me. I advised her that, if the IG called me, I would dutifully come in and tell them the truth. The next morning, Frank called me into his office.

"You know Kevin," he said.

"Some people have talked to the IG, and really regretted doing it."

"Really?'

"That's right. Some people have had their careers ruined by doing that."

"What is that supposed to mean, Frank?"

"Nothing. That will be all. You can go."

Frank ended the meeting. Walking out of his office, after receiving a direct threat, my decision to talk to the IG just solidified.

During my meeting with the IG, I was met by a very gracious and seasoned lady, a senior IG investigator. I answered her questions about Murdock and Anderson truthfully. She advised the IG staff was conducting an aggressive investigation and was outraged by their behavior. There was probably going to be official action taken against them.

The official gave me the IG contact code name "Martha." She advised when I got the telephone message "Martha" called, the IG was making its move to sanction Murdock and Anderson.

Three weeks later, I came into my office and found a note from my secretary. It contained the words, "Martha called." It had begun. The hammer came down on Murdock and Anderson. Almost fired, both men were removed from the office. Frank was given a small office shuffling papers and Larry was shipped off to the field; their titles stripped from them. I felt no sense of vindication. This sort of practice had become all too common in the CIA, which is veiled from oversight by organizations such as the Department of Labor. All personnel actions within the CIA are classified and can be withheld from investigators from other federal agencies. Some managers abuse this secrecy.

Chapter 10

Career Change

As an officer in the CIA Counter Terrorism Center (CTC), I received an exceptional performance award for "timely and relevant intelligence collection." I organized and conducted operations, gathering significant human intelligence overseas for the CTC, in some very dangerous places. It was fulfilling for me as an Agency officer and an American. I was called by the chief of the CTC division I served and asked to join the CTC and Directorate of Operations for the remainder of my career, to continue my work in human intelligence collection.

My assignments were taking a toll on my marriage and family. During missions, I had to be focused, have the "eye of the tiger," and be willing to kill or be killed. I had to "Do what the Romans do," drinking hard, working long days and nights, and leaving most of my personal morals at home. Essentially, I was paid to drink and steal. The value of human intelligence is critical to our national security. This cannot be overstated. And it has provided some of the most valuable intelligence to US policy makers. So, I do not want to belittle its importance. But, I found myself drinking too much, constantly around loose foreign women and in the company of other officers whose morals were slightly higher than a serpent. Many had sex with foreign women regularly and their wives never knew about it. Most lied, even to their co-workers, and the majority were functional alcoholics (I was no exception); albeit successful ones. My family was very important to me. I traveled to twenty countries, most of them less than tourist spots. Time with my kids had degraded to recording bedtime stories for my wife to play to them every night while I was gone, so they could hear my voice and remember what their father sounded like. I arrived home morally bankrupt and went to church, just to get a spiritual bath. On assignments, I became someone else. I was very effective. Finally, I looked myself in the mirror, and promised myself I would not live like that anymore.

When the offer of a promotion and permanent overseas assignment collecting intelligence came, I was flattered. But, I had already made the personal decision to put my family first. My marriage was on the rocks and my children barely knew me. My oldest son ██████████ had become the man of the house and was there more than I was. I knew when I retired from the CIA there would be a line of hungry officers ready to take my place. I would simply become a classified file in the basement of CIA headquarters. This would be at the expense of my marriage and my children. The divorce rate in the Directorate of Operations is about 60%. Alcoholism is a common problem.

The call came one afternoon in the spring of 1999, as I sat in my CTC office. I picked up the receiver.

"Kevin Shipp speaking."

The Chief of the CTC division was on the phone. He praised my work and offered me the opportunity to operate in human intelligence collection overseas for the rest of my career. I thanked him for the offer, but respectfully declined. He made the offer again. I declined again. He made the offer a third time and I declined a third time. He had previously expounded to me and a group of other officers that he and CTC management were the "Gods of your career."

During the conversation he became incensed.

"Do you know what you are doing? You are ruining your career! If you don't take this job, you will have no career in this Agency!"

"Sorry sir, but I have made my decision."

He abruptly hung up the telephone. Mentally drained, I walked out of my office. As I did, an older and well known officer came out of his office. He put his arm on my shoulder.

"I overheard your conversation," he said.

"Yeah, I turned the job down and took a bit of heat for it."

He gave me a gentle tug with his arm.

"It's about time someone told those bastards no! Good job," he said.

I appreciated that immensely, but I still felt emotionally drained by the event.

The pressures of my job had driven my marriage to the verge of a split. I loved my marriage and children more than any career. My kids were the most precious thing in life to me. After all, according to the doctors, I was not supposed to have children after I recovered from a terminal illness when I was twelve years old. It was a medical miracle. I knew when my Agency career was over they were all I would have left, with any real value. I had seen too many officers retire with ruined marriages and empty lives. Families and children are the only real wealth. Monetary wealth and "things" will only satisfy you temporarily. They have no lasting value and will never bring a person genuine peace and happiness. To remind myself, I routinely took a coffee mug with the picture of my kids on it to senior meetings. The majority of people in the room were either divorced, or did not have time in their careers for children. The mug served to remind me of what really matters.

Now that I had rebuffed CTC management and refused their offer, I had to seek another assignment within the Agency. This time I had made the decision to find a position, however mundane, that would allow me to spend time with my family. After putting my name in for several assignments, a call came from the management of the CIA Office of Security. A position had been created ██████████████████████ ████████ and needed an officer there to plug the holes in████████████████████operational security. I jumped at the chance. I attended the interview and was selected for the assignment. I was elated. My wife was reluctant at first. We had a beautiful house in The Plains, Virginia, on a little hill just behind the site where the International Gold Cup races are held. The place was wonderful and our family loved it. But, with the promise of a good salary █████████████████ ██████ we eventually agreed to make the change. ███████████████████████ ████████████████████ ███████████████████████████████████ ████████████████████████████████████ ████████████████████ .

Chapter 11
Wake-Up Call

By 1995 the CIA was in turmoil. An air of distrust among Agency employees hung over CIA headquarters. Careerism was at an all-time high. Officers fought for promotions and only the most ethical did so without back-channeling e-mails, closed door meetings or the shameless practice of doing anything their managers wanted, while stepping on those below them. This was becoming an acceptable internal procedure. Operational mistakes at the management level were covered up at all costs.

In the account that follows I must leave out the names of the actual offices, true names of people involved and the detailed results of the investigation I conducted because of the sensitivity of the information.

My first wake-up call came in 1995. I was an officer in the CIA's Office of Security performing an internal investigation on a sensitive CIA operation. During a routine study of internal processes, I and my fellow security officer, who initially raised concerns about the issue, but was on her way to another assignment, uncovered what appeared to be a significant, global vulnerability to our agents overseas.

At first, it seemed too bizarre to be true. However, the more research I conducted the more concrete my conclusions became. Because of an overlooked vulnerability, the lives of our agents, and their assets, were at risk. I drafted an extensive report on my findings and submitted it to my supervisor, who I will call Tom K. After Tom, a very fair, objective manager, reviewed my findings, he advised there might be something to the information in the report and recommended I present my findings to the Agency division involved. I called this division and advised I had developed some information that could be of concern to them. I had a several-page report detailing my findings.

They arranged a meeting with the Chief of the Division and his Special Assistant. During the meeting, I presented an overview of my findings. When the presentation was finished, I left them a copy of the report.

A second meeting was immediately scheduled for me to present my findings to a panel of senior Agency officers. The group was a little intimidating, but I was sure of my results. During the meeting, I gave a slide presentation on the findings of my investigation and disseminated several copies of my report. At first, the air of the meeting was suspicious. By the end of the meeting there was a sense of concealed alarm.

After giving the division a week to digest my memorandum, I called to find out what conclusion had been reached regarding my findings. The Special Assistant, who was at both meetings replied, "What memorandum?"

I reminded her of the memorandum I had distributed at the briefing. She responded, "Oh, I do not have that, we must have lost it."

I advised this was no problem, I would send her another one. I immediately did so. A week later, I called the Special Assistant again and asked if she had seen the memo. To my amazement she responded again, "What memo?" I reminded her of the memo I had given her two times. She replied she did not know what I was talking about and would have to check into it.

Several days later, I received a call from Charles N. (not his real name), chief of that division. In a threatening tone, he ordered me to drop the investigation, stating it was above my head (I was a GS 12) and was none of my business. I responded, respectfully, it would be negligent to do so and I thought we should continue. He angrily ordered me to drop the investigation and hung up the telephone. I was stunned.

It took me two days to go over the events in my mind and decide what I had to do and how much I was willing to risk my career. I finally reached the conclusion lives were at stake, and I had to pursue it.

I arranged a meeting with a senior officer at the Department of State who was heading the office in charge of embassy security. The CIA special assistant attended the meeting also. During the meeting, once again there was the familiar air of suspicion and superiority. I presented my findings to the group. The State officer advised there was no problem and the vulnerability had been corrected years ago, essentially mocking my findings.

Once again, I was shocked. My findings suggested otherwise. I respectfully advised I would do more research and close the matter if he was correct. He was not. More research revealed how potentially widespread the problem was.

Following the meeting, I went into the computer to access my memo from the server. The memo was gone. I called the Information Technology department to see if they could retrieve it from back-ups. They responded they could find no such memo on the backup server. Was this just a digital hiccup, or had someone intentionally deleted the file? Because I always kept important documents in hard copy, I retrieved a copy of the investigation memorandum from my files. I, along with another Agency officer, scanned the report back into the computer system. For several weeks I received nothing but silence from the officers I had briefed.

During the interim period my supervisor, Tom K., was attending a conference for Agency officers in the Senior Executive Service (SES). This is the highest career rank in the CIA. During offline discussions, Tom mentioned my findings to another SES officer; Mike O. Mike was the recipient of the CIA Intelligence Medal for heroism. He was one of the old school Agency officers who did his job for God and country. I had known him from his time in the CIA Office of Security. He was a man of authentic character. Tom mentioned to me Mike was going to give me a call.

Early one morning, I called another officer who was a good friend of mine. During the conversation he advised something had just been put on his desk he had to deal with and he would call me right back. Ten minutes later the phone rang. Thinking it was my friend, I answered, "Pizza Hut!" SES officer Mike O. was on the other end of the line (oops!). I had to explain to him I thought he was my friend who was supposed to call back. I deeply hoped he had a sense of humor.

Mike O. was now retired from the CIA and was working for the Department of State, Inspector General's (IG) Office. Because my findings involved US embassies, State IG had the authority to conduct an investigation. Mike requested I send him a copy of my report. Feeling a great sense of relief, I immediately sent him the information via secure fax.

Within a week Mike O. called me, advised he had thoroughly read my report and he was concerned there was a real problem. He requested a meeting at Department of State headquarters. During the meeting, I gave a verbal presentation of my findings to Mike and two senior IG officers. At the conclusion, they complimented me on my work and advised they would look into the matter. As I walked out of State headquarters, I felt a huge sense of relief. I could drop the matter now and move on.

After a global investigation, which included visiting several foreign embassies, Mike O. and the IG staff completed their study. Mike O. called me with the results. It was worse than even I thought. The vulnerability was real and could have resulted in the deaths of our agents. Mike scheduled an immediate meeting with the State IG and the CIA division responsible. During the meeting Mike O. and the IG officers sat at one end of the table, the CIA Chief of the division at the other, and me in the middle. The Chief of State IG officially reprimanded the CIA for putting the lives of agents at risk for more than ten years and ordered him to correct the problem immediately. I saw my CIA career fading before my eyes. Surely, this CIA office would not forget the embarrassment. It did not matter, I had done the right thing, and I could sleep at night.

A few months later, a lengthy report was published to the entire Intelligence Community, detailing the identification of the vulnerability and recommending corrective action. A special Agency office was set up with orders to correct the problem. I received an Exceptional Performance Award for my work.

After these events, I had a great sense of personal and professional fulfillment. I had been confronted with the choice between my career and what was best for my country and my fellow officers in the field. I had made the right choice. I continued to be stunned by my own Agency's serious cover-up of the problem, and especially its total disregard for the lives of its agents.

I lost a fundamental respect for the CIA's honesty and its ability to efficiently carry out operations. I had received a wake-up call trumpeting how weaknesses can occur because of arrogance and the lack of real scrutiny of the CIA.

Chapter 12

Detection of Deception

"He that has eyes to see and ears to hear may convince himself that no mortal can keep a secret. If his lips are silent, he chatters with his fingertips: betrayal oozes out of him from every pore."
—Sigmund Freud

The atmosphere in the polygraph examination room was tense. A quiet pressure loomed over the Subject of the test and me. You could hear a pin drop. I had asked the test questions regarding contact with a foreign intelligence service and concealing contact with a foreign national. He consistently reacted significantly, indicating deception. His respiration was erratic, his heart rate up and his Electro-dermal Activity (EDA) was soaring. Something was wrong. During original questioning, he had been confident and outgoing.

As I finished the test and began questioning him on concealing contact with a foreign intelligence service, his demeanor changed. He became defensive and made excuses for his reaction. I tested him again. He failed again. During the questioning that followed, he began to stumble over his own fabrications. First, he was reacting because he had foreign relatives he rarely sees. Then, it was his foreign uncle who was causing him concern. I questioned him further using the Behavioral Analysis Technique. Subsequently, he admitted this "uncle" was the member of a foreign government (an intelligence adversary of the United States). Over the next two hours, I pressed him. He admitted his "uncle" was working with two other foreign government officials whom he met at a "family function." He was getting tense and angry. He knew his story was unraveling and the truth was leaking out. Finally, he admitted his "uncle" and his government associates had sent him to the Agency to attempt to pass the polygraph test and gain inside access. As I left the room to examine his charts, he began to curse and swear. He was sweating profusely. The results of the test were "Significant Physiological Response," i.e., Deception Indicated to counterintelligence questions.

By the end of the test he admitted he had been coached by members of a foreign intelligence service and sent to attempt to gain access to the CIA. He was shown the door and his application for employment was denied. An investigation began on names of the agents he turned over. I was exhausted, we had stopped another one.

During my tours in the CIA Counterintelligence Center (CIC) and the Office of Security (OS), Polygraph Division (PD), I was trained to be an expert in the detection of deception. I gained extensive experience on human behavioral analysis and the polygraph instrument. Performing polygraph examinations was a grueling and exhausting process for us all. The stakes were incredibly high and the scrutiny by CIA management was intense.

Successful tests were extremely gratifying, both in catching the deceptive and clearing the innocent. It was a good feeling to get a new applicant to the CIA, nervous and scared about the process, successfully through the test and off to his or her new career. It was a mixed feeling of fulfillment and outrage to catch a foreign agent attempting to penetrate the organization, or an individual who had committed a crime such as child sexual abuse.

The global network of espionage is a dark underworld, full of ruthless individuals, a moral vacuum where ego and self-gratification generally rule. Billions of dollars flow invisibly across continents to fund operations pitting countries against each other, and fund uncover individuals working against their own government. Even on the good side, there are individuals who are career-hungry for the next catch, even a small one, to further their reputation. Fortunately, there are a few who do it purely out of patriotism, especially in America.

The polygraph has always been the subject of fierce controversy regarding its use in government applicant screening, criminal cases and private investigations. The polygraph test has both strengths and weaknesses. It is a significant mistake for any federal agency or law enforcement entity to entertain the misconception that it is one hundred percent accurate.

As an expert in Forensic Psycho Physiology, I was intimately familiar with the polygraph instrument and its use. The employment of the test has continually been under tremendous scrutiny, as it should be in a democracy. Government use of any intrusive system penetrating the privacy of individuals must always have a good Constitutional foundation, and continually be under oversight by vigilant representatives of the public.

The incident described at the start of this chapter is an example of the strengths of the polygraph. Love it or hate it, the polygraph has been used many times to prevent foreign intelligence penetrations of our Intelligence Community and to vet informants and assets, to ensure they are providing truthful information. A foreign asset or defector providing fabricated information, to get the financial benefit, can have catastrophic consequences if the information is acted upon by the US government.

Iraq is a prime example of this. False information provided by Iraqi military officers was taken as legitimate and acted upon, when it was inaccurate and fabricated. This mistake cost the American taxpayer millions of dollars in "payments" to these individuals.

A second strength of the polygraph is its use in criminal cases. Multiple criminal cases involving child abduction, murder, theft and other heinous crimes have been solved based on admissions made during a polygraph examination. My hat goes off to the brave law enforcement men and women who successfully ran those tests. Very seldom is it reported in the press that these cases were solved from information derived during a polygraph test.

There are, however, some significant weaknesses with the polygraph test. First, the test is only as good as the examiner performing it. In reality, the real effectiveness of the test rests with the skills of the examiner. Second, studies show the test is wrong about 20% of the time. This is way too high to be relied upon as the sole screening tool. It is also the reason it is not and never should be admissible in a court of law. If it was admissible in court, most subjects would not voluntarily take it.

The heavy reliance on the polygraph instrument in CIA applicant and internal investigation cases has caused erroneous investigation results in many cases and, in the case of the CIC internal investigation unit, which I used to be a part of, ruined many careers and many lives. Unfortunately, when the rest of a security system is weak, there tends to be an over-reliance on the polygraph test. This is a damaging mistake.

But, the CIA faces the daunting task of protecting extremely sensitive information. In recent years, the Agency has experienced serious internal espionage cases. There have been several since the 1980s, but two are significant in relation to the use of the polygraph.

CIA Officer Aldrich Ames Espionage Case

Despite its many successes, one of the most significant failures of the CIA polygraph program was the case of Aldrich "Rick" Ames. I was assigned to the newly reorganized CIC internal investigations unit, now collocated with the FBI Counterespionage Unit, in response to this crisis just after Ames' arrest. CIC was undergoing a massive reorganization and had become priority one in the Agency's internal investigation system.

Rick Ames was a former Counterintelligence officer assigned to Soviet Europe. Ames was disheveled in appearance and had several performance problems in previous positions. These were never documented, as his managers avoided this unpleasant task by transferring him from one position to the next with no paper trail revealing these problems. At the time, the CIC had been considered to be a dead-end job, much like it was in the FBI, until the Hanssen case.

In 1985, Ames began turning classified information over to the Soviets. He underwent his reinvestigation polygraph test in 1986. He failed the test.

During this period in the CIA, if a polygraph test brought results of "Deception Indicated" with no significant admissions, the person would be interviewed by a CIA security officer and undergo an Office of Medical Services (OMS) examination. If no noteworthy information was developed, the information was documented in the security file and the case was closed. Such was the case with Rick Ames.

Ames went through another polygraph test in 1991. He was coached by his Soviet handler before taking the test and knew if he made no confessions, there was nothing the Office of Security could do further. During this test, Ames exhibited a significant reaction to the question regarding concealing contact with foreign nationals. He explained this away, claiming it was because he had contact with foreign nationals as part of his professional duties. This explanation was accepted and Ames passed the test, despite the fact that he was on a CIA list of suspected moles.

Information previously collected by the CIA indicated secrets were being passed to the Soviets that could only have come from someone on the inside – a mole. Ames' 1990 background investigation revealed he was living an extravagant lifestyle, well above his government salary, and had paid $540,000 in cash for his house in Arlington, Virginia. This information was never passed to the Polygraph Division.

The case of Rick Ames generated outrage in the Congress and Senate. The FBI was quick to point out the CIA had blown Ames's polygraph test and it was clear the Agency could not conduct efficient counterintelligence investigations. A government security commission agreed and demanded a total restructuring of CIA counterintelligence.

CIA Officer Harold Nicholson Case

The second noteworthy case involving the polygraph was that of Harold James Nicholson. Nicholson broke all the profiles of a so-called spy. He was a high ranking GS 15 officer who had a sterling career record, a clean security file, no alcohol problems and no financial problems. He was popular and well thought of as a good instructor training incoming case officers. There were no external behavioral indicators that Nicholson was selling secrets to the Soviets.

In October 1995, Nicholson underwent his reinvestigation polygraph test. This would be the first of three tests he would take. He failed all three tests (using the new computerized instrument), with a score resulting in "Deception Indicated" to concealing contact with a foreign intelligence service, the most serious of the counterintelligence questions. Nicholson had been spying for the Russian government since 1994. The CIA was on to him during the time period he failed his 1995 polygraph examination.

Those who commit espionage often make several obvious mistakes, thinking they are too smart and will never get caught. Nicholson was arrested by the FBI for espionage as he transited Dulles Airport in November 1996. He had been coached by his Russian handler on ways to beat the polygraph test. Obviously, this coaching failed.

Following the Nicholson case, all CIA polygraph examiners were trained to recognize intentional attempts to beat the polygraph test. Despite websites that coach individuals on how to beat the test, we all caught them on a regular basis. These attempts ranged from tactics to penetrate the Agency for nefarious purposes, to young applicants who, for the thrill of it, wanted to see if they could beat the test. The training we all received, which I cannot discuss here, was exceptional and catching these people was relatively easy. All of them were immediately shown the door and can never apply to an intelligence agency again. My supervisor, whom I will call Mike D., a former Army CID examiner, and my co-worker, Henry M., also a former CID polygraph examiner, were extremely efficient at catching these sorts of people.

Attempting to beat the CIA polygraph test, despite what the internet pundits claim, is a silly thing to do, and only serves to document that the person cannot be trusted with our nation's most important secrets.

How the Polygraph Works

There are two questions most people ask about the polygraph test: What exactly is the polygraph test, and how does the polygraph instrument work? Webster's definition of the polygraph instrument is:

"Lie detector, n. 1. A polygraph for detecting physiological evidence (as change in heart rate) of the tension that accompanies lying."

First, it must be noted the polygraph instrument is not a "lie detector." The instrument does not detect lies; it simply monitors a subject's physiological responses during a specific set of questions. The polygraph's actual function is merely to monitor changes in the body's Autonomic Nervous System (ANS) activity. These physiological responses include changes in heart rate, blood pressure, respiration and skin conductivity. All these changes are signs of emotional arousal, not necessarily lying.

The polygraph instrument consists of three sets of components: two pneumatic tubes placed on the chest, which monitor changes in respiration; a medical blood pressure cuff, which monitors changes in blood pressure and heart rate; and a set of two finger plates attached to the fingers of one hand, which monitor Electro Dermal Activity (EDA) (formerly called Galvanic Skin Response, or GSR); electrical conductivity at the skin's subcutaneous level (see Figure 1).

Most polygraph examinations are now conducted using the new computerized polygraph system. Although the parameters are monitored via computer, the charts still must be scored by a trained examiner.

The polygraph examination consists of three major types of tests:

- The Guilty Knowledge test, or Peak of Tension test, consisting of questions to which only the guilty will react.
- The Zone Comparison Test, which compares responses of comparison questions with a significant issue question.
- The Relevant/Irrelevant Test, which compares responses to irrelevant questions with responses to significant issue questions. Many intelligence agencies use the Relevant/Irrelevant Test for applicant screening. These tests consist of a set of questions regarding the subject's lifestyle, or suitability, and a set of questions regarding counterintelligence. In my view, this is probably the most difficult test to administer and interpret because it is so broad in scope.

US military criminal investigation units largely use the Zone Comparison Test with relatively good success in ferreting out criminal activity. Law enforcement regularly uses the Guilty Knowledge Test. In my experience and based on studies I have read, the Guilty Knowledge Test is by far the most accurate polygraph test. It is the most focused and the easiest to administer. If all other tests are done away with in an organization, this is the one test that should remain and can withstand scientific scrutiny.

A Brief History of the Polygraph

The first attempts to discover technical methods to detect deception date back to the 1800s. Among the pioneers were Cesare Lomroso, who in 1895 used fluctuations in blood pressure to detect lying, Vittorio Benussi used variations in respiration as an indicator of deception in 1914, and after him William Marston used blood pressure, respiration and perspiration changes to detect deception. Marston was followed by John Larson, who developed an instrument to simultaneously monitor all three parameters. Finally, Leonard Keeler constructed the instrument that was the precursor to the modern polygraph instrument today. Modern polygraph procedures, question construction and chart scoring are the result of the work of John E. Reid, who is considered the father of modern polygraph.

Detecting Deception

Detecting deception can, at a more macro level, be observed through a person's body language as well. Studies show human communication is 65% nonverbal, 17% verbal, 12% voice quality, and 6% a mixture of interrelated chemical changes, body odors and miniscule variations too small to see with the naked eye. In fact, 90% of all of the decisions we make are based on emotion. We justify them with reason. Thus, nonverbal behavior communicates the majority of what we "tell," to use the poker player's term for reading behavior.

Although most people view lying as an immoral practice, lying is commonplace in our society. Parents lie to their children, adolescents lie to their parents, doctors lie to patients, teachers lie to students, husbands lie to wives, boyfriends lie to girlfriends and vice versa, clients lie to lawyers, witnesses lie to juries, salespeople lie to customers, and on and on it goes. This is an unfortunate reality of the human condition. Lying is a part of our society's culture.

Each of us displays a "psychological fingerprint." This fingerprint consists of four behavioral communication channels: nonverbal behavior; speech and words; voice quality; and "micro signals"—for example, fleeting facial expressions (a concept discovered by psychologist Paul Ekman).

In most normal people, deception causes stress, which is involuntarily displayed by the Autonomic Nervous System (ANS). There are 1,400 different responses involved in this process, including a complex chemical "dump" that occurs in the bloodstream.

Six negative stress responses are related to intentional deception: the fear/anxiety, or "flight" response; anger, or the "fight" response; depression, which is aggression turned inward; bargaining; disguising reality or trying to alter the other's opinion; and, acknowledgement— when the person is prepared to take responsibility for his or her actions.

Behavioral Clues to Lying

It is clear *behavioral clues will indicate the presence of the negative stress response.* These clues reveal themselves in behavioral "tells," as noted above. The signals show the presence of three stress response mechanisms. The first is the ANS physiological response, which is involuntary, uncontrollable, and results in dramatic changes in heart rate, blood pressure, body temperature, breathing and muscle tone.

The second behavioral clue is the emotional response, which is extremely difficult to control or falsify without overcompensating. And finally, the third behavioral tell is the cognitive response, which occurs when the person who is lying has to stall while he makes up a plausible lie in his mind, or obviously controls his responses as he thinks inwardly about how he is going to mislead the questioner without making a blunder. All of these activities generate observable behavioral activity. This is the same activity the polygraph instrument monitors on a much more micro scale.

Flight or Flight Response

A classic example of ANS activity generated by a person who is lying is the "fight or flight response." During this involuntary response, there are several changes that occur in the ANS. These changes result in an increase in heart rate (observed by flushed skin or pulsating arteries), respiration (observed by the increased raising and lowering of the chest), and perspiration (observed by an obvious increase of sweat on the upper lip, forehead and the palms of the hands). Other changes include pupil dilation (the involuntary widening of the dark center of the eye—the reason some poker players wear sunglasses), increase in blood flow to the capillaries in the surface of the skin (redness in the face, neck and upper chest), and tension in the visceral cavity muscles (affecting posture).

When people lie, they "leak." The involuntary ANS activity generated by conscious lying must leak out somewhere for the mind and body to gain relief. These leakage channels consist of the person's words and statements (incomplete or clipped words and sentences), the quality and pitch of the voice (usually higher during deception), the individual's body language (arms and legs crossed, body tilted towards the exit in an unconscious effort to flee, hiding the hands under the thighs or in the pockets, etc.), and written statements (adding or deleting certain words—for example, "I" or "we"—to attempt to avoid ownership of the issue).

Some polygraph parameters can be visually observed on the macro level by a trained eye. Increase in cardiac activity, respiration, perspiration and ANS-produced anxiety can be detected by a person who has mastered this skill and understands deception may be present if these changes happen when discussing a specific issue, while decreasing when the issue is changed. The polygraph simply records these changes more accurately, detecting changes smaller than can be seen by the naked eye, and using a computer program to amplify the signals picked up by the sensors.

The subject of detecting deception is a fascinating one and the topic of a large volume of research—too large to fully cover in this chapter. In a course I developed, titled the "Detection of Deception Seminar," I go into much more detail on the subject, covering sixteen hours of forensic psycho physiology.

Pre-Attack Recognition

As a result of my tours in the CIA/CIC, Counterterrorism Center (CTC) and Polygraph Division, I have developed a course titled "Criminal and Terrorist Behavioral Analysis and Attack Recognition." The research I conducted indicates trained observers, and potentially certain computer programs, can accurately read the ANS behavioral cues of a criminal or terrorist about to carry out a crime or an attack. I have used this technique successfully in the field, including large gatherings in sports stadiums for private clients. The material is too sensitive to describe in detail in this book (we do not want potential terrorists to have access to it). I am convinced it is an essential tool for law enforcement in crime prevention and in countering terrorist attacks. The information is available to counterterrorism, law enforcement and private security organizations by several credible professionals who are experts in this field.

In a variety of intelligence operations, detecting deception is critical. The CIA, FBI, Department of Defense, Department of Energy, and Department of State all gather intelligence of various types depending on their mission. It is extremely important that the veracity of, or the intentional deception by, the human source of the information is verified. In addition, part of detecting possible deception is examining the information provided by the source for validity and other external information surrounding the source, such as contacts, lifestyle, outside activities, etc.

In the case of the CIA, this could not be more important than in the evaluation of embassy walk-ins, or defectors. In the past, these defectors have provided both legitimate and false information. Federal agents dealing with these types of sources must be trained to be *experts* in the detection of deception and truth verification. The same applies to law enforcement officers conducting interrogations of subjects or debriefing witnesses. In these cases, the officer must have a distinct set of parameters he or she is trained to use to determine, with about an 80% certainty, the subject is being truthful or deceptive.

Finally, reporters conducting high-risk media interviews, such as the Susan Smith case involving the drowning of her children, must have these skills to assist them in making the decision whether or not to publish the interviewee's statements as truthful. In the Smith case, the reporter published her statements of innocence as fact when, in reality, Smith was guilty of the murders of her children. The indicators of Smith's deception were there in both her verbal statements and in her written accounts.

All of these examples point to the utility and value of expertise in detecting deception. As Shakespeare said, "All the world is a stage." A humorous sign posted in one of my CIA offices read, "Trust in God; polygraph everyone else." Our society is prone to falsity as a usual part of everyday life. In criminal and espionage cases, the purpose is nefarious and the consequences can be catastrophic.

Anxiety Response

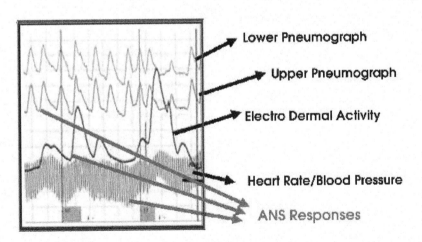

Figure 1: Computerized polygraph screen and psycho physiological responses the instrument monitors. These responses can also be detected by reading behavior, speech and body language at the macro level.

Chapter 13

Intuition and Reading/ Predicting Human Behavior

I was the advance agent on the protective detail of a member of Ronald Reagan's cabinet. The motorcade pulled into the Old Executive Office Building in Washington, D.C., and our agents escorted this official to a meeting with the President. As one of two agents responsible for the advance, the route of travel and protecting the motorcade upon its departure, it was my job to make sure our vehicle was in place and ready when the motorcade emerged.

Something inside me told me the agent driving the motorcade was going to depart from the building and take the wrong route. I requested the agent posted with me station another motorcade vehicle on the only other route the motorcade could take, in case the route of travel changed without notice. My co-worker thought I was being ridiculous and simply overreacting. The feeling I had was very strong. I again requested the agent post a second follow vehicle on the other route and he did so.

Sure enough, the motorcade emerged from the building and the agent driving took the wrong route without advising the advance team. We had the other car waiting, which picked up the motorcade and fell in as the follow car as if nothing was out of the ordinary. How did I know this? There was no conscious reason why I felt so strongly this was going to happen.

Years later, as I studied psychology and the subconscious mind relating to intuition, I realized my subconscious mind had fed me information from past assignments with the agent who was driving. No offense to him, of course, but there had been several times when he had not stuck to the predetermined motorcade or foot movements. That information had been processed by my subconscious mind and sent to my conscious mind as an alarm.

An identical incident occurred again with a high-risk official I was assigned to as a Team Leader for a movement in Washington. We placed a follow car at a location the senior Ops officers had not thought of. I just knew something was going to go wrong and it did, quickly and potentially disastrous. It was only because of the position of the follow car that we were able to stay with the official in a protective status during a very high threat operation.

This brings me to the discussion of a fascinating aspect of reading human behavior; intuition. For years intuition has been viewed as some sort of mystical force that only exists in the minds of the superstitious. Recent scientific studies have proven this is not the case. Intuition is a real and identifiable function of the human mind. It is the surfacing of a subconscious memory we misinterpret as a "feeling."

Intuition is a thought process that takes place at lightning speed in the subconscious mind. It is not mystical at all. It's really a huge, complex neurological database of information released in a flash when triggered by some sort of stimuli. Intuition is a natural function of our subconscious mind. Indeed, our subconscious mind controls over 90% of all we do during our daily activities. The conscious mind houses our morality, judgment, logical reasoning, subjectivity and awareness of self. The subconscious mind is a brain function that moves so fast our conscious mind cannot comprehend it.

During interaction between two or more human beings, there is a perpetual state of two-way communication, during which each party "leaks" behavioral information—such as emotion, attitude, amount of eye contact, body posture, tone of voice, speech patterns, etc. This information is rapidly fed into the subconscious mind, where it is stored for later use in the form of intuition.

How Intuition Works

Intuition is often called a "hunch," especially by law enforcement officers. Studies show this "hunch" is incredibly accurate. It is actually a rapid, millisecond processing of the surrounding environment, people and activities. These mental stimuli are compared and evaluated based on the huge stored database of past experiences. If something is wrong to the subconscious mind based on this stored information, an alarm is triggered and sent to the conscious mind. This is why veteran police officers are experts at spotting malevolent intent in individuals or potential danger in environmental surroundings. The more experience an officer has, the more data is stored in the subconscious. This subconscious thought is processed in a flash. Feelings based on intuition many times seem stronger than the immediate information before us. Those feelings are usually right. In this way, intuition assists in predicting human behavior. For example, a mother who has spent years with a child will know immediately if the child is lying to her.

The subconscious mind is essentially a huge amount of data stored on a "server" deep in the nervous system that processes the information with incredible speed, and in a very accurate fashion this "server" gathers information, stores it and retrieves it for use by the conscious mind.

Our subconscious mind will sound an alarm if we observe certain types of behavior; voice, posture, eye contact, appearance, tone of voice or body movements that have been associated with danger sometime in our past, going all the way back to early childhood. Honing your behavioral observation skills will improve this database housed deep within your subconscious mind.

Another personal example of intuition relates to the time I spent in ███████████████Bosnia, just after the Serbs unleashed their attack on ████████████I spent a lot of time closely working with the Bosnian government and several government and police personnel. They had been through an incredible amount of severe, long-term suffering. Back in the states, on several occasions I ran across an individual I had never seen before, but immediately knew he was from Bosnia. I could tell by the look in the person's eyes he had been there during what amounted to a holocaust. This happened in Detroit, Michigan, at a Domino's Pizza, and at a shopping center in Herndon, Virginia.

This was beyond my conscious thinking. I just knew it, strongly. When I asked them where they were from, sure enough I was right. In reality, my subconscious mind, full of data regarding the mannerisms, stance and especially the kind of sadness I had seen in people's eyes so many times during my time in ██████████████████had retrieved that data and sent it to my conscious mind. I didn't know quite how I could recognize these people, especially the ones that had suffered through the war, but I did and I verified it by asking them, with my co-worker standing there with me. It's quite amazing how the subconscious mind works.

A note of caution: be aware of your intuition, what it is and test it for accuracy. Intuition, like any other thought process, should be analyzed to make sure it is completely correct. Sometimes faulty information may have been fed into your subconscious memory. So, don't overlook your intuition, listen to what it is saying and verify its accuracy. Identify exactly what the "hunch" is and make sure it is bias free.

So, again, if you have a hunch about a person's voice quality, facial expressions, body movements, demeanor and/or the surrounding environment, pay close attention to it. If you have a strong sensing something is wrong, don't react too quickly; just be ready in case your intuition is right, which it is many times.

Experienced intelligence officers, counterintelligence officers and police officers are constantly receiving feedback from an individual's behavior, speech and voice. As any polygraph examiner will tell you, there are times when you know during the interview the Subject is lying and this is confirmed by the polygraph instrument and subsequent admissions made by the individual. There are times you will pick up deception in a conversation with a person without even thinking about what is going on consciously. There is a subconscious trigger.

Have you ever heard the phrase "a woman's intuition?" That's probably because it is true more often in women than in men. In our culture, women are given more freedom to access the database stored in their subconscious mind, which emerges as a feeling or emotion. Historically, women have practiced this from the time they were little. Men have been taught to "stuff it." It's amazing that, even in this context, intuition kicks into gear with men when they are approaching a dangerous situation.

My mother, Caroline Shipp, is one of the most classic cases of intuition I have ever seen. She will know when one of us is sick and will give us a call. When we were teenagers, we couldn't get away with anything. If we were out carousing with our buddies doing things we were not supposed to do, she would know about it. It was uncanny. For example, in 2009 she called to ask if my brother was OK after he had just come out of neck surgery he had not told her about. My brothers and I joke about this regularly. Mom has really developed the ability to intuitively read situations, and she caught us several times up to no good while we were growing up.

In summary, listen to your "gut feeling," especially in potentially dangerous situations. If you are a woman and have been asked out on a date or approached by a man who causes a sense something is wrong – don't do it! If you are with your family and are driving or walking through a neighborhood and you sense something is wrong, don't go there. If you are in a business deal and you sense your contact is deceiving you, listen to your intuition. Practice listening to this lightning fast retrieval of data, learn how to analyze it for accuracy and how to appropriately act on it. It could save your life.

Chapter 14

Attack on America

It was August 7, 1998. At approximately 10:30 a.m. a truck loaded with 1,500 pounds of TNT was detonated by suicide terrorists in the parking lot of the US embassy in Nairobi, Kenya. More than 200 people were killed; twelve of them Americans. Four minutes later, a second truck loaded with explosives was detonated outside the American embassy in Dar es Salaam, Tanzania. The blast killed eight people. Al Qaeda had begun the first of its large-scale attacks in the global Jihadist war against the United States. Twin bombings would become the modus operandi of an Al Qaeda operation.

Security at the embassy in Nairobi was poor. The building was located at one of the busiest intersections in the capital city, with no protection from the blast. There were no security devices in place to protect the building and its parking lot was also used by two adjoining commercial companies, the Cooperative Bank House and the Ufundi Cooperative Building.

Embassy security was contracted to a security company that employed local, unarmed guards. There was no embassy security control of the shared parking lot. Parking lot security was also provided by a private company contracted by the bank in the adjacent building. The security guards were poorly trained and paid paltry salaries.

The suicide bombers driving the truck altered the suspension so the vehicle could carry heavy explosives without being detected. A tarp covered the TNT. The attackers drove the truck over the curb aiming at the exit lane from the shared parking lot. A guard posted at the exit lane did nothing. A barrier, designed to protect the exit lane from entry, had not yet been installed, and the bombers were able to drive the truck into the parking lot.

A security guard, who observed the truck jump the curb, lowered the barrier to the underground parking garage. One suicide bomber immediately jumped out of the truck and ordered the guard to raise the barrier. The guard refused and the bomber threw a hand held Improvised Explosive Device (IED) at him. The bomber missed and threw a second bomb as the security guard ran around the corner of building. Another guard, hearing the ensuing chaos, locked the steel gates to the underground garage. The two suicide bombers, still in the truck stuck in the parking lot, set off the main charge. The explosion leveled the Ufundi building and destroyed the outer and middle structures of the US embassy.

Immediately after the US embassy suicide bombings, I was assigned to the newly created CIA/CTC Fusion Center. The Fusion Center had been created to be a central information conduit for all US intelligence and defense agencies to funnel information related to the bombings to the US government for immediate sharing, analysis and dissemination.

1998 Nairobi embassy bombing

Nissan Atlas truck similar to that used against US Embassy, Dar es-Salaam

The Fusion Center was an impressive operation to observe. For the first time in my experience working for US intelligence, I was part of an impressive, efficient (albeit stressful) and vibrant counterterrorism effort bringing all the US entities of intelligence and defense together. The Fusion Center and its approach appeared to be the answer to US agencies' inability to work together and share information. Classified and unclassified documents, secure and non-secure telephone calls, e-mails and hand delivered information poured into the Fusion Center in a constant, rapid twenty-four-hour stream.

The sheer outrage caused by attacks on US embassies and the loss of life brought US intelligence and defense together for one brief moment in history. Unfortunately, three short years later, the fusion concept had broken down. US intelligence agencies, primarily the CIA and the FBI, were once again refusing to disseminate vital intelligence to each other. Shortly thereafter, the 9/11 attacks occurred, due in part to a lack of sharing and acting on existing intelligence information, that could have possibly prevented the attacks.

The fusion center concept has since been adopted by other counterterrorism organizations, such as the New York Police Department (NYPD). The new technique of intelligent policing and the creation of law enforcement fusion centers are growing steadily in the US. In the case of the NYPD counter terrorism unit, its efficiency has exceeded that of the Department of Homeland Security. During NYPD's response to 9/11, politics, turf protecting, and bureaucratic laziness were all put aside and the counterterrorism mission placed as a priority. NYPD's management and officers had personally felt the pain and loss of their own officers during the 9/11 attacks. Political delays could simply no longer be tolerated [A point worth noting is, because intelligence fusion involves the collection of information from multiple sources, privacy and civil rights concerns must be addressed and adequately balanced].

The CIA and the New Global Jihad

Global terrorism, essentially a multi-tentacled World War IV (if you count the Cold War as World War III), began with the rise of Ayatollah Khomeini. The unpopular US-supported Shah of Iran was overthrown by the Iranian people in a violent coup. The people of Iran saw the government of the Shah as a rich, hedonistic dictatorship, which ignored the needs of the ordinary masses. While US intelligence slept, Khomeini took control of Iran and declared global Jihad against the United States and Israel.

US intelligence did not take the threats of global Jihad seriously. Khomeini's violent brand of Islam rapidly spread across the world, creating silent radical Islamic groups preparing themselves for battle. Only a few years later, the United States had underestimated the ability of these groups to stage a successful attack against the US, especially on American soil. Despite pieces of information gained, but not shared, by different parts of the US Intelligence Community and specific warnings by other foreign intelligence services, the threat of global terrorism had not been realized by the US.

By the time the danger was understood, it was too late. Attacks against the United States began to materialize with fury, eventually culminating in 9/11, the greatest intelligence failure in US history, trumping Pearl Harbor.

Events leading up to the 9/11 attack bore several similarities to the Japanese attack on Pearl Harbor. In 1947 the CIA was founded by President Harry S. Truman in response to the 1941 Pearl Harbor attack. Prior to that attack, there was significant credible intelligence indicating an attack by the Japanese was imminent. Failures in disseminating and analyzing information resulted in one of the worst domestic attacks in US history and a significant loss of life.

Despite intelligence failures involved in the attack, there was significant American opposition to the creation of a secret intelligence organization. Many government officials were concerned it could evolve into a kind of Gestapo. The FBI, the Department of Defense and the Department of State all considered the CIA a competitor and a threat to their authority. This climate of distrust lasted fifty-four years, continuing all the way up to the 9/11 attacks.

Sixty years after Pearl Harbor, the impetus for the creation of the CIA, the same errors in intelligence occurred again, with a similar, but more horrific loss of American life, this time civilians. Similar to Pearl Harbor, there was credible intelligence available to conclude an attack on US soil was imminent; information that could possibly have prevented the attack.

The CIA had become a huge monolith structured to confront the Soviet global threat. Sadly, after the fall of the Soviet Union, not only was the Agency in total disarray, with morale at an all-time low, but it did not have the functional capability to go after an amorphous enemy such as global terrorism. It was in serious need of redesign. Unfortunately, because of intense internal resistance to change, and political pressure from the executive branch, redesign never took place, in part paving the way for 9/11.

Errors before a Catastrophe

Both the CIA and the FBI made serious errors in their analysis of possible terrorist attacks on American soil. The CIA failed to analyze the potential of airliners being used as flying bombs. This was despite concrete intelligence regarding the famous 1995 Bojinka plot, which was engineered by Ramsi Yousef, the same man who masterminded the 1993 attack on the World Trade Center. Yousef developed a complex plan to attack targets in the US, which included the Pentagon, Wall Street and CIA headquarters itself.

In addition, Philippine intelligence provided the CIA with information indicating Yousef was also planning to hijack and explode eleven US airliners, with 4,000 passengers aboard, traveling from Asia to the US. The CIA was unable to uncover the connection between Al Qaeda leader Osama Bin Laden, his deputy Ayman al-Zawahiri, and Ramzi Yousef.

The relationship between the architect of the 1993 World Trade Center bombing, Khalid Sheik Mohammad, and Al Qaeda was never examined. The CIA had also been provided reports that Sheik Mohammad was sending terrorists to attack targets within the US on orders from Bin Laden. The fact that Ramsi Yousef was a cousin of Sheik Mohammad was overlooked.

The CIA had information connecting Sheik Mohammad's plans to use airplanes during terrorist attacks, information indicating he was planning attacks on US soil and he had direct connections to Al Qaeda. Foreign intelligence services were providing the CIA with regular information warning of an attack on US soil, but none of this information was taken seriously. ████████████████ warned the CIA just prior to 9/11 that terrorists were planning to hijack aircraft for use as weapons against the US.

████████████ issued a warning to the FBI and the CIA that Al

Qaeda was planning an attack on US targets. ███████████ intelligence warned the CIA that Bin Laden had engaged in discussions with the Taliban regarding hijacking US commercial aircraft. FBI agents in Phoenix, Arizona, had reported to the CIA that several Arab individuals were seeking flight training, including instruction on how to fly large commercial aircraft. The CIA conducted no analysis of this information.

The FBI field office in Minneapolis, Minnesota, briefed the CIA on the flight training attempts of Zacharias Moussaoui and briefed the DCI on the attempts of "Islamic Extremists" to learn how to fly. No warning was issued by the CIA Director or other Agency officials. In addition, a report provided to the Intelligence Community by the Library of Congress warned Al Qaeda suicide bombers had the capability to fly aircraft loaded with explosives into the Pentagon.

Prior to 9/11, officers from the CIA, FBI, and NSA (which had collected several communication intercepts that pointed directly to 9/11, but never communicated these to the rest of the Intelligence Community) had access to cable traffic documenting the travels of the two Al Qaeda hijackers, al-Hamzi and al-Mihdhar, but none of these agencies contacted the others to analyze the information. Although the CIA knew about the presence of the two operatives, it did not turn the information over to the FBI until just a few weeks before the attacks. The FBI, when it received the information, did not act on it.

Although these hijackers had associated themselves with an FBI informant, the FBI was not monitoring their activity. The CIA also neglected to notify the Department of State that al-Mihdhar was in possession of a multiple-entry visa to the US, should have been placed on a watch list and should have been prevented from re-entering the country.

After 9/11, I went back and read the Department of State's assessment of the 1993 World Trade Center (WTC) bombing. It was chilling. When taken together with the above warning signs, a second attempt at the WTC was obvious. Even previous terrorist attacks and basic common sense made it clear that if Al Qaeda failed to complete an attack on a high value target, it would return to finish the job. Thousands of Americans went back to their offices in the WTC under the assurances from the government they were safe. Nothing could have been farther from the truth.

Because the CIA had no focus on Al Qaeda and no penetrations of its organization, no assessment of Al Qaeda was prepared. Congressional intelligence oversight committees did not see the need to hold hearings on the existence of terrorism. No warnings were issued to the White House regarding a possible attack on the United States. America's intelligence and counterterrorism apparatus was under-funded, disjointed and asleep at the switch. In addition, the Agency focused all of its attention on terrorist attacks against US interests abroad and did not consider the likelihood of a domestic attack. FBI reports indicated Al Qaeda was not sophisticated enough and did not possess the logistics and resources necessary to carry out an attack on American soil. In the years leading up to 9/11, there was no collection and analysis of information regarding the potential of turning airliners into weapons and there was inadequate information collected and analyzed regarding Al Qaeda's plans to attack the United States.

To summarize, the NSA had collected several communication intercepts that pointed directly to 9/11, but never communicated these to the rest of the Intelligence Community. The CIA had information that two of the 9/11 hijackers had entered the US in January of 2000 but failed to place the individuals on the terrorist watch list until just before the 9/11 attacks. Although these hijackers had associated themselves with an FBI informant, the FBI was not able to monitor their activity.

During the subsequent investigation by the 9/11 Commission, the FBI, Department of Defense and Department of State declassified their reports for review by the panel and the American public. The CIA refused to declassify reports delineating its failures prior to 9/11. The need for review of information that led to the attack was critical in preventing it from ever happening again. Apparently, to the CIA, this did not matter. What mattered most was, once again, protecting the organization's negligence under the guise of "secrecy."

In short, the 9/11 tragedy was the result of the same historical disparity between the CIA and the FBI. It was the failure of the entire Intelligence Community to work together, actively sharing information; a total departure from the fusion center concept.

Turmoil Within

As mentioned earlier, during the Cold War, the CIA had become a giant, secretive monolith built to confront the Soviet threat. After the fall of Soviet Communism, the Agency was in serious disarray. Entire divisions, along with their staffs were being cut from the organization. Employees were being told in meetings their jobs might be in jeopardy as the CIA cut programs tied to the Soviet threat.

With morale at its lowest point ever, infighting and back-channel attempts to save careers, at the expense of others, were intense. The giant structure that had been built since 1947, and flourished under the Reagan administration, could not adequately deal with the growing threat of global Jihadist cells.

In the midst of the CIA's turmoil caused by the change in its mission, the drawing down of entire divisions and attempts to restructure the organization to meet the new threat of terrorism, multicultural diversity training and sexual harassment courses became a central focus of the Agency's operation. Overlooking the real value of true diversity, especially in an organization with an international mission, the Agency began creating pseudo-diversity assemblies under pressure from groups inside and outside the organization.

The CIA began allowing multiple, internal racial and ethnic groups to have tacit authority to promote the advancement of their members by putting pressure on CIA management, career panels, etc. These groups began demanding promotion of their members based on status in the group, rather than merit. Some of the groups began to oppose each other. CIA employees who had earned promotions through high performance, but did not fit into a particular "diversity group," were denied promotions based on this reason alone.

The CIA had become divided. High level positions that once required the successful completion of high standards mentioned earlier were changed and those requirements dropped to allow for the commanded demographical change. The CIA no longer possessed the employee unity it had while defending America against the real threat of communist expansion. Focus on the intelligence mission, especially counterterrorism, began to wane. The CIA was becoming weak.

In 1995, I wrote an essay on real multicultural diversity, the kind of diversity our Constitution and Bill of Rights protect, and the false diversity occurring at CIA headquarters. I placed the article titled, "Will the Real Multicultural Diversity Please Stand Up," in an Agency unclassified, open discussion database. The article caused a barrage of responses. Postings regarding the article set an all-time record in the internal discussion site. Ninety-nine percent of the responses were supportive and expressed appreciation for putting into words what the vast majority of CIA employees, of all races and ethnic groups, were feeling. The database was shut down one month later.

Essentially, the CIA had divided its workforce into opposing groups, granting or withholding promotions for reasons other than EEO-based merit, and its internal operations were being weakened in the process. Multitudes of managers, case officers and security officers had left the organization because of this impact on morale and career potential.

While this and confusion over restructuring were going on, the CIA had paid little attention to the rising global jihadist movement, and CIA analysts reached the mistaken conclusion that radical groups were merely fronts for Soviet aggression—so they could not exist without Russian sponsorship. While the CIA continued to operate via this conclusion, jihadist groups all over the world began to develop and begin operations.

Because of US government actions, and primarily CIA operations occurring in Africa and the Middle East, fundamentalist Islamic groups were convinced the US government was bent on the conquest of the Muslim world. While the CIA failed to realize this perception, these groups mobilized themselves, preparing for a global war against the "crusaders and infidels."

The 9-11 World Trade Center attack. Warnings after the 1993 attack were ignored.

Chapter 15

Backfire: 9/11 and the Loss of American Freedoms

Just forty-five days after the 9/11 attacks, President George W. Bush signed the US Patriot Act into law. The Patriot Act gave more sweeping powers to the federal government. The document was 342 pages long and filled with complex legal technical jargon that amended over twelve federal laws. Most congressional representatives commented they did not even read the massive document before passing it.

Members of Congress and their constituents, the American people, had no idea the act contained legislation that turned the CIA, the FBI and the INS into what amounted to be a secret police. The definition of "terrorism" was so broad it could include political dissenters (groups that are working for change for political or ideological reasons) that use a broad definition of "force" to further their cause. This definition could include nailing a protest poster to a courthouse, participating in a picket line, engaging in anti-abortion protests, taxpayer protests, protests staged by environmental organizations such as Greenpeace, and political actions by the National Rifle Association.

The most appalling aspect of the Patriot Act was the power given to the government to conduct "sneak and peek" searches of American homes and businesses. Government agents were now able to enter citizen's homes, examine all their personal documents, search their computer files, look through their possessions and take possession of files and documents, without a warrant and without ever notifying them they had been there.

After claiming this portion of the act was never used, under pressure from Congress, the federal government admitted to engaging in these searches approximately forty-seven times. Under further pressure, the number went up to two thousand. Finally, the FBI claimed it was not certain of the number of times the searches had been done.

In addition to searching your home, federal agents could now secretly access your financial records, education records, Internet provider's records, bookstores, video stores and credit information—as long as the government could assert the search was related to a terrorism investigation under the broad definition given. All the agent had to claim to the public holders of this information was they were conducting "a terrorism investigation." Your financial institution or school could not tell you the records were accessed *without facing criminal prosecution.* These document searches and seizures could be targeted at private businesses as well. Company management, as well as all the holders of your business and personal information, had to turn the records over and were bound by the act from notifying you.

Another power under the Patriot Act is allowing the government to conduct roving wiretaps. Any judge can authorize federal agents to wiretap an individual's cell phone, telephone line, Internet connections and e-mail system to follow that person, even if the individual's name is not disclosed. This is called a "Doe" target. All that is necessary is for the government to label you as a "terrorist." Using the new FBI data mining system known as Carnivore, the FBI can search all of your electronic forms of communication using this Internet spying tool.

Thus, the Patriot Act gutted important provisions in the US Bill of Rights. It also violated the fourth Amendment of the Constitution by authorizing secret searches and seizures. In the words of Senator Russell Feingold (D-Wisc.), we will lose the war on terrorism "without firing a shot if we sacrifice the liberties of the American people."

The original provisions of the Patriot Act expired in 2009. Led by Senator Russ Feingold, a request from the White House to extend the sweeping powers of the Act was delayed for two months. In a vote of 95-4, a bipartisan debate was ended and a new version of the act was approved. The bill made most of the laws in the act permanent. However, two sections of the act and a third section that is part of the intelligence reform law of 2004 expired in 2009.

Changes that brought most of the opponents of the bill to agreement were:

- Entities that receive secret court orders to turn over information on an American citizen cannot disclose those orders, but can challenge the seal on the information after a year
- Libraries, including those offering Internet access, do not have to turn over records to the FBI without the approval of a judge
- Recipients of the FBI's "national security letter," demanding personal information on an individual or business would not have to disclose the requested information to the FBI if they consult a lawyer
- Unlike the original act, subjects of no-notice "sneak and peek" searches must be notified within 30 days after the search

Senator Feingold, still opposing the powers given to the government that remain in the act, commented the changes in the bill were "nowhere near enough." Other senators, such as John Sununu (R-NH) called the changes "significant steps forward." Sununu claimed several senators opposed the Patriot Act, but backed down from confronting the White House.

Since the passage of the Patriot Act, 234 cities, towns and counties have passed their own resolutions, ballot initiatives or local ordinances prohibiting their local police from complying with the Patriot Act.

Government Holds Secret Interpretation of the Patriot Act

In 2011, Senators, Ron Wyden (D-OR) and Mark Udall (D-CO) began warning the government is using a secret legal interpretation of the Patriot Act. This interpretation is so broad it amounts to a law totally different than the one revealed to the public. "There is a significant discrepancy between what most Americans – including many members of Congress – think the Patriot Act allows the government to do and how government officials interpret that same law," wrote Senators Wyden and Udall. "We believe that most members of the American public would be very surprised to learn how federal surveillance law is being interpreted in secret." The Senators have been prevented from specifying what aspects of this secret Patriot Act have them seriously concerned. Information surrounding their protests indicates some of their concerns involve the "business-records provision" of the Patriot Act. This provision gives the FBI extensive power to force medical offices, banks, businesses and other organizations to turn over all "tangible things" it claims are relevant to a security investigation. If the organization reveals it has turned this information over, it can face criminal prosecution. Wyden and Udall continued, "In our view, the executive branch's decision to conceal the U.S. government's official understanding of what this law means is unacceptable, and untenable in the long run. . . . Intelligence agencies need to have the ability to conduct secret operations, but they should not be allowed to rely on secret laws."

The Senators introduced an amendment to compel the Director of National Intelligence and the Attorney General to provide a "detailed assessment of the problems posed by the reliance of government agencies on interpretations of domestic surveillance authorities that are inconsistent with the understanding of such authorities by the public."

The Senate Select Committee on Intelligence, overseen by Vice Chairman Senator Saxby Chambliss (R-GA), rejected an amendment by Wyden requiring the Justice Department to estimate how many American citizens the US government has eavesdropped on in violation of the Foreign Intelligence Surveillance Act (FISA) Amendments of 2008.

Senator Ron Wyden (D-OR).

Senator Mark Udall (D-CO).

Senator Saxby Chambliss (R-GA),
Vice Chairman, Senate Select
Committee on Intelligence.

Authority and 'No Limits'

Immediately following the attacks of 9/11, President Bush anointed the CIA with unthinkable authority. The Agency was given the go-ahead to kidnap suspects, also known as, "rendition," even on the soil of allied countries and without that country's knowledge; then turn the suspects over to foreign intelligence services, who engaged in severe torture and interrogation. No limits were set on what the CIA could do, including establishing secret prisons in foreign countries without the consent of the local government.

The Agency began to function as the organization feared by opponents of its creation after Pearl Harbor; a global military police organization. Thousands of "suspects" were "snatched and grabbed" in over a hundred foreign countries and incarcerated in secret prisons. Hundreds of these individuals had no important connections to Al Qaeda.

As noted above, the CIA had now been given legal powers to spy on American citizens. It could read secret Grand Jury testimony without a judge's approval and collect private information or "intelligence" on citizens, businesses and financial institutions. The CIA had been given authority to spy on US citizens for the first time in American history. The traditional constraints which permitted the Agency to spy only on non-US citizens or foreign governments had been removed.

General Hayden, Director of the NSA, submitted a plan to use the NSA's massive resources to eavesdrop on suspected terrorists within the United States without a warrant. On October 4, 2001, the President ordered Hayden to execute the plan. Now both the CIA and the NSA were spying within the United States.

The most chilling aspect of the CIA's new sweeping powers was the proposal by its Assistant Director of Intelligence, James Monneir Simon, Jr. Simon proposed to Attorney General John Ashcroft that a national identity card be created and required for every American citizen. This card would contain the individual's fingerprint, specially digitized photograph, retinal scan, voice sample and a sample of DNA. Because of the possibility of Americans' losing the card, the proposal was made to insert the microchip into the person's body. Fortunately for us all, this chip concept never materialized. The fact that a senior CIA official proposed this to the White House was a signal of the dangerous lengths the CIA was willing to go with its new powers.

In addition to its newly acquired control, the CIA continued to use huge amounts of taxpayer dollars to run its new operations. Millions were handed out to Afghanistan and Iraqi sources. No accounting of these expenditures was made to Congress or the American people. The Agency had managed to keep its budget secret and hidden its activities, even from the Government Accountability Office.

Finally, the Department of Homeland Security (DHS) had been attempting to gain approval from Congress to use Intelligence Community spy satellites to surveil individuals within the US for law enforcement purposes. DHS Secretary Michael Chertoff briefed members of Congress on the program on February 13, 2008. According to a Congressional memorandum to Chertoff dated April 7, 2008, Chertoff advised the charter for the National Applications Office (NAO) would be completed in a week. When Congress received the charter, it did not contain any Standard Operating Procedures or the legal framework Congress had recommended to protect the privacy and civil liberties of Americans. The NAO had already begun advertising to fill positions in the organization. The charter had been finalized without any input from the Congressional Committee on Homeland Security, the Government Accountability Office or the "privacy and civil liberties community." Eventually, news programs reported the Attorney General had decided to scrap the proposal.

President Harry S. Truman. As a result of the Pearl Harbor attacks, Truman established the CIA in the midst of strong opposition from the FBI and Department of State.

Lt. General Hoyt S. Vandenberg, first Director of Central Intelligence and one driving force behind the creation of the CIA.

Senator Russ Feingold (D-Wisc.)

Chapter 16

Countering Terror

I spent my last years at the CIA in the Counterintelligence Center (CIC), Counterterrorism Center (CTC) and as a Polygraph Examiner. In these positions I witnessed the rapidly-growing specter and global expansion of Jihadi terrorism. Ayatollah Khomeini had unified hatred against the west, especially the USA. His particular brand of revolutionary and murderous Islam had spread rapidly throughout the world.

As a Counterintelligence officer I witnessed repeated attempts by Iran and other countries to penetrate US intelligence and steal US secrets. Most concerning was reports that began to indicate the surveillance gathering and intelligence operations of Iran were as good as those in the west. To make matters worse, a new, well-funded enemy had just arrived on the global scene: Osama Bin Laden. It was clear Iran was sharing its surveillance and operational techniques with terrorist organizations. It was also providing them with materials and funding.

Osama Bin Laden personified how CIA operations can breed their own later failures. The CIA trained the Afghanistan Mujahedeen in guerilla warfare, supplied them with military equipment and arms, and most notably, stinger missiles. The CIA claims the Mujahedeen tribe it trained was a different tribe than the one Bin Laden was part of, a statement so ridiculous it is almost funny, if it were not so tragic.

When the Afghanistan war was over, there is no question the Mujahedeen, and probably Bin Laden himself, used CIA training, arms and equipment to turn on their trainers, the CIA and the US government. Several Stinger missiles supplied to the Mujahedeen were missing and cannot be accounted for to this day. It is apparent some of these missiles may have wound up in the hands of Iran.

The Soviet Union had been defeated in Afghanistan. In doing so, we had created an enemy that was just as lethal and did not play by the rules of nuclear Mutually Assured Destruction (MAD) or any other political deterrent. This new enemy was bent on world conquest, even if it included self destruction.

As a Counter Terrorism ████████████████ Team member, I learned how sophisticated terrorist groups were becoming. They were now being trained by state sponsors and provided funding from other countries determined to see the destruction of the US and its allies. Their primary modus operandi, before and after each attack, is conducting surveillance. They were becoming very professional at it. However, this is also their chief weakness and one the US government, police departments and American citizens need to be aware of and exploit. There are many good surveillance detection training programs offered by government and private security organizations.

One of my functions while visiting overseas embassies was training all embassy personnel in methods of detecting the various types of terrorist surveillance. The more US government and private industry employees, and US citizens, who understand these concepts; the more pairs of eyes we have detecting terrorist activity before it occurs.

Indonesia: The New Al Qaeda Front

Following my days at the CIA, I was appointed as the Program Manager for the Department of State, Diplomatic Security, Antiterrorism Assistance (DOS/DS/ATA) program in Indonesia. Later, I became corporate Program Manager for all global ATA training programs.

Indonesia, the only Muslim democracy in the world, is a fascinating country and an important ally of the US. I took over the Indonesia Antiterrorism program just after the suicide bombings at the Jakarta Marriott and Paddy's Pub in Bali. It was becoming clear that, with the loss of Afghanistan, Al Qaeda and other groups were migrating to Indonesia and the Philippines for training and to carry out attacks. This was becoming the new front in the war against terror.

In Indonesia the Al Qaeda backed Jemaah Islamaiya (JI) group was now organized and carrying out operations. JI was structured and led by Dr. Azahari Husin, an engineer and explosives expert, and Nordin Top, a charismatic figure and chief JI recruiter.

During my visits to Indonesia, I became good friends with the Chief of the Bali Counterterrorism Unit (C/CT). I am withholding his name for his protection. He was a Muslim and a good friend of the US. The Bali bombings were a classic Al Qaeda technique; the detonation of one suicide bomb, and as people ran from the explosion, the detonation of another. It was a horrible act of murder. The bombings killed 202 people, many of them Australians.

Memorial site at the original location of Paddy's Pub in Bali, Indonesia.

The suicide bombers used a Mitsubishi L300 van loaded with explosives.

Memorial containing the list of victims killed in the Bali attack.

The Bali C/CT and I had lengthy discussions about suicide bombers and their modus operandi. With the assistance of ATA training and a professional Indonesian CRT unit, his team was able to locate and kill Azahari, thereby seriously crippling the JI. After the operation succeeded, I received a jubilant message from him stating they had achieved their mission and neutralized Azahari. I heartily congratulated him on his successful mission. He and his team certainly deserved it. The Indonesians are, without question, one of our closest Muslim allies in the global war against terror and their units were always the most fulfilling students to train.

Suicide Bombers

My days in CTC and the ATA program provided me with insight into the latest successful and deadly weapon in the hands of modern terrorists. This weapon is the suicide bomber. Suicide bombers are, in effect, smart bombs. They are walking explosives with human brains. They can use reason to plan their attack, change plans if they perceive detection, dress and look like their targets and need no escape plan.

Azahari bin Husin, Jemaah Islamiyah technical mastermind and bomb engineer behind the 2004 Australian embassy bombing and the 2002 and 2005 Bali Bombings.

Noordin Mohammend Top, Key Jemaah Islamiyah bomb maker, fancier and recruiter

Most suicide bombers have been taught from the time they started walking to hate the west. Psychologists will tell you what a child learns from ages one to six will stay with the person for the rest of his or her life. This is reinforced throughout their education and radical religious training. In essence, they are sociopaths. Their training is intentionally void of any morals outside of their radical theology. They will use children, women and even persons with Down's syndrome to act as what are called "mules" to carry explosives, without knowing they will be remotely detonated when they reach the target. Al Qaeda and related groups also recruit widows with no hope of a future, the poor and destitute and youths who feel they have no future outside of pleasing their handler and conducting a suicide operation.

Al Qaeda has perverted the Koran (transliteration of Quran or Qur'an), which decries suicide, twisted Islam's teachings and led certain groups of people to believe suicide is "martyrdom." I explain more about suicide bombers and the religious motivations behind them in Chapter 18.

Suicide bombers, on foot, in vehicles and, as we have seen so horribly, in planes, represent the most serious threat to the US in the war on terror. The US and, especially our Muslim friends, must attack the problem at its root first; that is, aggressively eliminating the teaching of religious murder in madrasahs and other schools. This violation of the Koran's prohibition of suicide must be publicly exposed. Democratic countries must use humanitarian aid to counter the Al Qaeda lie that the West is stealing their futures.

US and allied counterterrorism forces must continue to develop mechanisms for interrupting suicide missions in the planning phases and detecting the actual attacks before they occur. Finally, American citizens need to be aware of good, basic surveillance detection skills to aid law enforcement in detection. In my next book *A Million Pairs of Eyes. The Personal Guide to Spotting Terrorism* I present many of these surveillance detection techniques.

The Author (center) on an antiterrorism team.
(Photo courtesy of the Author)

The Author's sleeping companions during antiterrorism assignments. (Photo courtesy of the Author)

The Author preparing firearms for an antiterrorism assignment. (Photo courtesy of the Author)

Photo of the Author teaching a university course on terrorist crime scenes. *(Photo courtesy of the Author)*

The Author teaching tactical firearms in an austere environment. *(Photo Courtesy of the Author)*

The Author as an antiterrorism tactical firearms instructor. *(Photo courtesy of the Author)*

Chapter 17

The Rise of Al Qaeda

"We—with God's help—call on every Muslim who believes in God and wishes to be rewarded to comply with God's orders to kill the Americans and plunder their money..."
—Osama Bin Laden

Eventually, the US Intelligence Community began to find Al Qaeda was not a small band of terrorists operating only on the purse strings of Osama Bin Laden. A larger picture began to unfold; Al Qaeda had set up a global network of associated terrorist groups, guerilla groups, cells planted in multiple countries and Islamic organizations that, on the outside, appear to be legitimate Muslim educational organizations or charities, but are a sophisticated part of the organization. These Al Qaeda networks include associated groups that share the organization's goals for global Jihad and function as Islamic societies located in Muslim communities in several countries around the world.

There are approximately seven million radical Muslims in the world today. Many of them are prepared for armed global Jihad, including mass murder. As noted previously, countering this type of decentralized structure is extremely difficult using the previous cold war structure of the CIA. In addition, because of years of failing to anticipate the threat, the CIA has not been able to recruit and retain officers fluent in Arabic, Farsi and other languages necessary to penetrate these organizations and analyze the huge amounts of communications intercepts that come in daily. Because of its de-centralized structure, Al Qaeda can react rapidly to attacks that dismantle one of its nodes or front organizations and "grow" new cells at an alarming rate. This is much like some species of spiders or sea cucumbers; cut off one appendage and the organism simply grows another.

Al Qaeda is the offshoot of the "Muslim Brotherhood" and converted this organization's political agenda of global Jihad into defined operational activity. A significant reason the cells of this entity are difficult to penetrate is the fact that they operate through family relationships. These relationships are extremely close and the results of disobedience could result in death. Recruitment is usually done from within families, friends and those of the same nationality attending local mosques. Members of Al Qaeda who are not part of the immediate family are, like in the Muslim Brotherhood, referred to as "brothers." This family/brotherhood bond extends to other organizations around the world with the same Muslim Jihadist beliefs.

CIA Statement on the Muslim Brotherhood

On February 10, 2011 during a hearing on Capitol Hill, Director of National Intelligence James Clapper testified that the Muslim Brotherhood "has pursued social ends" and "betterment of the political order." Clapper downplayed the Brotherhoods radical religious underpinnings. He went on to say, "The term 'Muslim Brotherhood'… is an umbrella term for a variety of movements, in the case of Egypt, a very heterogeneous group, largely secular, which has eschewed violence and has decried Al Qaeda as a perversion of Islam."

Counter terrorism experts around the world were stunned at Clapper's statements, which demonstrated a serious lack of intelligence and simple understanding of the Muslim Brotherhood. Apparently, Clapper and the CIA had missed the Brotherhoods' public statements regarding its ultimate goal of overturning Western governments and the establishment of a global Islamic caliphate. Clapper's statements forced the Obama administration to later correct his claim that the Muslim Brotherhood is "secular."

The brotherhood connection is the bond that enables Al Qaeda to survive, reorganize, morph into a new cell after an attack and gain the necessary funding and international logistics the overall organization needs. This international network, or brotherhood, gives Al Qaeda huge resources with which to operate. Resources come from some state actors, personal donations, donations from Mosques and large donations from Islamic charities, including several in the US. Al Qaeda can function in the United States, North Africa, Russia, East Africa, Europe and Canada with the same flexibility.

Al Qaeda can even farm out its different operational needs to different geographical cells. For example, one cell in a certain country can generate false documents, such as passports and credit cards, another can handle training new members of the organization and another can supply the funds needed for operations.

Former Al Qaeda Deputy Chief, now leader of the organization, Ayman al-Zawahiri designed the current cell structure for Al Qaeda operations. Cells are designed to be small, anywhere from two to fifteen members. Cell members are given only the operational information they need to know for an attack, and nothing more. Thus, if a cell is raided and the members interrogated, they will not know the larger plans of the attack. Many times cell leaders do not even know the identity of their direct reports. Cells are typically separate from others in the organization and members of cells do not communicate with each other. In many cases they do not even know the other cell exists.

Al Qaeda operations are much like those of an intelligence organization. It uses an agent recruiting, handling and deployment mechanism much like other state intelligence services. It is possible they have, indeed, been trained by formal intelligence organizations from countries such as Iran. In these Al Qaeda operations, an agent handler is at the top of the chain of command. The cell leader reports to this handler, who is residing in the local area. The handler reports to a senior member of the organization, usually not living near the attack site. Upon receipt of orders from the organization, the handler activates the cell leader who proceeds to deploy members of the cell for surveillance, target identification, or the actual attack itself.

As noted, Al Qaeda has developed a system of agent recruitment, handling and deployment similar to, and as efficient as, modern intelligence organizations. This includes intelligence sections within the overall organization. Agents have been tasked with penetrating local government establishments, security forces, police departments and military organizations. Al Qaeda relies heavily on gaining the support of the local Muslim communities to provide assistance for their operations; including within the United States.

Overall, Al Qaeda's operational network of cells and affiliates carry out sophisticated surveillance and reconnaissance operations, as well as information collection using the internet. The organization uses this intelligence to conduct assassinations, large-scale bombings, suicide bombings, ambushes and counter surveillance operations.

It is in the surveillance and reconnaissance phase the cell must come out of the shadows in one way or another. The CIA, using good surveillance detection and counter surveillance operations, has disrupted several attacks before they have occurred. This is true success. Catching the terrorist after the attacks is important but, at that point, intelligence operations have failed.

I developed and taught surveillance detection and counter surveillance programs for the Agency, US embassies and personnel from several private security organizations. Strategic and innovative surveillance and counter surveillance techniques are of critical importance, because they are a preventative action. In addition, there are some exceptionally effective counter surveillance techniques that bring the cell out into the light of day, where the members can be intercepted.

Al Qaeda has developed a communications operation fire-walled from technical security penetrations. The organization uses the oldest form of communication that has existed, the human courier. In addition, Al Qaeda has learned to use encrypted software for using e-mail when necessary. These two aspects have made it more difficult for the NSA to intercept Al Qaeda's communications.

The majority of Al Qaeda attacks involve three significant phases. First, operatives conduct surveillance and target identification. Next the attack is rehearsed, usually several times. These are two weak points in their operations and are the phases that can be exploited by counter surveillance teams. Finally, the organization transports cell members with the responsibility to provide support to the attack team. This includes careful selection of the safe house, procuring weapons and explosive material, disguises, maps and local vehicles that blend in with traffic.

In older attack plans, Al Qaeda and other terrorist organizations would employ an attack team that would rehearse an escape route for use after the attack. This tactic is now diminishing in favor of a more efficient modus operandi, the suicide attack (discussed more in the next chapter). Suicide attacks need no escape plan.

The Killing of Osama Bin Laden

In the dark early morning hours of May 1, 2011, two stealth US Special Forces helicopters descended on a three story, fortress-like compound in the city of Abbottabad, Pakistan, north of the capitol city of Islamabad. The helicopters flew in low, undetected from Afghanistan. Twenty to twenty-five members of the elite US Navy Seal Team ████were on board the aircraft. Under orders from the Joint Special Operations Command in cooperation with the CIA, members of Seal Team ████ were dropped by one of the helicopters, then stormed the compound. A firefight ensued and two of Bin Laden's couriers, one of his sons and a woman, reportedly used by Bin Laden as a human shield, were killed. Other women and children were present in the house, but were not harmed. The Seals proceeded to the third floor, where they found Bin Laden in hiding. Once the Seals identified Bin Laden, he was immediately shot in the head and killed. One of the helicopters, a CH47 Chinook equipped with classified stealth technology, was lost in the operation due to "mechanical failure" and was destroyed by the crew, leaving behind the tail section of the aircraft. In all, the operation took only forty minutes.

The operation marked the end of the hunt for the world's most notorious terrorist and mass murderer. Overall, the operation was a resounding success. It was the final result of billions of dollars and years of investigation, research and cooperation with other foreign countries. The killing of Bin Laden was also a symbolic gesture to the world that the US will not stop countering terrorist attacks against US citizens, no matter what the cost.

A senior US security official told *Reuter's* news agency, under conditions of anonymity, the Seals were under orders not to capture Bin Laden and the mission was "a kill operation." President Obama's top terrorism advisor, John Brennan, stated capturing Bin Laden alive was considered remote before the assault. Brennan stated Bin Laden and his associates in the building resisted the assault by the Seal team, implying that because of this Bin Laden was not taken alive.

Abbottabad, a city of ninety thousand is located in the Orash valley, north of Islamabad, the Pakistani capitol. It is home to the Pakistani military academy, three Pakistan army regiments, thousands of military personnel and is the location of multiple military occupied buildings. The military academy, located just blocks from Bin Laden's hide out, was the equivalent of Pakistan's West Point.

The building Bin Laden had been living in was valued at approximately one million dollars. It had no telephone or Internet service. The compound was "extraordinarily unique," eight times larger than other homes in the area. Few windows faced outside. Security measures included twelve to eighteen foot outer walls topped with barbed wire. Internal walls sectioned off different parts of the compound. Residents of the structure burned their trash rather than placing it out for collection.

US forces took Bin Laden's body into custody after the firefight and flew it to Afghanistan by helicopter. His identity was confirmed there. DNA testing and photographic analysis confirmed the body was that of Osama Bin Laden. Since Bin Laden was a Saudi citizen, the Obama administration offered to turn the body over to Saudi Arabia, but the government refused. The Obama administration had to seek another option.

Burial at Sea

According to Obama's top terrorism advisor, John Brennan, "It was determined it was in the best interest of all involved in accordance with Islamic law," to have Bin Laden's body buried at sea.

Osama Bin Laden's body was transported to the US aircraft carrier USS Carl Vinson which was operating in the north Arabian Sea.

Islamic law strictly dictates the body must be bathed three times in a very specific, ritualistic procedure, while covered with a cloth. When possible, the bathers should be same-gender family members of the deceased. After bathing, the body must be wrapped in a kafan, a white cotton cloth, to protect the deceased's modesty. Prayers of forgiveness are then said for the deceased. Although burial customs vary by region, Islamic tradition also stipulates the body must be buried the same day as death, in other words within twenty-four hours. The deceased body must be buried in the ground with no casket. The grave is given a marker that does not rise more than twelve inches above the ground.

US officials stated burying Bin Laden's body at sea would prevent his gravesite from becoming a shrine and discourage vandalism and desecration of the grave.

There is a mandate in Islamic law that if it is likely an enemy of the deceased may try to dig up the body or destroy the grave site, burial at sea is allowed.

On the USS Carl Vinson, Bin Laden's body was washed, placed in a weighted bag and a military officer read prepared religious remarks. The remarks were translated by an unidentified native Arabic speaker.

The body was then placed on a prepared flat board, tipped up and Bin Laden's body eased into the sea.

A Sunni Muslim official of the most prestigious Sunni educational institute described burial at sea as a "sin" and contrary to Islamic custom. A representative of the Al Azhar Academy of Islamic research in Cairo stated when someone drowns the body must be recovered and buried in the ground.

Information Leading to Bin Laden's Hide Out

The controversy continues regarding how US officials obtained the information that led to the site where Bin Laden was hiding. Up until the summer of 2011, US officials believed Bin Laden was hiding in the mountains along the Pakistan-Afghanistan border. In August 2011, US intelligence officials received a tip providing information on Bin Laden's whereabouts in Abbottabad. The CIA began monitoring the compound and surveilled it for months.

Analysis by the CIA of the compound revealed there was a "high level of confidence" the compound housed a high level terrorist target with a "strong possibility" it was Bin Laden. This led to the planning of the operation.

Accounts by the Obama administration produced conflicting information. One account claimed Bin Laden was armed and fired at the Seal team. Another account claimed Bin Laden was unarmed, but shoved his wife at the assault team to defend himself. Pictures disseminated to members of the Congress and Senate by administration officials turned out to be false. Because so much inaccurate information was being disseminated, president Obama eventually ordered that no information would be disseminated to the public.

In my opinion, based on conflicting statements made by administration spokesmen, Bin Laden was unarmed at the time of the shooting. That being said, I understand why the Seal team assaulted the compound with such speed and firepower, immediately terminating Bin Laden. Bin Laden's previous statements, the modus operandi of Al Qaeda, and the majority of Al Qaeda's attacks involved terrorists wearing suicide vests, to be detonated in an instant. Based on this information, the Seal team did not know if the compound was rigged with explosives. In addition, it was possible Bin Laden's security guards, and even Bin

Laden himself, were wearing suicide equipment that could have been detonated, killing the team members. I am sure the operational goal was to take out security and Bin Laden before they had the chance to push the button.

Defenders of the Bush administration's practice of rendition, secret foreign prisons and, specifically, the procedure of water boarding were quick to flood the media with statements that water boarding directly led to the location and killing of Osama Bin Laden. News reports of the success of water boarding touted the CIA logo in the background and connected Bin Laden's capture directly to the procedure. It was an attempt by the CIA to rebuild its reputation after serious constitutional issues had arisen regarding the Agency's operations.

Some politicians claimed the information leading to Bin Laden's location came from self-proclaimed 9/11 mastermind Khalid Sheikh Mohammed - during water boarding; which led to the identification of a Bin Laden courier. Representative Steven King (R-Iowa) issued a tweet stating "Wonder what the Obama administration thinks of water boarding now." Attorney General Eric Holder and the Obama administration previously ruled water boarding was torture and was illegal. Upon taking office, President Obama issued an Executive Order barring the use of interrogation techniques not already legally authorized by the US Army Field Manual.

In an interview with *Newsmax*, Former Defense Secretary Donald Rumsfeld stated the information that led to the killing of Bin Laden was obtained through "normal interrogation approaches." When asked if harsh interrogations at Guantanamo bay played a part in locating Bin Laden's whereabouts Rumsfeld responded, "First of all, no one was water boarded at Guantanamo Bay. That's a myth that's been perpetrated around the country by critics." Rumsfeld went on to say, "The United States Department of Defense did not do water boarding for interrogation purposes to anyone. It is true some information that came from normal interrogation approaches at Guantanamo did lead to information that was beneficial in this instance. But it was not harsh treatment and it was not water boarding." Rumsfeld, who was there during the use of "enhanced interrogation" methods, directly contradicted statements made by former members of the Bush administration. The Obama administration provided no information on who conducted the enhanced interrogation interviews and where they took place.

During a Judiciary Committee hearing on the killing of Bin Laden, Attorney General Eric Holder stated, "Well, I think that, as has been indicated by other administration spokesmen, there was a mosaic of sources that led to the identification of the people that led to Bin Laden." Representative Dan Lungren (R-California) asked Holder, "I understand that, but were any pieces of that mosaic the result of enhanced interrogation techniques?" Holder responded, "I do not know." Keep in mind this is the Attorney General of the United States who is (or should be) fully briefed in exactly what methods were used to locate Bin Laden.

Intelligence Committee Chairwoman Senator Diane Feinstein (D-California) stated, "To the best of our knowledge, based on a look, none of it came as a result of harsh interrogation practices." At a news briefing, Obama spokesperson Jay Carney stated, "The fact is that no single piece of information led to the successful mission that occurred on Sunday and multiple detainees provided insights into the networks of people that might have been close to Bin Laden."

During an NBC interview CIA Director Leon Panetta stated "Enhanced interrogation techniques" were used to extract information that led to the mission's success. Panetta stated those techniques included water boarding. Panetta's statements were in stark contrast to the official comments of other White House officials who possessed no incentive to bolster the reputation of their committee or organization.

The CIA water boarded Khalid Sheikh Mohammed one hundred and eighty three times during the 2002 to 2003 timeframe. The administration finally admitted the CIA did not obtain information that led to Bin Laden until 2005 or 2006. The information attributed to the identification of the courier came years later, after "enhanced interrogation" had been stopped.

The one fact that was clear was the identity of the courier and the location of Bin Laden came to light years later, after the enhanced interrogation was ceased. Administration officials conceded it was multiple sources of intelligence and years of work that led to the location of Osama Bin Laden.

What concerns me, once again, is the CIA's willingness to conceal, alter or falsify information to protect its own interests and justify some of its potentially unconstitutional actions.

The New Leader of Al Qaeda

On June 16, 2011 an announcement posted on several jihadist websites declared Bin Laden's successor and the new senior leader of Al Qaeda had been chosen. Ayman al-Zawahri, an Egyptian surgeon, had been selected to lead the organization. Al-Zawahri had been Bin Laden's top deputy for several years. He met Bin Laden in the mid-1980s while supporting the Mujahedeen guerillas fighting the Soviets in the northwestern Pakistani city of Peshawar. In June 2001, Zawahri coordinated the merger of Al Qaeda and the Egyptian Islamic Jihad, Zawahri's own terrorist organization responsible for the 1981 assassination of Egyptian President Anwar Sadat. He is described as having a contentious personality and lacking the charismatic qualities of Bin Laden. Documents retrieved from Bin Laden's hideout revealed incidents of infighting and back-stabbing by senior Al Qaeda members as they vied for leadership of the organization.

Zawahri is suspected of planning the 1997 attack that killed sixty-seven foreign tourists in Luxor, Egypt. He was instrumental in the operational planning of the 9/11 attacks on the World Trade Center. Zawahri approved the July 7, 2005 suicide bombings in the London transport system which killed fifty-two innocent civilians. He has been indicted in connection with the 1998 bombings of US embassies in Kenya and Tanzania.

Zawahri is expected to attempt to orchestrate a significant attack in the West to demonstrate Al Qaeda is a legitimate force in the radical Islamic war against the United States, its allies and Israel. A website connected to Al Qaeda is now calling on "lone wolf" terrorists to target and kill Americans at their homes in the US. The website contains a list of the names of forty prominent Americans, with photos attached to twenty-six of them. The list is made up of US officials, business and political leaders, executives of think tanks and defense contractors.

In Figures 2 and 3 I have depicted in graphic form the Al Qaeda organization. Of note in the Al Qaeda organizational structure is the formation of the Worldwide Islamic Front of Jihad against the Jews and the Crusaders. This organization, for the first time, brought together both Sunni and Shi'a Muslims, formerly philosophical and political enemies, under the same cause of global Jihad.

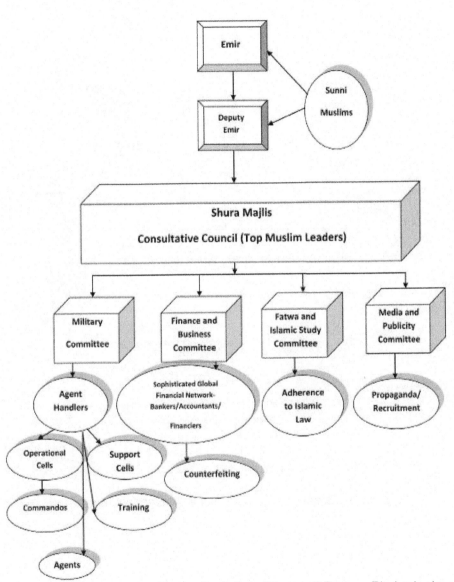

Figure 2: A breakdown of Osama Bin Laden's consultancy council. Bin Laden formed the counsel to create a global Islamic and Military organization. This organization includes thirty or more radical terrorist organizations.

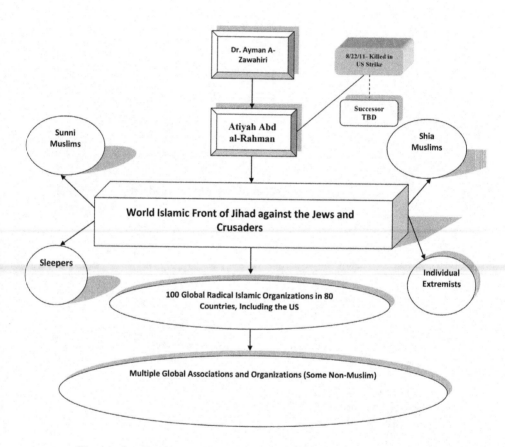

Figure 3: Breakdown of the global Al Qaeda organization

Al Qaeda's Second in Command

Al Qaeda then appointed its second in command, Atiyah Abd al-Rahman. Rahman was the network's former operational leader. On August 22, 2011 Rahman was killed in the Pakistani tribal region of Waziristan. US officials declined to comment on how he was killed. A CIA drone strike was reported in Waziristan. At the time of this writing, Rahman's replacement is unknown.

Al Qaeda's New Amorphous Strategy –Death by a Thousand Cuts

With the damage done to the organization's structure by the US and allied war on terror, Al Qaeda has been forced to alter its operational modus operandi. In a special addition of the propaganda magazine *Inspire*, an English publication produced by al Qaeda in the Arabian Peninsula, or AQAP, the organization described its new strategy in conducting terror attacks on the US and its allies. The publication states this is a strategy of "attacking the enemy with smaller, but more frequent operations is what some may refer to as the strategy of a thousand cuts. The aim is to bleed the enemy to death."

Using this terror philosophy Al Qaeda has developed a more decentralized amorphous structure. This structure is aimed at using the internet, propaganda, front organizations and front charities to inspire spontaneous terrorist cells and lone wolf terrorists to carry out their own attacks, not directly affiliated with the Al Qaeda organization, around the world.

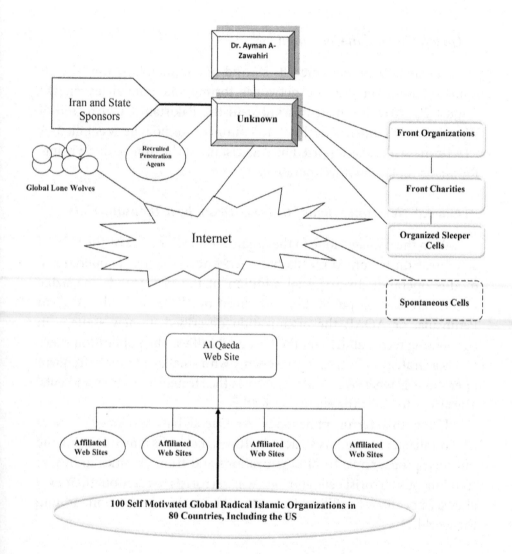

Figure 4 depicts this new amorphous, digitally operated structure.

Osama Bin Laden (Now deceased)

Ayman al-Zawahiri
(New leader of Al Qaeda)

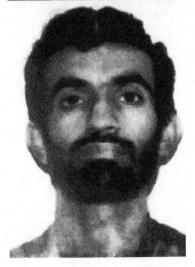

Ramzi Yousef, one of the planners
of the 1993 World Trade Center
Bombing and the Bojinka plot, a plan
to blow up 11 Airliners with 4,000
passengers on board on flights from
Asia to the US.

Chapter 18

Smart Bombs: The Advent of the Suicide Bomber

Up until the early '90s US intelligence and warfare tactics faced a traditional kind of threat. Typically, the threat involved military or guerilla fighters planning attacks on America and its allies, which included providing a way of escape. Today, this has all changed.

Hamas, Al Qaeda and a host of splinter terrorist groups have begun to employ a new and deadly weapon in their campaign against the West and Israel, the suicide bomber. Al Qaeda, and its affiliate groups, recruit, by the thousands, radical Islamic converts to act as suicide bombers; promising them the rewards of martyrdom in the afterlife. This trend continues to be the single most deadly and difficult threat to counter in international security today.

I want to begin with a discussion of the basic religious tenets behind suicide attacks. These terrorist groups proclaim suicide attacks are supported by Islam's holiest book, the *Koran*. This could not be farther from the truth. In reality, the *Koran* is direct and clear in its teaching that suicide is forbidden. This is found in 4:29 of the *Koran*. The *Koran* does teach in several passages the martyr can expect a reward and eternal life in "paradise" (3:170-174 and 22:58).

Osama Bin Laden and the leaders of Hamas have duped young Islamic converts into believing suicide attacks are a form of martyrdom and guarantee them a reward in the afterlife, which includes seventy-two virgins waiting for them in paradise. This has been a gross distortion of the teachings of Islam and the *Koran* itself.

The Koranic view of martyrdom was derived from the historic example of the Islamic martyr, the third Imam, Husayn, the grandson of Mohammed. Husayn was murdered by followers of the Caliph Yazid and the Umayyads in the year 680. Husayn's shrine is one of the great pilgrimage sites in the Muslim world. The issue of his martyrdom is one of the greatest divisive subjects, more than Islamic law or theology, in modern Islam.

The greatest split in Islam was created by Ayatollah Khomeini in Iran. Shi'a Islam is the dominant form of the religion in that country. Although Husayn has been historically portrayed as a peaceful, suffering martyr, Khomeini altered this interpretation and portrayed Husayn as a political activist and a hero of social change. This helped fuel the Iranian revolt and the overturn of the Shah of Iran. Since then, certain sectors of Shi'a Islam, most notably Al Qaeda, have portrayed Husayn as the example of political revolt against oppression.

Although the Koran forbids it, Bin Laden and others have mutated Koranic teaching and Husayn's death to teach suicide bombings are an act of Islamic martyrdom, guaranteeing the attacker a reward in the afterlife. Thus, as many modern Islamic groups are aware, but afraid to decry publicly for fear of death, Khomeini, Bin Laden and others have radically changed the beliefs of traditional Islam itself.

Essentially, suicide bombers are an innovative weapon of warfare. They are, in effect, smart bombs. They have perfect guidance systems, intelligence, the ability to change plans based on circumstances and can blend in with the intended target. These are typically young men, and now women bred and trained to be weapons of mass murder. They can identify their target with 100% accuracy. They can abort and move to a secondary target without programming. They have perfect guidance systems.

Suicide bombers and their handlers conduct research and intelligence before choosing their target. They are trained and educated to acquire the skills necessary for each particular attack, such as 9/11. The lethality of their attacks is without limitation. Studies show that approximately 1,000 new suicide bombers are recruited every quarter.

Several analytical reports have indicated there are similarities in the majority of suicide bombers. Some of these similarities are:

Grand Ayatollah, Ruhollah Khomeini, Supreme Leader of the Islamic Republic of Iran. Leader of the 1979 Iranian revolution. Initiated Islamic suicide terrorism.

Physical appearance:

- Healthy, strong and undistinguished in appearance and manner
- Physical fitness enhanced by extensive commando training
- Scars on their knuckles, hands and forearms from commando training
- Medium height and build – easily blend into crowds
- No abnormal physical and peculiar features that would cause their identification – e.g., no tattoos
- Dress and hair styles are inconspicuous
- Trained to talk and behave like average people
- Well dressed if in the first-class section of an airliner targeted for hijacking
- Employ disguises or plastic surgery
- In their twenties, healthy and strong – relatively few are older
- Leaders are older, in their thirties to sixties
- Younger terrorists are used to hijack jetliners, infiltrate government buildings, throw grenades into sidewalk cafés, assassinate heads of state, or detonate body-bombs on buses
- Appropriately dressed (or disguised) - acting normal before initiating the attack
- *Suicide terrorists must approach a target inconspicuously* by blending in
- The necessity to appear like a normal citizen also applies to the Revolutionary Armed Forces of Colombia (FARC), the Liberation Tigers of Tamil Eelam (LTTE), the Kurdistan Workers Party (PKK) and other guerrilla organizations

An example of the preferred physical appearance used by terrorists is Imad Mughniyah (head of Hezbollah's special operations) who was described as "someone you would pass in the street without even noticing or giving a second glance."

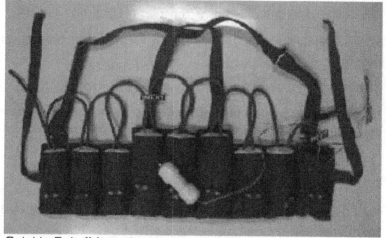

Suicide Belt (Manual switch detonation)

(Photo courtesy of Inert Products, LLC)

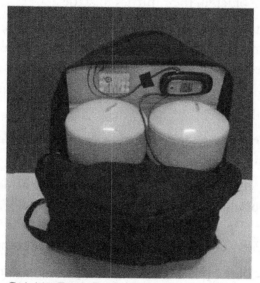

Suicide Back Pack (Remote detonation via cell phone) (Photo courtesy of Inert Products, LLC)

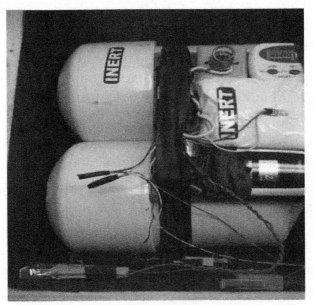

Suicide Car Bomb (Remote detonation via cell phone) (Photo courtesy of Inert Products, LLC)

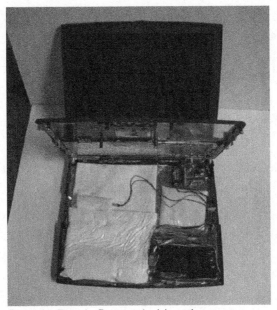

Suicide Bomb Concealed in a Laptop Computer. (Photo courtesy of Inert Products, LLC)

Other Common Terrorist Characteristics:

- Religiously motivated terrorists are more dangerous than politically motivated terrorists

- Religiously motivated terrorists are the groups most likely to develop and use weapons of mass destruction (WMD) to fulfill their messianic or apocalyptic visions

- Women make formidable terrorists because of their coolness under pressure. They have proven to be more dangerous than male terrorists. Security check points have been hesitant to conduct body searches on women, and some of these suicide bombers carry explosives under a disguise that makes them appear pregnant

- Hezbollah, the LTTE, PKK and other groups have used attractive young women as suicide body-bombers with devastating effect

- Chechnyan rebels utilize female suicide bombers, known as "Black Widows." They are carrying out suicide attacks as reprisal for the Russian killing of their husbands. Some of these Black Widows are elderly women

- They can work together with other suicide bombers - increasing the devastation; superior to any weapons system made

- Suicide body-bombers are trained to be totally at ease and confident when approaching their target

- Average marital status: 75% to 80% unmarried. Family responsibilities hinder requirements for mobility, flexibility, initiative, security and total dedication to cause

Aftermath of a Hamas suicide attack on the Sbarro pizza restaurant in Jerusalem. 15 innocent Israeli civilians were killed and 130 wounded. After the bombing, every restaurant the Author visited had a tense, guarded atmosphere. Israeli citizens could no longer relax and enjoy eating out without fearing another attack.

Signals and Warning Indicators

Case studies show not all suicide terrorists are able to act normally in approaching their target. In most cases psycho physiology, behavioral analysis and trained observation are useful in detection. For example, stress, or euphoria (in the case of the smiling terrorist convinced he is going to heaven to receive seventy-two virgins) chemicals are released by the autonomic nervous system and revealed in physical behavior. Antiterrorism training in *Behavioral Analysis and Attack Recognition are Critical.*

Early warning indicators of a terrorist attack include:

- Intelligence information on the individual, such as a "watch list"

- Unanticipated stress and nervousness may be exhibited - a hazard of the profession, involuntary and difficult to control

- The terrorist has higher levels of stress, resulting in involuntary psycho physiological responses

One of the challenges presented to law enforcement and counter terrorism professionals is the fact that most terrorists are trained to cope with nervousness. Female terrorists are particularly cool under pressure. A terrorist will look, dress or behave like a normal person—for example, a university student—until he or she executes the assigned mission. Terrorist profiling, based on personality, physical and sociological traits has limitations and is not as effective as other counterterrorism tactics such as intelligence and counter operations.

There are several motivations for a terrorist organization to carry out an attack. They include, but are not limited to:

- Political

- Religious

- Ideological

- Issues specific to their cause

- Criminal/Narcotics

- Environmental/Animal rights

Terrorist organizations share similar characteristics, such as:

- Ability to conduct *sophisticated* surveillance

- Ability to act on surveillance information

- Intensive, high risk, expert training

- Weapons, equipment, money and logistics support

- Educated, professional experts - engineers/explosives technicians

It is also important to know the historical characteristics of a potential victim of a terrorist attack. Some of these characteristics are:

- Position/fame/threat to the group's cause

- Personal/professional habits

- Quality and quantity of security

- Predictability of daily routes and routines

- Location and security of home/office

There is a plethora of terrorist organizations in the world today. Some of these are currently more active than others. The following is a list of current terrorist organizations. I have indicated the most active, lethal organizations that target the US, its allies and Israel in bold print.

Terrorist Organizations:

Abu Nidal Organization (ANO) – worldwide

Abu Sayyaf Group (ASG) – Philippines

Al-Qaida – Worldwide network

HAMAS (Islamic Resistance Movement)

Breton Liberation Army (ARB) – France

Armed Islamic Group (GIA)

Armenian Secret Army for the Liberation of Armenia (ASALA)

Armed Forces of National Liberation (FALN)

Army of National Liberation (ELN)

Aum Supreme Truth (Aum) – Japan

Basque Fatherland and Liberty (ETA)

Devrimci Sol (Revolutionary Left)

Democratic Front for the Liberation of Palestine (DFLP)

Front de la Liberation de la Bretagne (FLB)

Front de la Liberation de la Cote de Somalie (FLCS)

National Front for the Liberation of Corsica (FNLC)

Harakat ul-Mujaheddin (HUM)

Al-Gamaa't al-Islamiyya (Islamic Group, IG)

Hezbollah (Party of God)

Islamic Resistance Movement

Jaish-e-Mohammed – India

Japanese Red Army (JRA)

Kach and Kahane Chai – Israel

Kurdistan Workers' Party (PKK)

Liberation Tigers of Tamil Eelam (LTTE)

The Lord's Resistance Army (LRA) – Uganda

Mujaheddin-e-Khalq Organization (MEK or MKO)

The Palestine Islamic Jihad (PIJ)

Palestine Liberation Front (PLF)

Popular Front for the Liberation of Palestine (PFLP)

Popular Front for the Liberation of Palestine – General Command (PFLP)

Revolutionary Armed Forces of Colombia (FARC)

Revolutionary Organization 17 November (17 November)

Revolutionary People's Liberation Party/Front (DHKP/C)

Revolutionary People's Struggle (ELA)

Revolutionary United Front (RUF) – Sierra Leone

Sendero Luminoso (Shining Path, SL)

Tupac Amaru Revolutionary Movement (MRTA)

Alex Boncayao Brigade (ABB)

Continuity Irish Republican Army (CIRA)

Irish Republican Army (IRA)

Islamic Movement of Uzbekistan (IMU)

Loyalist Volunteer Force (LVF)

New People's Army (NPA)

Orange Volunteers (OV)

The Party of Democratic Kampuchea (Khmer Rouge)

Provisional Irish Republican Army (PIRA)

Qibla and People Against Gangsterism and Drugs (PAGAD)

Real Irish Republican Army (IRA)

Red Hand Defenders (RHD)

Sikh Terrorism

Taliban

Army of the Guardians of the Islamic Revolution
(Iranian Revolutionary Guard - supporter of Hezbollah and Hamas, responsible for terrorist attacks against American troops in Iraq)

Department of State List of Designated Terrorist Organizations:

- Abu Nidal Organization (ANO)
- Abu Sayyaf Group (ASG)
- Al-Aqsa Martyrs Brigade (AAMS)
- Al-Shabaab
- Ansar al-Islam (AAI)
- Asbat al-Ansar
- Aum Shinrikyo (AUM)
- Basque Fatherland and Liberty (ETA)
- Communist Party of the Philippines/New People's Army (CPP/NPA)
- Continuity Irish Republican Army (CIRA)
- Gama'a al-Islamiyya (Islamic Group)
- HAMAS (Islamic Resistance Movement)
- Harakat ul-Jihad-i-Islami/Bangladesh (HUJI-B)
- Harakat ul-Mujahidin (HUM)
- Hizballah (Party of God)
- Islamic Jihad Union (IJU)
- Islamic Movement of Uzbekistan (IMU)
- Jaish-e-Mohammed (JEM) (Army of Mohammed)
- Jemaah Islamiya organization (JI)
- Jemmah Anshorut Tauhid (JAT)
- Kahane Chai (Kach)
- Kata'ib Hizballah (KH)
- Kongra-Gel (KGK, formerly Kurdistan Workers' Party, PKK, KADEK)
- Lashkar-e Tayyiba (LT) (Army of the Righteous)
- Lashkar i Jhangvi (LJ)
- Liberation Tigers of Tamil Eelam (LTTE)
- Libyan Islamic Fighting Group (LIFG)
- Moroccan Islamic Combatant Group (GICM)

- Mujahedin-e Khalq Organization (MEK)
- National Liberation Army (ELN)
- Palestine Liberation Front (PLF)
- Palestinian Islamic Jihad (PIJ)
- Popular Front for the Liberation of Palestine (PFLP)
- PFLP-General Command (PFLP-GC)
- al-Qaida in Iraq (AQI)
- al-Qa'ida (AQ)
- al-Qa'ida in the Arabian Peninsula (AQAP)
- al-Qaida in the Islamic Maghreb (formerly GSPC)
- Real IRA (RIRA)
- Revolutionary Armed Forces of Colombia (FARC)
- Revolutionary Organization 17 November (17N)
- Revolutionary People's Liberation Party/Front (DHKP/C)
- Revolutionary Struggle (RS)
- Shining Path (Sendero Luminoso, SL)
- United Self-Defense Forces of Colombia (AUC)
- Harakat-ul Jihad Islami (HUJI)
- Tehrik-e Taliban Pakistan (TTP)
- Jundallah
- Army of Islam (AOI)
- Indian Mujahideen (IM)

One of my assignments as an Agency officer was subject matter expert and instructor of surveillance and counter surveillance. Part of my duties included training several Agency officers and US foreign embassy personnel in techniques to detect pre-attack terrorist surveillance. The following is the typical modus operandi used in the majority of terrorist attacks, also known as the "Terrorist Attack Cycle." The most exploitable cycle steps are in bold print. For the sake of security, I will not go into operational detail on each of the steps of the cycle.

It is my conviction that, if Americans and citizens in other countries of the free world know how terrorist groups operate, it will enable them to spot unfolding terrorist attacks before they occur. There will be a larger number of "eyes on the ground" potentially picking out terrorist activity, especially in the planning stages, and reporting it to authorities.

Steps of the Terrorist Attack Cycle (TAC):

1. Select/indoctrinate/train attack teams
2. Collect intelligence on potential targets
3. Identify list of possible targets
4. **Initial surveillance of listed targets**
5. Analysis and final selection (a soft target, i.e., the easiest to hit)
6. **Additional surveillance and planning**
7. Final victim/site selection (usually the softest target)
8. Attack escape planning (rapidly being eliminated by the deployment of suicide bombers, but still conducted by their handlers)
9. **Attack rehearsed/timed**
10. **Attack team deployment**
11. **Target identification/final surveillance**
12. Attack event (historical accounts indicate that in this phase there is only a 20% chance of survival)
13. Escape – No longer an option for the suicide bomber
14. Connected secondary attack, directed at law enforcement and emergency response personnel - a common operational signature of Al Qaeda

In my view the global war on terrorism represents the potential of World War IV. The clear intent of Islamic Jihad is the destruction of Western democracies and their replacement with a world Islamic Theocracy.

Now, two Asian countries (India and Pakistan), fortunately allies of the US to date, possess nuclear weapons. Both of these countries are at political odds with one another, and Pakistan's government is in a state of instability with the Taliban exerting tremendous pressure on the capital, Islamabad, at the time of this writing. The leaking of nuclear secrets by Pakistani nuclear scientist Abdul Qadeer Khan, considered to be the father of Pakistan's nuclear bomb program, to Libya, Iran and North Korea in 2004 is alarming.

The fervent efforts of current Iranian president Ahmadinejad represent a grave threat to the free world. Of particular concern is Ahmadinejad's strongly held and publicly declared belief in the coming of the Muslim equivalent of a Messiah, called the "12th Imam." In his public statements Ahmadinejad has made it clear his political and military intentions revolve around his deeply held belief in the imminent return of the 12th Imam.

The Shiite form of Islam is the predominant religion in Iran. In Shiite teaching an Imam is an anointed leader or theocratic ruler. Shiites believe only Allah can appoint an Imam (whereas Shias believe an Imam can be a prayer leader or cleric and Sunnis believe an Imam can be a prophet, a belief also held by Shiites).

Shiite Islam includes prophecies that foretell there is coming a 12th Imam, who is the great spiritual savior of all Muslims. This religious figure is known as Abu al-Qasim Muhammad and is also called Muhammad al Mahdi. Mahdi, as he is commonly called, is said to have been the son of the 11th Imam, Hasan Al-Askari. Shiite teachings give an account of Mahdi going into hiding as a five-year-old child during the 13th Century. Shiite Islam teaches Mahdi has been "in hiding" in caves since his disappearance and will supernaturally return just before Allah's Day of Judgment.

According to Shiite teaching, the Hadith, the signs of the 12th or Hidden Imam, are:

- A descendant of Muhammad and the son of Fatima
- Physical appearance will have a broad forehead and pointed nose
- Will return just before the end of the world
- Appearance will be preceded by a number of prophetic events during three years of horrendous world chaos, tyranny and oppression
- Will escape from Madina to Mekkah; thousands will pledge allegiance to him
- Will rule over the Arabs and the world for seven years

- Will lead a prayer in Mekkah, with Jesus at his side and following his prayer
- Will eradicate all tyranny and oppression bringing harmony and total peace

Ahmadinejad possesses a deeply held belief that he is personally responsible for preparing the world for the coming of Mahdi, the Muslim Messiah. In order to prepare the way for the coming of the 12th Imam, Ahmadinejad believes the world must be in a state of chaos. He believes he has been "directed by Allah to pave the way for the glorious appearance of the Mahdi." This is nothing short of an apocalyptic view that drives Ahmadinejad's politics, and very possibly his motivation to acquire nuclear capability.

Considering Ahmadinejad's threats to "wipe Israel off the map," his denial of the Holocaust, a soundly documented historical event, his philosophical hatred of America and his deeply held messianic and apocalyptic world view, if Iran acquires nuclear capability the threat of a global terrorist nuclear World War IV could become very real.

Ahmadinejad's recent announcement that Iran is beginning a manned space program could simply be designed to conceal the development of ballistic missiles capable of carrying nuclear payloads for long distances. At the time of this publication Ahmadinejad and Iran are considered the single biggest threat to international security. Sanctions imposed by the United Nations are not working and, frankly, never will against a Theocracy such as Iran. I shudder to think what will happen to the US and Israel if Iran is allowed to continue its nuclear weapons program over the short period of time necessary to develop and deploy a nuclear warhead.

Mahmoud Ahmadinejad, President of the Islamic Republic of Iran. Considers himself called to pave the way for the "12th Imam," through initiating world chaos.

Arak heavy water nuclear reactor in Iran

Chapter 19
Radical Islam

Moderate Islam

Moderate Islamic philosophy and teaching is diametrically opposed to the militant, radical version of Islam that began its global spread under Iran's Ayatollah Khomeini in the 1980s. Militant Islamicists represent only a relatively small population compared to the world's moderate Muslim community.

According to moderate Muslim scholars, the history of the prophet Muhammad contradicts the views of Muslim extremists. These scholars teach that Muhammad, after receiving his message, founded a state in Medina that is now located in Saudi Arabia. Medina was home to people of several faiths who coexisted peacefully. Originally, Muhammad directed his teachings of faith and worship toward the geographical birthplaces and origins of the teachings of Moses and Jesus. Muhammad taught there was a connection between Judaism, Christianity, and Islam. His goal was to show these religions Islam was not hostile to them and to educate them on the message of Islam. Islamic history portrays Muhammad as a peacemaker, extending his hand to Jews and Christians in whatever location he settled.

When Islam was established as a religion, he turned the attention of this worship to Mecca, still living alongside Jews and Christians. This is the belief of moderate Muslims today. Although many of them would like to speak out and decry extremist teaching and the perversion of the Qur'an by the followers of Khomeini, Bin Laden and now Zawahiri, they are afraid of being targeted for persecution, or even death. Unfortunately, their concerns are valid. The threat of radical Islam is just as much a threat to moderate Muslims as it is to Americans. Both of these groups must join together to protect each other and form a larger national community unified in the fight against militant Islamic extremists and the groups that provide them support.

Radical Islam

A large segment of today's radical Islamic extremist groups derive their beliefs from the Islamic Wahhabi movement. The Muslim scholar Muhammad ibn Abd al-Wahhab originated the religious philosophy, now known as Wahhabism, in eastern Saudi Arabia in the eighteenth century. Wahhabism is a religious movement and a branch within Sunni Islam. Abd al-Wahhab advocated the purging of Islam from impurities. This pure form of Islam is the primary form of Islam in Saudi Arabia, which provides global funding of mosques, schools and social programs to spread its doctrine. And al-Wahhab questioned medieval interpretations of Islam and claimed to rely only on the Qur'an and the Hadith. He attacked the "perceived moral decline and political weakness" of current Islam and condemned idolatry in all forms. Wahhab declared that all those who did not hold his views were not true Muslims, giving his tribe justification for attacking other Muslim tribes, ignoring the Qur'an's command not to fight other Muslims.

From the 1920s until today, Wahhabism has been steadily growing and spreading its radical ideology. It was the religion of the al-Saud family when they brought unity to Muslim tribes on the Arabian Peninsula, seized power, and established the Kingdom of Saudi Arabia. The Wahhabis began by destroying moderate Islamic shrines and sacred burial places, claiming they were idol worship and a corruption of "true Islam." There was no legitimate basis in Islamic law or doctrine for their beliefs. Today, the United States government sends billions of dollars a year to Saudi Arabia for oil. Through these billions of dollars of payments for oil, the US government is financing a country that holds the basic global view that America must be eliminated and replaced with Wahhabi Islam. It's clear much of this American money is going to propaganda programs promoting Wahhabism and winding up in the hands of militant terrorist organizations. We are, essentially, funding our own eventual destruction because of our dependence on Saudi oil.

Today, adherents to Wahhabism are directly connected to radical Islamic militants. These militants believe Islam must be reformed, and this must be done with war and violence. A noteworthy and courageous moderate Muslim scholar, Sheikh Muhammad Kabanni, has risked his life to come out and publicly expose militant Islam. Sheikh Kabanni practices the traditional form of Islam known as Sufism. Sufism originated from the teachings of Muhammad. Its religious tenets include the perfection of character and purification, which agree with the Islamic requirements of law and religious doctrine. Muslim extremists are, as one would predict, strongly opposed to the teachings of Sufism. Kabanni claims eight percent (8%) of Muslim mosques and charities in the United States have been taken over by militant Muslim groups. These organizations raise money in America and send it to terrorist organizations under the guise of "humanitarian aid." Several other moderate Muslim scholars have courageously opposed militant Islamic teaching and exposed front organizations operating under the cover of mosques and humanitarian operations. Many of these Muslim teachers have received death threats and are forced to live in constant fear of assassination by extremist groups sent to America to silence them.

Modern radical-political Islam is completely incompatible with democracy. The goal of radical Islam is complete world domination and the total annihilation of democratic governments. It has a single aim: establishing a universal Islamic state. This universal Islamic state would require a religious and political system that dictates all aspects of life through a stern, and sometimes deadly, set of laws and dictates. This totalitarian form of government would eliminate the right to privacy of its citizens, controlling all thought, speech, and conduct.

Radical Islamic extremists see the West as the supreme enemy of Islam. Their radical organizations, such as the Muslim Brotherhood, also call themselves "Salafists." Saudi Wahhabism is often referred to interchangeably as "Salafism." Salafism originated as "Salafiwa," which had moderate elements. The core belief of Salafism is that Islam was taught by Muhmmad, and his companions practiced his teachings. Second and third generations following them practiced this form of Islam, which was believed to be pure, unaltered and the ultimate authority for interpretation of the Qur'an (or Koran) and the Sunnah (sayings and living habits of Muhammad). Salafists consider this the eternal model for all following Muslim generations. However, from the nineteenth to the late twentieth century, Salafism gradually became conservative and ultra-orthodox; this is the Wahhabism that exists today. A branch of Salafism, Salafist Jihadism, consists of adherents to the belief that Muslims must spread this form of Islam through violent jihad.

Radical Islam teaches jihad is an apocalyptic war between the Islamic "sons of light" and the infidel "sons of darkness." Its proponents participate in what is called "dawa," the aggressive propagation of radical Islamic ideology using missionary advances. Other radical groups teach jihad through armed conflict. Some militant groups consider jihad to include both missionary work and armed conflict. Dawa can include a kind of stealth jihad where the proponents do not publicly propose armed conflict, but support it covertly in private and through funding. Dawa teaches Muslims to completely separate themselves from Westerners and form autonomous Muslim districts. Because the government of France did not take this practice seriously, there are now Muslim sectors in France even the police will not venture into. France has a serious internal security problem and is facing a slow collapse.

Radical Islam's goal is not the peaceful takeover of the world, but the perpetration of an apocalyptic struggle between the Islamic world (Dar al Islam) and the heretical world (Dar al Harb), reaching the ultimate level of chaos that will usher in the end of time, or last judgment. Jihadists consider this their ultimate goal. They believe the initiation of world chaos will begin the eventual fight between good (Islam) and evil (the West), causing the triumph of Islam and ushering its martyrs into their reward in paradise.

Included in this radical Islamic teaching is the concept of "takiyya." Takiyya involves the hiding of a Muslim's true religion and background to achieve the ultimate goal of conquest. Takiyya teaches Muslims living in a non-Muslim area can live in hiding to conduct a secret fight against the "unbelievers." Essentially, this amounts to radical Islamic sleepers, both cells and individuals, covertly operating dawa and jihad in America and other Western nations against the "unbelievers." Everything radical jihadists engage in, from hiding their beliefs to suicide attacks, is based on their total adherence to radical Islamic principles. They covertly use propaganda techniques to inspire members and recruits to engage in acts of terrorism without detection by Western authorities. In this way, they remain hidden from detection, conceal their jihadist philosophy, and hide their connections to the attackers themselves. They also use the Western, constitutional protections of privacy, freedom of speech, freedom of religion, and hate crime legislation to their benefit, causing widespread social change and silencing all criticism of radical Islamic speeches and activities.

Chapter 20

Sharia Law

"Indeed we believe that one day the flag of Islam will fly over the White House." —Anjem Choudary

On October 7, 2010, ABC's Christianne Amanpour held a panel discussion on Islam. Following a discussion by Franklin Graham on the facts of Islam, Anampour left her role as moderator and began an attack on former presidential candidate Gary Bower, essentially accusing him of racism, discrimination, and inciting violence against Muslims. Bower had said nothing of the kind, but was there to support peaceful Muslim and Christian relations. Amanpour's goal was to portray Islam as a peaceful and moderate religion. Moderate Islam is indeed that, but Amanpour avoided discussion of militant Islam, which directly threatens America and global security. Toward the end of the discussion, she opened the floor to Anjem Choudary, a Muslim cleric from London. Choudary made it clear that any practicing Muslim wants Sharia law to hold preeminence all over the world, including in America. At the end of his comments, Choudary made the chilling statement, "Indeed we believe that one day the flag of Islam will fly over the White House." Based on US law; that is called sedition.

During a March 2, 2010, CBN interview, Choudary made the following statements:

"You can't say that Islam is a religion of peace. Because Islam does not mean peace. Islam means submission. So the Muslim is one who submits. There is a place for violence in Islam. There is a place for jihad in Islam."

Anjem Choudry is the leader of the Islam4UK group. Choudary wants Sharia law to rule the United Kingdom, and he is actively working toward bringing that to pass. His group has been banned in Britain under counterterrorism laws. He said:

> "The Koran is full of, you know, jihad is the most talked about duty in the Koran other than tawhid – belief. Nothing else is mentioned more than the topic of fighting."

Several former members of Choudary's group have been arrested on terrorism charges.

Essentially, Choudry is actively working to overturn the US Constitution, replacing it with Sharia law. Overtly and covertly, radical Muslims in the US are engaging in the same activity.

"Sharia" means the "way" or "path." It is the sacred law of Islam. Muslims believe Sharia originated from two primary sources: divine revelations in the Koran (Qur'an) and the sayings and examples set by the prophet Muhammad. Islamic jurisprudence interprets the law and extends its application to address issues not mentioned in the two primary sources. These secondary sources include the consensus of religious scholars and analogies taken from the Qur'an. Sharia is adhered to by all Muslims who believe it is God's law. However, modernists, traditionalists, and fundamentalists hold different views of Sharia. There are several variations of Sharia in different countries and cultures. The European Court of Human Rights has ruled that the punishments prescribed by Sharia in some Muslim countries are barbaric and cruel.

Fundamentalist Sharia law cannot coexist with a democratic form of government because it includes the following judicial mandates:

- Courts do not utilize lawyers and the plaintiffs and defendants represent themselves

- Only a judge conducts the trials. There is no jury system

- Sharia law excludes pretrial discovery. It forbids cross-examination of witnesses and there is no penalty for perjury. Judicial rulings do not set binding precedents and no codified statutes are used

- Sharia law rests solely on medieval Islamic jurist's manuals and non-binding legal opinions, called "fatwas." Fatwas are issued by scholars. They can be made binding at the discretion of the judge

- In Sharia court, oral testimony has priority, and forensic, written, and documentary evidence is excluded

- The only admissible testimony is a confession, an oath, or a witness testimony. Written evidence is only admissible based on the testimony of several witnesses, with the final decision based solely on the judge's opinion

- Testimony is accepted only from at least two witnesses. Muslim male witnesses who are not related to the plaintiff are preferred

- Forensic evidence, such as fingerprints, ballistics, blood samples, and DNA, as well as circumstantial evidence, is rejected in favor of eyewitnesses. As a result, women plaintiffs claiming rape have significant difficulty proving their case

- Only half the weight of a woman's testimony is accepted compared to that of a man. Testimony from non-Muslims may be excluded by the judge if the charge is against a Muslim

- Oaths are not only used to ensure truthfulness by the defendant, they replace written documentation as evidence

- Plaintiffs lacking other evidence to support their claims may demand that defendants take an oath swearing their innocence; refusal thereof can result in a verdict for the plaintiff

- Sharia courts do not include appeals courts, prosecutors, cross-examination, complicated documentation, discovery, or juries. Almost all of the infrastructure found in US legal proceedings is absent, including exclusionary rules, case law, forensics, and standard legal codes

- Sharia applies the death penalty for crimes such as adultery, leaving the Muslim faith (apostasy), and homosexuality. It orders amputations for theft and whipping for public intoxication or fornication. It also opens the door for honor killing (killing wives or children for leaving or dating outside the Muslim faith)

Sharia law mandates the following social and religious beliefs and practices:

- **Democracy violates Islam** – All systems of man-made laws are prohibited under Islamic law

- Supremacy of Islam – Islam is superior and must replace all other faiths, cultures, governments, and societies. Allah ordains that those systems must be conquered and dominated

- **Zakat** – All Muslims are required to pay zakat. Zakat is one of the five pillars of Islam. It is an offering or payment that can only be given to Muslims. Jihadists use the custom of zakat to require Muslims to contribute money to charities that in turn finance militant Islamic groups. This is the practice of "Sharia-compliant finance." In September 2008, the US government used $180 billion of taxpayer dollars to bail out American International Group (AIG). AIG is the largest seller of Sharia-compliant insurance products in the world

- **Apostasy** – Apostates, or those who leave Islam, are to be killed wherever they are found

- **Lying** – Muslims are permitted to lie, especially to non-Muslims, to protect themselves and Islam

- **Abrogation** – Violent Medinan verses in the Qur'an that were written later supersede earlier, more moderate verses

- **Persecution of Jews, Christians, and other non-Muslims** – Based on genocidal practices, radical Muslims killed an entire Jewish population in the Arabian Peninsula. Following are quotes from the Qur'an used by radicals to justify persecution of Jews, Christians, and other non-Muslims:

  o *"And certainly you have known those among you who exceeded the limits of the Sabbath, as we said to them: Be as apes, despised and hated"* (Q 2:65)

  o *"And you will most certainly find them [the Jews] the greediest of men for life, greedier than even those who are polytheists..."* (Q 2:96)

- o *"O you who believe! Do not take the Jews and the Christians for friends; for they are friends but of each other; and whoever amongst you takes them for a friend, then surely he is one of them; surely Allah does not guide the unjust people"* (Q 5:51)

- o *"Fight those who believe not in Allah nor the Last Day, nor hold that forbidden which hath been forbidden by Allah and his apostle, nor acknowledge the religion of truth, even if they be of the People of the Book [Christians and Jews], until they pay the jizya [tax] with willing submission and feel themselves subdued"* (Q 9:29)

- **Slander and blasphemy** – Slander and blasphemy are not protected as free speech and, thus, are not allowed. In Sharia, slander means anything that might offend a Muslim

- **Gender persecution** – Women are inferior to men. Allah gives permission to Muslim men to beat their wives and commit marital rape whenever they please. Muslim men can marry up to four wives and have concubines of any number. A Muslim woman may marry only one Muslim man and is forbidden from marrying a non-Muslim. A woman may not travel outside the home without the permission of her husband or a male relative. Muslim women claiming they have been raped must present four male witnesses. If they cannot, they may be charged with adultery and may be stoned. A Muslim woman who remarries after divorce loses custody of her children

- **Honor killing** – Under Islamic law, Muslim parents face no legal penalties for killing a child or grandchild. Honor killing is permitted when an offspring leaves Islam or marries a non-believer

- **Underage marriage** – Sharia law permits the marriage of pre-pubescent girls as young as eight or nine years old. There is no minimum age for marriage

- **Adultery** – Unlawful intercourse (extramarital or premarital) is punishable by whipping or stoning to death

- **Female genital mutilation** – Women are obligated to be circumcised the same as men
- **Hudud punishments** – Allah commands hudud punishments for violations of Islamic law, including amputation, crucifixion, beating, and stoning

In the US, recently appointed Supreme Court Judge Elana Kagan had military recruiters removed from the Harvard Law campus, but welcomed Muslim recruiters looking for legal talent to implement Sharia-compliant financing.

The overt and covert activity by radical Muslim groups in the US to implement Sharia law represents an attempt by these groups to use the Constitutional protection of privacy, religion, and free speech, combined with the exploitation of hate crime legislation, to overturn the Constitution itself.

Chapter 21
Stealth Jihad

"The Ikhwan [Arabic for 'brothers'] must understand that their work in America is a kind of grand Jihad in eliminating and destroying the Western civilization from within and 'sabotaging' its miserable house by their hands and the hands of the believers so that it is eliminated and God's religion is made victorious over all other religions."
—Muslim Brotherhood

"I have no doubt in my mind, Muslims sooner or later will be the moral leadership of America. It depends on me and you, either we do it now or we do it after a hundred years, but this country will become a Muslim country."
—Islamic Association of Palestine

In 1991, Mohammed Akram published a document known as the *Explanatory Memorandum*, which contained the first quote above. Akram is a senior member of Hamas. He is also a member of the board of directors of the Muslim Brotherhood in North America. The publication states that the Islamic effort in the US is a plan by the Muslim Brotherhood to implement a "settlement process" and build a population in America. Once the settlement is established, it is to undertake a "grand jihad" aimed at "eliminating and destroying the Western civilization from within."

Muslim Brotherhood Operations

The Muslim Brotherhood and other radical Islamic organizations, such as the Islamic Association of Palestine, use US constitutional protections to promote Sharia law and establish sectors of Sharia-compliant financing. The Brotherhood is slowly and methodically building a large population of Islamic extremists prepared to act, non-violently or violently, to overturn the US Constitution and force America to be Sharia-compliant. This amounts to sedition and treason. It ignores article VI which states that the Constitution is the "supreme law of the land." Under the guise of multiculturalism the Brotherhood is demanding American society tolerate its activities.

The modus operandi of the Muslim Brotherhood includes:

- Spreading propaganda demanding tolerance and acceptance of radical Islam and Sharia law

- Engaging in covert sedition under the protection of US First Amendment rights and freedom of religion

- Holding teachings in mosques, conferences, and seminars that stress the Islamic mandate to overthrow the Constitution, establish Sharia law, and replace democracy with an Islamic state, all under the US Constitutional protections of free speech

- Implementing Sharia-compliant financial procedures in the US, which provide funding for advancing Sharia law and financing radical Islamic organizations

- Co-opting the US government into accepting their goal under the guise of religious tolerance and appeasing other Muslim countries unhappy with the US invasions of Iraq and Afghanistan; the US government will consult with the Muslim Brotherhood on Muslim matters

- Supporting Islamic institutions and mosques to publish student textbooks that teach Sharia law

- Preventing US law enforcement and intelligence from investigating their seditious activity under the protection of religious freedom

- Supporting the practice of Saudi officials who are practitioners of Wahhabism and connected to the Muslim Brotherhood; giving millions of dollars to leading US universities for Middle Eastern study programs designed to influence textbooks and programs
- Participating in "interfaith programs" with other religions to mask their operations
- Penetrating Wall Street and promoting Sharia-compliant finance with the support of the US government, including the use of tax payer dollars to bail out Sharia-compliance practicing companies such as American International Group (AIG)
- Influencing the Obama administration to declare that there is no "War on Terror," never mention Islam when speaking about terrorist attacks, and declare that Islam has nothing to do with terrorism Note: President Obama's counterterrorism advisor, John Brennan, stated that Obama does not accept that there is a "Global War" with militant Islamic extremists. The Obama administration adheres to the policy of the Organization of the Islamic Conference (OIC), which decrees that Islam has nothing to do with terrorism. The OIC is comprised of 56 predominantly Muslim nations and the Palestine Authority. OIC nations promote Sharia law and, thus, do not define jihad as terrorism. Furthermore, the US government is providing no training to US intelligence and law enforcement officers on the threat and operational activity of stealth jihad.
- Indoctrinating Muslim children in Sharia using mosques and madrasahs
- Refusing to report criminal or abusive activity condoned by Sharia, such as honor killings, domestic abuse, and marital rape
- Using lawsuits to intimidate its opponents, including American counterterrorism organizations
- Disseminating propaganda to the news media
- Trumpeting accusations of racism against any individual or organization that exposes its activities

A classic example of the effect of stealth jihad in the US is the November 5, 2009, mass killing of thirteen people at Fort Hood, Texas, by Army Major Nidal Hasan. Hasan had clearly described his intentions previously to Senior Army officers for years before the attack. In 2007, Hasan gave a fifty-slide briefing to his medical school class titled "Koranic View" as it Relates to Muslims and the US Military." In the briefing, Hasan lectured that Muslims are required under Islamic law to conduct jihad against non-Muslims. Being deployed to the Middle East against Muslims was cause for Hasan to engage in jihad. His presentation was a regurgitation of Islamic law. Hasan was the imam for Fort Hood. He was clearly influenced by Sharia law and stealth jihad. This fact was ignored by investigators of the Obama administration and was withheld from the public because of political correctness. The US Army had records of Hasan's radical Islamic statements well before the attack.

Stealth jihad is similar in many ways to the Soviet Union's attempts to overthrow US democracy. Radical Islam seeks to take over American culture, thought, religion, education, and government. Like the Soviets, it grooms and plants it "agents" on US soil, indoctrinating and training them for as long as necessary, even decades, as "sleepers" engaged in "civilization jihad." They are ready and waiting for the command to activate and engage in violent jihad if and when it becomes necessary. The Muslim Brotherhood uses information warfare, conducts covert operations, engages in psychological warfare, subverts the American culture, and penetrates American foundational institutions. It uses fear and intimidation to silence law-abiding Muslims and stages "outreaches" to the Muslim community designed to coerce them into thinking they must comply with Sharia law in its puritan form. This form of subversion is much more insidious than that of Communist Russia. The population of radical Muslims that perpetrate this view in the US is significant in size. It has crept into almost every facet of American society. It will not hesitate to use violence, including self-

US Army Major
Nidal Malik Hasan

destruction, if necessary. Its widespread message is recruiting operatives from the Muslim community and reaching out to "lone wolves" looking for a reason to engage in violence. In reality, the Muslim Brotherhood is the modern front organization for radical Islamic jihad and the fight for global supremacy. Shockingly, it has penetrated the top levels of the US government, our legal system, educational institutions, the news media, and US intelligence.

The Brotherhood and Sharia Law

Earlier in this book, I discussed the foundational tenets of Sharia law. Understanding Sharia law is critical to understanding the modus operandi of the Muslim Brotherhood and stealth jihad. The unyielding goal of Sharia law is the overthrow of the US Constitution and, eventually, the US democratic system of government.

The Muslim Brotherhood and other jihadist organizations utilize Sharia law as their weapon to coerce moderate Muslims into compliance with jihad and penetrate US financial, social, educational, and government institutions.

Sharia law is used as a cover for radical Islamic extremists to conceal covert criminal activity and funnel mandatory Muslim contributions to terrorist organizations.

Muslim Brotherhood Seal

Al-Qaeda's Plan

Al-Qaeda augments the Muslim Brotherhood's stealth jihad with a campaign of active, violent jihad. It has implemented an intense campaign to recruit US-born terrorist operatives. This can be seen in the increasing number of terrorism incidents occurring in the US.

One of al-Qaeda's strategies is to saturate the US with multiple small and large-scale terrorist plots to tie up the FBI and state and local law enforcement in lengthy, complex investigations and trials. An alarming sixty-three American citizens have been arrested, charged, or convicted for attacking or plotting to attack their own homeland. According to FBI Director Robert Mueller:

> *"Groups affiliated with al-Qaeda are now actively targeting the United States and looking to use Americans or Westerners who are able to remain undetected by heightened security measures."*

Al-Qaeda is exploiting the weakened US economy and lack of federal funding needed to expand counterterrorism programs. Al-Qaeda, in conjunction with the Muslim Brotherhood, actively seeks to inspire lone wolves to break out on their own and stage jihad attacks, taking law enforcement's focus of off the bigger picture of impending attacks using weapons of mass destruction. The organization knows that it can never match the US military and defeat it. Thus, it seeks to tie up the US military, law enforcement, and intelligence in overseas conflicts and defense of America and its allies against aggressive radical Islamic regimes. It also encourages US dependence on Middle Eastern oil and causes the US government to remain embroiled in complex and expensive internal counterterrorism programs and operations.

Chapter 22

Radical Islamic Front Organizations

As already discussed, the Muslim Brotherhood, al-Qaeda, and several other radical Islamic groups are waging a far reaching, complex "civilization jihad" on American soil. These groups have established several well-organized and interrelated front organizations that carry out and fund their operations. Through these they engage in systematic propaganda efforts to portray radical Islam as moderate, mainstream, and the subject of religious persecution and racist attacks by "Islamophobes." Through "conferences" and "seminars" they educate American Muslims and prospective converts on the tenets of Islam and, in particular, Sharia law. These groups establish Muslim charities that fund the creation of textbooks and other periodicals that portray radical Islam as part of multiculturalism. Funds from these front charities, under the guise of "humanitarian aid," are used extensively to provide money to foreign terrorist organizations like Hamas who carry out attacks and suicide missions against Israel and Western targets overseas. This extensive network of organizations provides substantial funding and support for global al-Qaeda operations. Saudi Arabia sends millions of dollars to mosques in the US to promote Islamic Wahhabisim and Sharia law.

The following section covers the majority of these front organizations and how they operate.

SAAR Network

- Based in Virginia
- Also known as the Safa Group
- The subject of federal raids fifteen times

- A complex network of companies, Islamic charities, and non-profit corporations
- Ingeniously designed to conceal the radical Islamic activities of its members
- US Immigration and Customs Enforcement alleges that the network is involved in a huge money-laundering operation that finances terrorist groups
- Some of the organizations are real and others are only on paper
- Management of personnel and financial records overlap, making the group's activities difficult to detect
- Most organizations are registered at the same Virginia address with no physical office
- Funds are transferred to secret offshore accounts
- Formed by a group of Muslim businessmen, scientists, and scholars from the Middle East and Asia
- Federal investigations allege SAAR is composed of up to one-hundred for-profit and non-profit organizations that "facilitate the funding of terrorist operations"

The Muslim World League (MWL)

- Connected to the SAAR Network
- Established by the Saudi Royal family
- Established to promote Islamic Wahhabism
- Virginia office was raided by federal authorities
- Has ties to al-Qaeda and Hamas
- Operational arm for radical Islam

International Islamic Relief Organization (IIRO)

- Operational arm of SAAR
- A branch of the MWL
- Connected to al-Qaeda and Hamas
- Suspected of funding training camps in Afghanistan

Sana-Bell

- Located in Virginia
- Part of the SAAR network
- IIRO financial management company
- US branch of MWL

Bait ul Mal, Inc. (BMI)

- Islamic investment firm founded in New Jersey
- Investors include a top Hamas official and a Specially Designated Terrorist connected to Osama Bin Laden and al-Qaeda
- Part of the SAAR network and connected to Sana-bell and IIRO

United Association for Studies and Research (UASR)

- Located in Springfield, Virginia
- Part of the SAAR network
- Several connections to Hamas

World Assembly of Muslim Youth (WAMY)

- Based in Virginia
- Raided by federal agents
- Suspected by the federal government to have ties to terrorism
- Several leaders are members of al-Qaeda

Council on American-Islamic Relations (CAIR)

- Invited to visit the US State Department
- Originated from the Islamic Association of Palestine (IAP)
- IAP suggested CAIR branch off to concentrate on anti-Muslim discrimination
- Takes the public position that it condemns terror
- Website invites complaints of profiling Muslims
- Has sponsored rallies including anti-Jewish rhetoric; one rally portrayed Jews as "descendants of the apes"

- Refuses to condemn the Taliban
- Supports Hamas
- States that it is against suicide bombing, then justifies it at seminars
- Conducts intensive press campaigns to convince the press not to overreact to acts of terror, warning them not to speculate about Islamic connections to terrorism
- FBI counterterrorism chief stated that the organization brands anyone who investigates or exposes acts of terror, including the US government as "anti-Muslim"
- Affiliated with the Muslim Brotherhood
- Holds the radical Islamic ideology of the Muslim Brotherhood
- Conceals their ideology from their members
- Claims to be moderate to drown out legitimate Muslim moderates
- Has access to and influence of top US lawmakers in the Congress

Muslim Public Affairs Council (MPAC)

- 501c(4) non-profit social welfare organization
- Claims to be a "public service agency working for the civil rights of American Muslims"
- Sponsors events and rallies supporting terrorist activity
- Radically anti-Israel
- Speeches have encouraged crowds to violence in the name of Allah
- Encourages militarizing the Muslim public
- Affiliated with the Muslim Brotherhood

Islamic Society of North America (ISNA)

- Largest Muslim organization in the US
- Oversees hundreds of Muslim organizations in America
- Many affiliated organizations support the doctrine of the Muslim Brotherhood, Hamas, and the PIJ
- Publishes Islamic Horizons, which promotes militant Islam

- Holds conferences that promote violence and anti-American and anti-Jewish hatred
- Affiliated with the Muslim Brotherhood

Kind Hearts

- Incorporated in Toledo, Ohio
- Operates in several states: Oklahoma, Nevada, Colorado, Pennsylvania, and Indiana
- Claims to be a non-profit, charitable organization engaged in humanitarian aid
- Closely tied to the Holy Land Foundation and other organizations engaged in terrorist financing
- Federal government froze assets in 2006
- Connections to Hamas
- Following the shutdown of HLF, associated itself with the IAP

American Muslim Council (AMC)

- Tax-exempt organization created to "educate [the] public about Muslims"
- Publicly supports Hamas terrorists
- Issues anti-American and anti-Jewish statements
- Supports multiple militant Islamic groups, including American Muslims for Jerusalem and the Kosovo Task Force
- Headquarters of the Islamic Salvation Front, which is suspected of supporting terrorism and attacking moderate Muslims

Muslim Arab Youth Association (MAYA)

- Sponsors conventions that host several Islamic militants
- Basic tenet is that America is corrupt and evil
- Has hosted Hamas and the Muslim Brotherhood
- Encourages the propagation of militant jihad
- Sells books at conventions stating that Americans and Jews are the enemy

Islamic Circle of North America (ICNA)

- Operated by Muslims of South Asian descent
- Publicly supports the imposition of Sharia law in America
- Publicly supports Islamic fundamentalism and encourages terrorist attacks
- Affiliated with the Muslim Brotherhood

Holy Land Foundation for Relief and Development (HLFRD/HLF)

- Headquartered in Richardson, Texas
- Received large donations from Hamas
- Alleged to have sent millions of dollars to finance Hamas operations
- Supported Hamas' goal of the elimination of Israel
- Shut down by federal authorities

The Benevolence International Foundation (BIF)

- Located in the US since the early 1990s
- Assisted al-Qaeda with setting up organizations in Chechnya, Bosnia, and Sudan
- Designated as a "specially designated global terrorist organization" by the US government
- Possible money laundering organization for al-Qaeda

The Global Relief Foundation (GRF)

- Organized in 1992 as a non-profit, charitable organization
- One of the largest Islamic charities in the US
- Registered with the Taliban
- Supporter of the Mujahedeen and al-Qaeda
- US government froze its assets and deported its chief executive
- Has offices in several other countries

- Annual contributions in the US of $5 million, the majority of which is sent overseas
- Connections to Osama Bin Laden

Islamic African Relief Agency (IARA)

- Also functions under the names Islamic Relief Agency (ISRA) and the Islamic American Relief Agency
- US branch was founded by students of the University of Missouri where it is now headquartered
- In 2004, the US government added IARA to the list of specially designated global terrorist organizations

The International Relief Organization (IRO)

- Founded in 1992 in Virginia
- Significant branch of the Saudi evangelical charity al-Rabita al-Alami al-Islmiya (Muslim World League)
- Large network of Saudi Islamic evangelical charities
- Identified by Osama Bin Laden as one of al-Qaeda's major funding sources
- Promotes Wahhabi Islam worldwide

Mercy International

- Formed in Denver, Colorado, in 1986 and now located in Garden City, Michigan
- Muslim charity
- Formerly known as Human Concern International (HCI), which funded the Afghan resistance against the Soviets
- Speeches have promoted attacks against Israel

American Muslim Alliance (AMA)

- Formed in California in 1994 as a non-profit organization to "raise the political awareness of Muslims in America"
- Now functioning as a political action committee (PAC) at the state and national level

- Supporter of Hamas
- Actively works to influence US politics
- Contributed $50,000 to Hillary Clinton's Senate campaign; Clinton returned the funds when she learned that the organization supports Hamas
- Leaders publicly support armed Islamic resistance
- Anti-Semitic and has distributed propaganda disputing the holocaust

This list is just a few of the organizations in the US that advocate Sharia law, promote radical Islam, and support terrorist organizations. There are still others in America and groups continue to emerge to covertly promote the subversion of America and replace terrorist-supporting organizations that are shut down by the federal government. I have only focused on groups that operate in the US. There are many others that operate in Canada, Britain, Australia, France, Germany, and other Western democracies.

As the famous Biblical verse in the gospel of Matthew states, "You shall know them by their fruits." Many of these groups proclaim to the news media and lawmakers that they are peaceful organizations established to educate the public on Islam and protect Muslims from discrimination. However, when you examine what they do, you find that they promote radical Islam, Sharia law, replacing the US government, push for the destruction of Israel, promote terrorist acts in the US, and finance foreign terrorist organizations.

Access to the United States Government

Members of the Muslim Brotherhood and affiliated organizations have been successful in influencing and penetrating the US government. These are some of their current activities:

- Participating in taxpayer-funded Department of State diplomatic programs
- Courting members of the House and Senate, including forming current relationships with Republican and Democratic members of Congress
- Pushing out moderate groups and silencing their message

- Lobbying Congress and testifying at congressional hearings
- Meeting with Capitol Hill staffers
- Meeting personally with the last three US Presidents Clinton, Bush, and Obama, as well as White House officials and Cabinet officials
- Using the cloak of democratic principles, including freedom of speech, religion, assembly, hate-crime legislation, and the Middle East peace process, to conceal radical ideology
- Concealing radical ideology through well-funded public relations campaigns
- Hosting the first lady Hillary Clinton at the convention for the Muslim Public Affairs Council (MPAC)
- Giving speeches at the State Department on emerging Islamic trends, with Muslim Brotherhood and Wahhabi ideologues portraying radical Islamists as "reformers"
- Receiving US-taxpayer dollars to conduct "sensitivity training" for federal, state, and local law enforcement officers
- Employing hidden radical ideologies derived from the Muslim Brotherhood
- On April 4, 2012 White House officials hosted a delegation from the anti-Western Islamist organization, the Egyptian Muslim Brotherhood. A White House spokesman stated, "we have broadened our engagement to include new and emerging political parties and actors."

Radical Islamic Figures Attend Prayer Sessions on Capitol Hill

On November 11, 2010, Fox News broke the story of radical Islamic figures attending prayer sessions on Capitol Hill. The Congressional Muslim Staff Association (CMSA) has been holding standard weekly Friday Jummah prayers on Capitol Hill for over ten years. There is no public record of exactly who attends these events. Rep. Keith Ellison (D-MN), one of the two Muslims currently serving in Congress, sponsored the group to obtain official status in Congress in 2006. Congressman

Andre' Carson (D-IN), the second Muslim Congressman, co-sponsored the group after his election in 2008 (this is not to imply that the Congressmen are by any means radical).

The following radical Islamic figures attended Capitol Hill events under the Clinton, Bush, and Obama administrations:

- **Randall "Ismail" Royer** – Previous communications associate for the Council on American-Islamic Relations (CAIR). Royer confessed to receiving jihadist training in Pakistan in 2004. He is now in prison serving a 20-year prison term

- **Anwar al-Awlaki** – Considered one of the most dangerous terrorists in the world and was included on the government's capture or kill list, he led a prayer service on Capitol Hill just after the 911 attacks

- **Anwar Hajjaj** – Previous president of the Taibah International Aid Association (TIAA). The US and the U.N. designated TIAA as a terrorist organization in 2004.

- **Salam al-Marayati** – President of the Muslim Public Affairs Council (MPAC). In 1999, Marayati was removed from his national terrorism committee post for pro-terrorist comments

- **Esam Omeish** – Previous president of the Muslim American Society (MAS). In 2007, Omeish was forced to resign from the Virginia Commission on Immigration for calling for "the jihad way" and other radical Islamic remarks

- **Johari Abdul Malik** – An imam at the Dar Al Hijrah Islamic Center in Northern Virginia. Made public statements in support of suspected and convicted terrorists that attended his mosque

- **Nihad Awad** – Served as the executive director of CAIR. In 1993, he attended a Hamas meeting in Philadelphia that was wiretapped by the FBI

- **Abdulaziz Othman al-Twaijri** – Leader of a division of the Organization of the Islamic Conference (OIC). The OIC is considered a foreign agent by the US government

- **Tariq Ramadan** – A Muslim scholar. He was alleged to have given donations to terrorist groups. Beginning in 2004, Ramadan was banned from the US for six years. Secretary of

State Hillary Clinton lifted the ban in January 2010

Several of these figures had direct ties to Anwar al-Awlaki, now known to have been behind several violent terrorist plots against the US. Al-Awlaki was a senior recruiter and operational planner for Al Qaeda. He was killed by a US drone missile strike in Yemen on September 30, 2011.

Anwar al-Awlaki (Now deceased)

Chapter 23

CIA and Intelligence Operations

As a CIA officer, one of my assignments at Langley was senior briefer to new employees and members of the Intelligence Community Entering-On-Duty (EOD) with the CIA for the first time. These new employees ranged from clerical personnel to college graduates joining the CIA, case officers, senior members of the FBI, DEA, Department of State and ranking officers from each of the branches of the military. It was my job to provide a detailed, three-day lecture on the CIA, the Intelligence Community and an introduction to CIA operations.

In the paragraphs that follow, I will present an overview of the structure of the US Intelligence Community in general and CIA operational techniques in particular. This will serve as a good, concise explanation of how US intelligence agencies and, in particular, the CIA function.

The US Intelligence Community is, without a doubt, the most sophisticated, complex and sizable intelligence apparatus in the world. The CIA utilizes the most professional, refined, cataloged process of the collection, analysis and dissemination of information. This data, once analyzed and validated is called "intelligence." A common mistake, especially in the private sector, is to call raw information gained from a source or document "intelligence," before it is studied, analyzed, properly reported and properly disseminated. This can lead to serious embarrassment and has done so for several government and private organizations in very costly instances in the past. This oversight is made primarily because of a lack of understanding of the true nature of intelligence and the intelligence process.

What Makes Up the Intelligence Community?

The US Intelligence Community consists of seventeen large government organizations. This includes the newly created office of the Director of National Intelligence (DNI), the CIA, the National Security Agency (NSA), the National Reconnaissance Office, the National Geospatial Intelligence Agency (NGA), the Defense Intelligence Agency (DIA), the Department of State Bureau of Intelligence and Research (INR) and intelligence branches of the Army, Navy, Marine Corp and Air Force. Four members of the Intelligence Community are considered national intelligence organizations due to the fact that they perform operations on behalf of the federal government as a whole. These national intelligence organizations consist of the CIA, NSA, NRO and NGA.

Other intelligence activities of the US government are conducted by smaller branches of executive civilian organizations. These consist of the Department of Homeland Security, the Department of State, the Department of Energy, the Department of Treasury and the Justice Department (FBI and DEA). For the purpose of this book, I will focus on the functions of the Director of National Intelligence (DNI) and the four national Intelligence Community (IC) organizations.

The DNI was created after the 9/11 attacks as a result of the 9/11 Commission's investigation. The creation of the DNI abolished the single, powerful position of the Director of Central Intelligence (DCI) which controlled US intelligence. The DNI has more broad sweeping powers than the DCI, but is not involved in management of the Agency's day-to-day operations. The DCI continues to function in that capacity.

The CIA was created by President Harry S. Truman (Ironically, Truman may be my distant relative. The "S" in Truman's middle name stands for "Shipp/Solomon;" his two grandfathers Anderson Shipp and Solomon Young) originally as the Central Intelligence Group (CIG), in the midst of much controversy over a secret intelligence service within a democratic government.

The National Security Act of 1947 created the CIA as an organization independent from the other national organizations within the executive branch reporting directly to the President of the United States. The CIA's role is to serve the National Security Council (NSC) as an advisor, collect, analyze and disseminate intelligence to the NSC and perform "other operations the NSC may order the CIA to conduct." This last function of the CIA is very broad and eventually paved the way for CIA covert operations.

Since the 1947 Act, the CIA has grown substantially in its power and interpretation of the 1947 Act and become the foremost Agency for covert human intelligence collection, analysis and covert operations. Executive Order 12333, issued by President Ronald Reagan, gave the CIA authority to covertly collect foreign intelligence within the US as long as the operation was not targeting domestic citizens or organizations.

The National Security Agency (NSA) was created in 1952 by President Truman to oversee communication intelligence activities. It is the most secret of the seventeen intelligence organizations. NSA's primary responsibility is to collect signals intelligence and produce signals intelligence information, or SIGINT. NSA's SIGINT responsibility includes communications intelligence, or COMINT, the interception and analysis of foreign radio, wire, or any other means of electronic communication and the decryption of these transmissions. SIGINT also includes non-communications information obtained from electromagnetic information produced by atomic detonation or sources of radiation. This type of information is called electronics intelligence, or ELINT.

The National Reconnaissance Office (NRO) was formed in 1992. The NRO was created as the organization that would tie together the reconnaissance efforts of the Air Force, CIA and the Navy. This includes reconnaissance information derived from classified aircraft systems, SIGINT satellites, and imagery satellites which produce information designated as imagery intelligence, or IMINT. The NRO has also established its own Counterintelligence staff to counter foreign intelligence threats to its information, personnel and facilities.

The National Geospatial Intelligence Agency (NGA) was created in 1996 based on the recommendation of DCI John Deutch and Secretary of Defense William Perry. The NGA's mission is to the meet the imagery mapping needs of the US government.

The Defense Intelligence Agency (DIA), established in 1961, performs the function of supporting the Secretary of Defense, the Joint Chiefs of Staff and the commanders of the four military branches. The DIA was created to solve the problem of the significant overlap of military intelligence functions among the various military branches.

Up until that point, several Defense Department intelligence activities were being duplicated and distribution of intelligence was inefficient. Consequently, important intelligence information was not getting to the military organizations in the Department of Defense.

The DIA established a centralized military intelligence function to ensure intelligence is collected in a coordinated fashion and disseminated properly throughout the Department of Defense and the military branches. In addition, the DIA did not approve of the CIA's collection performance. The DIA has its own human intelligence, or HUMINT element and MASINT, or measurement and signature intelligence. MASINT consists of technically collected information resulting in intelligence that tracks, locates, identifies or reveals distinctive characteristics, or signatures, of fixed or mobile target sources. An example of this would be the precise location, size and structural characteristics of a targeted building. MASINT excludes information derived from IMINT or SIGINT sources.

The Intelligence Cycle

The intelligence process defines the methods used specifically by the CIA to produce finished intelligence. This process is known as the "Intelligence Cycle." Let's begin by discussing the different types of intelligence. Again, a critical point is that "intelligence" is not just merely raw information. It is material that originates from vetted, credible sources, has been properly analyzed, and a report of that data has been prepared by trained professionals. The final product of this process is "intelligence."

There are several types of intelligence collected by the US Intelligence Community. These types of intelligence consist of military intelligence (the capabilities of hostile nations), political intelligence (political climate and policies of foreign nations), economic intelligence (the condition, trends and weaknesses of foreign economies), and scientific and technical intelligence (the technical capabilities of the civilian and military sectors of foreign governments).

The overall process of intelligence collection begins with information deemed necessary by the President of the United States, the National Security Advisor, the Vice President, the National Security Council, the Department of Defense, the Department of State, the Department of

Homeland Security, military Joint Chiefs of Staff, the Attorney General, the leaders of the national unified commands and the four branches of the military. For example, the President or his National Security Advisor generate what is called a "requirement" for intelligence information necessary for them to make important US policy decisions.

Finished intelligence for dissemination to policymakers is produced by the systematic Intelligence Cycle. First, a definition of the requirement is determined, including planning and direction (i.e., by the White House or the National Security Council). The cycle consists of four *primary* steps:

1. **Collection** of existing intelligence and raw information from all available open sources (credible Internet sites, multiple publications, target Internet sites, research libraries and videotaped programs) and identifying and filling gaps in information by covert collection methods. Collection involves target analysis—that is, studying the target of information collection to identify where the information being sought is located and can best be exploited

2. **Analysis** of the information and preparation of the final intelligence report. Analysis is conducted using a strict set of guidelines by trained, unbiased professionals. Analysis may identify additional requirements

3. **Reporting** derived from processing the information, converting it from large amounts of data into a logical collection of information

4. **Dissemination** of the finished intelligence report to US policy makers. This intelligence process may, in turn, produce additional requirements for information and, hence, the cycle begins again

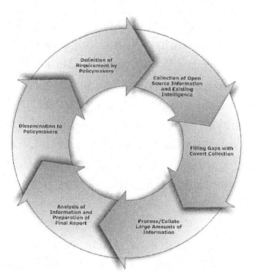

Graphic: Expanded View of the Intelligence Cycle

The Collection Process

Once the requirement for intelligence has been issued, the collection process begins. In CIA HUMINT operations, the collection process is initiated with asset or agent recruitment. The CIA uses what is called the "Recruitment Cycle" to target, interview and recruit agents, attachés, detainees, émigrés, diplomats, defectors and in some cases, travelers who have visited, reside in or have relatives in targeted areas.

The CIA learned the hard way that good human intelligence cannot be replaced by technical collection such as SIGINT or IMINT. A recruited asset with direct access to target conversations, blueprints, operational plans, technical manuals, weapon system manuals and the motivations and intentions of the target is far more effective than technical methods.

In the late 1970s, under the direction of DCI Stansfield Turner, the decision was made to draw away from recruiting human assets in favor of using what he viewed as the safer, more efficient technical means of collection. Entire branches at the CIA were eliminated and the Directorate of Operations staff significantly reduced. Turner became so unpopular among the Directorate of Operations populace that morale suffered. One agent told me they had to regularly wipe the spit off Turner's painting hanging in the hall of DCIs in CIA headquarters.

As mentioned earlier in the book, to make intelligence collection even more difficult, later came the Clinton administration's order forbidding CIA officers from associating or recruiting any asset, including members of terrorist cells, with any human rights violations. These two historical events severely hampered US HUMINT operations for years and did decades of damage to the CIA's HUMINT capability. When 9/11 occurred, the CIA had almost no valuable penetrations of Al Qaeda or other dangerous terrorist organizations.

Covert Operations

The CIA foreign agent recruitment cycle consists of spotting, assessing, developing the agent and the final recruitment pitch. The process of spotting a possible recruit begins with analysis of the target. This includes identifying the information required, the location of that information, individuals with access to that information, technical means of collecting the information and, finally, the identification of the specific individual(s) or technical targets, with direct access to the information. All of this requires complex operational planning regarding the system that will be used to recruit the agent or initiate the technical collection. All good operational plans will have contingency procedures built into them. So, if Plan A fails or is discovered, Plan B goes into effect, etc.

In the operational courses I taught, I always included a kind of tongue in cheek, but true, discussion of "Murphy's Law": "If something can go wrong, it will go wrong." During my course, I used the example of an operation I was conducting to prevent a hostile foreign intelligence service from carrying out the assassination of a principal figure I was appointed as the team leader to protect. My job was to detect and stop any attempt by this service to surveil, track or attack my protectee.

As the operation unfolded, I was to communicate orders to the rest of the team via radio and advise them of any developments or necessary changes in their position. When the time came for this contact, I activated the radio I had been given by the Command Post. The radio was dead. I replaced the battery with the spare battery I was given. The spare battery was dead. I jettisoned the radio and went to the operational cell phone I also carried. The cell phone was dead. Lastly, I jumped into a pay phone with the back-up quarters I carried, and used the pay phone to call the other agents and organize our next movement. It really does pay to have a Plan B, C, or D. "Murphy" was right!

The CIA uses highly trained professionals called "case officers." They are not called CIA "agents." This term is a misnomer. Case officers are generally well educated men and woman fluent in foreign languages and tasked as "handlers" of operations designed to recruit foreign spies to act on behalf of the US.

As part of the collection process, the CIA uses various types of cover to carry out its operations. A case officer will utilize two specific types of cover when conducting operations. The first, "cover for status," affords the case officer with a legitimate reason to be in that country. This is usually in the form of "official cover" in which the case officer works as ████████████████ This provides the officer with some measure of diplomatic immunity.

A case officer may be assigned overseas under a deeper cover for status known as nonofficial cover, or NOC. In this capacity the officer will act as a businessman, student, etc. NOCs typically utilize the second form of cover known as ████████████ ████████████ which typically involves the use of an alias name and documentation disguising the person as a journalist, university professor or member of a foreign diplomatic service.

During my career I utilized several forms of cover to allow me to carry out the mission I was ordered to complete. On other assignments, I was dispatched as an overt CIA officer. Working under a solid cover provided a much safer feeling and kept me out of the view of the local intelligence service. On some overt missions while I was assigned as a protective agent for Agency officials, I was followed, my hotel room was discreetly entered, my luggage was searched, and sometimes I was generally harassed.

Once the operational plan is finalized the recruitment cycle continues. The next step in the cycle is called "spotting." When spotting a potential asset or agent, the case officer is looking for an individual with access to the information being sought.

Spotting is followed by the next step in the cycle called "assessing." In this step, the goal is to identify the target's vulnerabilities, character and belief system, ego motivations, any disgruntlement and susceptibility to recruitment.

The next step is to "develop" the target for recruitment. This includes working the target by appealing to his or her motivations to change over and become an agent of the US government. There are many motivations that convince an individual to spy for the US. These include money, revenge, ego and the need to feel important, religious beliefs, or close friendship with the case officer.

The final step in the recruitment cycle is the "pitch." This is the sensitive point at which the case officer is convinced that the target's vulnerabilities or motivations are significant enough to cause him or her to accept the invitation to obtain sensitive information or access for the case officer.

There are two types of agents a case officer may target. The first is an "access agent." This type of agent is an individual who can gain access to people or information that the case officer cannot. A good example of this is a terrorist cell, where cell members are largely family members or close friends and allies.

The second type of target agent is called a "penetration agent." This agent is an individual with direct access to the internal areas of a target location or with access to highly protected information or materials.

An important part of collecting information from a source or agent is the process of vetting the individual. Using all available information about the individual and corroborating the information he or she provides, the case officer and the Station must make the decision that the source is credible, the information is legitimate and the source is not a double agent.

Another very valuable source of CIA recruitment is the defector. The CIA protects and debriefs significant defectors, sometimes over a period of months or years. Legitimate defectors are provided healthy salaries, nice homes and resettlement in the US. Defectors have provided the CIA and US policy makers with some of the most valuable and important foreign intelligence information. A classic example of this is Stanislav Levchenko. Levchenko, a KGB officer, defected from Russia for religious and philosophical differences with the Russian system of government. Levchenko provided the CIA with a treasure trove of information on the internal operations of the KGB.

Analyzing the Information

Once the CIA has collected and disseminated information back to headquarters, the process of analysis begins. The CIA possesses six different types of analysts: political (observe and assess political developments), leadership (monitor and assess foreign leaders), economic (assess foreign economic conditions and policies), military (assess foreign military capabilities), science and technology (monitor and assess information warfare, foreign technology advances, weapons proliferation, chemical and biological weapons and foreign energy issues) and targeting (use analysis of networks and sophisticated analytical tools and processes to locate, identify and provide information on key figures in the target organization).

Analytical techniques used by the US Intelligence Community include data mining (algorithms used to discover previously undetected patterns), social network analysis (locating individuals through connection in their social networks), automated database input (which automatically adds target information to databases), link analysis (which ties known activities with unknown individuals), clustering (allowing the utilization of the most valuable information first), time series analysis (identifying trends over time), and visualization (presenting complex information in understandable formats).

In the reporting phase of the intelligence cycle, finished intelligence is documented in report format for dissemination to policymakers. Finished intelligence reports fall into five categories: current intelligence, warning intelligence, analytical intelligence, periodicals, databases and maps. The CIA open source *World Fact Book* is a good example of an unclassified finished intelligence product.

Finally, the finished intelligence product is disseminated to the appropriate policymakers. Examples of finished intelligence products are the *President's Daily Brief*, the *Senior Executive Intelligence Brief*, the Secretary of State's *Secretary's Morning Summary* and the Defense Department's *Military Intelligence Digest*. With these publications the intelligence cycle is complete until new requirements arise.

A last type of intelligence CIA officers joke about at Langley is what we called rumor intelligence, or "RUMINT." This consists of the constant hallway and smoking court chatter that always hums under the surface at CIA headquarters. RUMINT, although rarely true, many times affects careers, office morale, career decisions and the like.

CIA headquarters is a hornet's nest of politics and career positioning and RUMINT was certainly a part of that. Many of us took dangerous assignments just to get away from the politics of CIA headquarters and some of its back channel practices. It was a humorous and unfortunate reality.

New CIA headquarters building in Langley, Virginia

CIA seal on the lobby floor of headquarters.

Chapter 24

Counterintelligence

In 1994 I was assigned to the CIA's newly reorganized Counterintelligence Center (CIC). My position was in the recently created internal counterintelligence investigations branch. The Aldrich Ames espionage case had recently occurred and the Agency was still reeling from the long-term effects of the damage Ames had caused to the CIA and US intelligence. It was our job to ferret out any other "moles" in the Agency.

During my tour in CIC, I was assigned the case of a high level Agency employee who had failed the polygraph question on concealing contact with a foreign intelligence service. The employee was belligerent and uncooperative during interviews designed to determine why he was reacting to a counterintelligence question. Because of my recent successes in handling employees who were upset by becoming a case in CIC, the case was assigned to me. During the interview with the individual, we established a good rapport and I convinced him to go back and take a subsequent polygraph on the same subject. He did so, and failed the test a second time.

After further interviews, CIC became convinced the employee had engaged in espionage. Information that had come in through other sources indicated there was a second mole in the organization. After my last interview with him, the case was briefed to the President of the United States. As soon as the case appeared to be another Ames, CIC officers, who previously were disinterested in the case, jumped on the bandwagon.

The Deputy Chief of the Counter Espionage Group (CEG), when he saw the case could be another historical one, came to me and advised he was taking over the case. This was fine with me; I could see the case was going to be a significant mess. The officer under suspicion had friends in high places in the CIA and they were beginning to assault CIC for investigating his activities.

Just a few months later, amidst a storm of resistance from the Directorate of Operations (DO), new information surfaced indicating the officer under investigation was not a potential mole at all. In fact, the CIC had moved too quickly on the case, without examining all the information. The individual was eventually cleared of being a spy. The DO now demanded justice and recompense for CIC's mishandling of the case. A high level meeting was arranged with DO senior management to confront the CIC. As soon as these events unfolded, the Deputy Chief of CEG came back to me and ordered me to take the case from there. I smelled a rat. It turned out I was right.

The Deputy Chief of CEG was supposed to represent CIC to the upper management of the DO in the upcoming meeting. He directed me to attend as well. Five minutes before the meeting, he called and advised another meeting had come up and he could not go with me. He directed me to represent CIC at the "meeting." The meeting turned out to be a frontal assault by DO management on CIC for bungling the investigation and DO management confronted me about the handling of the case. Knowing I had been set up by the cowardice of the Deputy Chief, I calmly represented the facts of the case I had gathered before CIC management took it over and related that actions after that period were out of my hands.

In the place of CEG management, I was ordered to deliver a letter of apology to DO management, which I dutifully did. Frankly, this did not bother me at all and I understood the DO's frustration over the matter. Personally, I was always glad when an Agency officer was cleared of counterintelligence issues. However, I had seen first-hand the kind of cowardice, displayed by the Deputy Chief of CEG, which was beginning to run rampant in the CIA.

The new CIC was instituted based on the recommendation of the Security Commission, created to address the damage Ames had done, develop new measures that would locate any existing moles within the CIA, and institute practices that would prevent such a thing from ever occurring again. The final recommendation of the Security Commission was the creation of the Counter Espionage Group (CEG), which co-located CIA counterintelligence officers with FBI counterintelligence agents. This was the first time these two competitive and sometimes opposing organizations were forced to work together, whether they liked it or not. Many FBI agents and CIA officers abhorred the idea.

My experience in CEG revealed to me that international counterintelligence and espionage are part of a dark underworld, teeming with thousands of agents operating for multiple countries, with a constant undercurrent of covert activity taking place in the shadows of every society. Most of this culture's operators are void of any ethics or morals, their identity is derived from what they do. This underworld involves billions of dollars flowing through international economies at a constant rate. Operations are hidden from public view, in the invisible world of espionage and counterintelligence.

On February 21, 1994, a cadre of FBI agents moved in and arrested Aldrich Ames as he drove his Jaguar from his home. He was imprisoned in the Alexandria county jail. As noted in a previous chapter, investigation revealed Ames had been spying on behalf of the Russians for a shocking nine years.

Ames, a disgruntled alcoholic with a long-term poor performance record, had actually been promoted by his CIA managers to the position of Chief of Counterintelligence for the Soviet Union and Eastern Europe. The culture of the Agency at the time was to shuffle poor performing high level officers off to other assignments, just to get rid of them and not have to go through the pain and paperwork of official sanctions. Despite Ames' problems, he was never held accountable; he was just moved from office to office. Eventually, Ames was given access to CIA files on every agent spying for the US in the Soviet Union.

In 1985, under the guise of his position, Ames met with a Soviet intelligence officer from the Soviet embassy in Washington, D.C. For $50,000 he provided this Soviet agent the names of Soviet citizens who were working for the CIA. At a later meeting he provided the name of every agent he knew who was secretly working for the CIA. One by one the CIA spies in the Soviet Union were rounded up, arrested, tried for treason and executed. The CIA had betrayed its deepest agents.

Ames also revealed the names of many of his CIA co-workers and their operational positions in the CIA. The damage done by the compromise of CIA intelligence operations, revelation of the identities of covert CIA personnel and penetration agents in the Soviet Union was of nightmarish proportions.

In 1994 a Security Commission was created by Congress to address the future of the CIA. Among the horrible discoveries made by the Commission was the CIA knew its Soviet operations were being compromised, but ignored the fact for eight years, and even deliberately concealed these compromises from the President and the NSC. Simply put, senior CIA officials lied to the President of the United States about information that was compromising US security and costing agents their lives.

Previously noted was the recommendation of the Commission to overhaul CIA counterintelligence, collocating it with FBI counterintelligence in a new office in CIA headquarters. CIA officers were now taking directions from the FBI. Internal investigations of Agency employees exploded. Hundreds of CIA employees at all levels became the subject of investigation. Careers were being ruined at an alarming rate. An atmosphere of distrust existed between FBI agents and CIA officers in the newly created CEG. The case loads of internal espionage investigations were almost impossible for counterintelligence officers and FBI agents to keep up with. Most graduates of the FBI academy shunned counterintelligence work, seeing it as a career dead-end. Many of the agents were new and inexperienced in the field. Most seasoned FBI agents wanted to make their careers by catching criminals and in one agent's words, "go after bank robbers."

I interacted well with most of the FBI agents I worked with and found them to be men and women of honor. The heated animosity existed at the FBI and CIA management levels. The FBI routinely reminded CIA officers that the Agency could no longer conduct adequate investigations and had botched the ones it handled in the past. It also bragged the FBI had never had a mole and an FBI agent had never engaged in high treason. The FBI was, essentially, a superior organization. Memos were written after meetings documenting what was said, so neither organization could misrepresent any actions on an internal case. On at least one occasion, someone in the FBI leaked a case it had botched to the press, blaming the mistakes on the CIA. I knew the case well. It was handled by one of my fellow officers who had done a thorough job.

On February 18, 2001 the unthinkable happened. The FBI learned one of its own high level agents had been spying for the Soviets; for years. Robert Hanssen was arrested at a park in the Virginia suburb of Vienna.

Hanssen was caught secretly hiding a package containing highly classified national security information at a "dead drop" site, to be retrieved by his Russian intelligence handlers. Hanssen was charged with espionage and conspiracy to commit espionage. These charges could possibly carry with them the death penalty.

Beginning in 1985, while he was assigned to the FBI as a supervisor in the intelligence division of the FBI New York field office, Hanssen had volunteered to provide KGB intelligence officers, assigned to the Soviet embassy in Washington, D.C., with highly classified information. Hanssen provided the KGB and its post-Cold War successor, the Russian SVR (Sluzhba Vneshney Razvedki), with dozens of classified US government documents, to include "Top Secret" and "Codeword" information, via placement at "dead drop" sites - on twenty different occasions.

He compromised several covert human intelligence sources, resulting in the execution of US penetration agents in the Soviet embassy in Washington, D.C., when they returned to Moscow, and provided information on extraordinarily sensitive technical operations being conducted by the US Intelligence Community. Hanssen also provided over two dozen computer disks, containing huge amounts of classified information. He turned over information on FBI counterintelligence operational techniques, operational sources and methods, and compromised the FBI's ongoing espionage investigation of Department of State foreign service officer Felix Bloch. In total, Hanssen turned over more than six thousand pages of some of the US government's most sensitive information, especially information involved in targeting Russian intelligence. In exchange, Hanssen received diamonds and six thousand dollars in cash.

During the period Hanssen was engaged in espionage against the US, he was assigned to New York and Washington, D.C., where he held high level counterintelligence positions. Hanssen had direct, unrestricted access to massive amounts of classified information on US intelligence programs and operations.

Hanssen was able to cover his activities using his FBI training, experience and expertise as an FBI counterintelligence agent, to prevent detection by the FBI or the CIA. This included withholding his true identity from his Russian handlers and avoiding the use of "tradecraft" that would have been detected by his peers or the Russians themselves. Computer forensic analysis techniques, extensive covert counterintelligence surveillance, authorized searches and operational techniques documented Hanssen had regularly accessed classified FBI records, copied those records and provided them to Russian intelligence.

Because of his assignments to national security positions, Hanssen had been given full access to the most sensitive information regarding the former Soviet Union and Russia. FBI Director Louis Free called Hanssen's actions "the most serious violations of law and threat to national security." That was no exaggeration. The damage to US national security and counterintelligence operations was at the highest level, and described by Free as "exceptionally grave." "Grave" is the highest classification of damage to US national security.

The only positive aspect of the Hanssen case was the revelation that Hanssen was discovered when the FBI was able to obtain Russian documents detailing an American spy, who matched the description of Robert Hanssen, was operating within US intelligence. The uncovering of this information and the eventual arrest of Hanssen was the direct result of the joint FBI, CIA counterintelligence effort working to identify penetrations of the CIA and other agencies of the US Intelligence Community. The FBI conducted the entire investigation with the direct assistance of the CIA. The identification of Hanssen, the ensuing investigation and his eventual arrest were the direct result of the new joint FBI, CIA relationship and the Counter Espionage Group (CEG). The Security Commission's recommendation and the collocation of FBI agents and CIA officers in the new Counterintelligence Center were working. It remains a model of the success of FBI and CIA cooperation.

The climate in the CEG had changed. The FBI had just uncovered the most destructive and far reaching espionage case in US history. It was one of its own internal agents; a mole in the FBI. FBI agents in CEG were now deeply embarrassed and displayed shock and dismay. It was the largest piece of professional humble pie ever delivered. Those of us who were CIA officers were in total disbelief it could happen again. We knew the agony you feel when a trusted insider betrays his co-workers, his agency and his country. We had been there. We felt sympathy for the embarrassment caused to the FBI, a valuable and honorable organization.

The damage to national security caused by Hanssen made Aldrich Ames look like a Sunday school teacher. To this day, the American public is not aware of the colossal and far-reaching damage to US intelligence caused by Robert Hanson.

Counterintelligence Strategy

Counterintelligence is not to be confused with counterespionage. Counterespionage is narrowly concerned with stopping foreign governments from stealing US secrets. Counterintelligence has several more aspects of its function. Counterintelligence, or CI, is concerned with gaining accurate and extensive knowledge of foreign intelligence service procedures and operations and developing sources and methods to neutralize them.

Counterintelligence as a US mission was instituted by President Ronald Reagan in Executive Order 12333. This order was far reaching in its definition of the CI mission. The purpose of US CI operations was to meet the goals of the 2005 "National Counterintelligence Strategy of the United States." The objective of the strategy was to protect intelligence collection and analysis from foreign intelligence penetration, denial, influence and/or manipulation, ensure the effective execution of US intelligence operations, safeguard the nation's vital national security secrets, protect emerging technologies and sensitive assets from theft and exploitation by foreign governments, and to identify, analyze, exploit and neutralize the intelligence activities of foreign powers and terrorist organizations that seek to damage the US.

The creation of a national counterintelligence strategy was a necessity, not just a case of political forward thinking. The CIA, FBI, Office of Naval Intelligence and several other US security organizations had been penetrated by Soviet, Chinese, Israeli, North Korean and Cuban intelligence services. Espionage cases had abounded, involving the treasonous activities of internal employees within these US intelligence services.

Counterintelligence operations are designed to collect information regarding foreign intelligence and security services. The data is collected and analyzed; much like the intelligence cycle described in the previous chapter, and is used to conduct operations to neutralize the activities of these entities. The material collected in counterintelligence operations includes information on foreign leaders, members of the intelligence organizations and their operations worldwide, how they communicate their activities and details regarding the targets of their operations.

As discussed previously, defectors have played a significant role in US counterintelligence operations. High ranking intelligence officers who have defected to America from the Soviet Union, China and Cuba have provided US intelligence with significant intelligence information and revealed counterintelligence operations that have been of high value to US intelligence. Much of the information provided from debriefings of these defectors involves counterintelligence information on the structure and function of their intelligence services, enabling the CIA to develop programs to neutralize those activities.

The vetting and interviewing of these defectors has been an extremely sensitive part of US counterintelligence operations. The defector's information has to be analyzed and corroborated to ensure the defector is who he or she says they are and the person truly has the access they claim. In the past, defectors have deceived their US handlers by providing false information to gain asylum and money, or by providing disinformation designed to direct US intelligence operations away from the legitimate target.

The CIA Counterintelligence Center is the primary member of the US Intelligence Community tasked with collecting and analyzing information on foreign intelligence services. One recent revelation by the CIA is the discovery of the sophistication and active operations of the Iranian intelligence service, spying on Americans and American facilities.

I am convinced much of the operational expertise of the Iranian service has been shared with anti-American terrorist organizations such as Al Qaeda. Counterintelligence reporting on Al Qaeda has indicated the organization is quite sophisticated in its intelligence and surveillance activities.

The CIA and the DIA also run double-agent operations against foreign intelligence services that have approached Americans as a target of recruitment. These double agents are tasked with providing seemingly valuable, but false information with the goal of interrupting the foreign services operations and leading their efforts in the wrong direction.

The overall, wide ranging and complex role of counterintelligence in protecting US national security information is critical. A robust counterintelligence effort is the best defense against foreign espionage efforts and aids in the protection of critical US secrets, operations and personnel.

Aldrich Ames, CIA officer convicted of committing espionage.

Harold Nicholson, CIA officer convicted of committing espionage.

Robert Hanssen, FBI agent convicted of committing espionage.

Chapter 25

Tyranny of Secrecy

"The very word 'secrecy' is repugnant in a free and open society; and we are as a people inherently and historically opposed to secret societies, to secret oaths, and to secret proceedings."
—John F. Kennedy

"For too long, judges have allowed the government to hide its mistakes behind claims of national security." —Barry Siegel

"Secrecy does not assure either security or success. Executive lies and deception inflict severe and long-lasting damage to the nation."
—Louis Fisher

Secrecy, when used in the context of the Constitution, is an important safeguard for our nation's interests. It defends America from the theft of national security information by foreign enemies bent on the destruction of our form of government. It protects the lives of our service men and women who serve on the front lines of war. It guards the lives of intelligence assets who have chosen to assist our country in the defense of democracy. But, secrecy is a powerful weapon and must be under the appropriate controls. Because secrecy contains, in itself, an inherent power, there must be checks on when it is used, and it must continually be under vigilant oversight by those who properly represent the American public.

Secrecy is only valuable in protecting democracy when it answers to that democracy. Without proper Constitutional checks, secrecy, by its nature, will tend to corruption; much like absolute power in the hands of any individual or group will do the same. When a nation uses the threat of a foreign enemy to justify the use secrecy to spy on itself, it is on the path to tyranny. In principle, democracy, a free society and the truth itself are opposed to the notion of unbridled secrecy. Hence, its use must be the subject of intense scrutiny and public accountability.

A democratic government is under the control of its people, not the other way around. When the executive branch of government, using secrecy, manipulates the judicial branch, the balance of powers has been interrupted and important democratic principles subverted. When the Judicial Branch blindly subjects itself to the executive branch, or is intimidated by it, it abdicates its Constitutional function.

Origin of the State Secrets Privilege

In October 6, 1948, an Air Force Boeing B-29 Superfortress Bomber departing Robbins Air Force base crashed shortly after takeoff near Waycross, Georgia. Nine of the thirteen men, including three RCA engineers, were killed in the crash. Four members of the crew parachuted to safety. On August 9, 1950, a lawyer for the widows of the three civilian engineers who died in the crash requested the Air Force's accident report to explain the disaster. A judge issued a summary judgment of $225,000.00 against the government and in favor of the widows. The government argued the report could not be released without damaging national security. Air Force affidavits claimed the aircraft was engaged in a "highly secret mission." In response to the judge's challenge, the Assistant Attorney General stated, "We contend that the findings of the [Executive Branch] are binding...upon the judiciary. You cannot review it or interpret it. That is what it comes down to." The judge did not agree and found the government in default. An appeals court unanimously agreed with the lower court's decision.

When the case came before the US Supreme Court in 1953 the lower court's decision was reversed; for the first time officially recognizing a "state secrets privilege." Fifty years later an FOIA request revealed the crash had been caused by faulty landing gear and did not involve a secret government system. The government had simply used the privilege to cover up its negligence. The privilege gave the government the absolute right, much like that of a monarchy, to conceal evidence, refuse to disclose documents and block legitimate lawsuits.

Air Force Boeing B-29 Superfortress Bomber.

Robbins Air Force Base, Houston County, Georgia

The Violation of Constitutional Balance of Powers

Since 1953, the definition of what constitutes a states secrets privilege has expanded, including "bits and pieces of seemingly innocuous information" the government claims can be woven together. Since the Supreme Court decision, known as "*US vs. Reynolds*," judges have ruled blindly in favor of the executive branch, without looking at the documents involved in the dispute, supposedly supporting the government's state secrets privilege claim. Out of fear of ruling against "national security," they have chosen total deference to the government's assertions. Although the executive branch claims the privilege maintains the balance of powers, enabling it to take independent action, this assertion is contrary to the actual Constitutional doctrine. Because the executive branch and the CIA pressure judges to invoke the privilege (most notably in cases involving US citizens), convincing them they do not know enough about intelligence to render a decision, and judges comply with no review of the case facts, this does the opposite of what the government claims. It clearly subverts the Constitutional doctrine of balance of powers, tilting important First and Fourth Amendment decisions in favor of the executive branch. By deferring to the executive branch with no case review, the judiciary has retreated from its Constitutional responsibility.

From 1953 to the present the federal government, and most notoriously the CIA, has used assertion of the state secrets privilege to block cases of negligence, discrimination, shut down whistleblower claims, prevent other branches of the government from conducting investigations and block contractors from resolving business conflicts with millions of dollars at stake involving classified government contracts.

In particular, the CIA's recent abuse of the state secrets privilege to deny access to evidence and information was accelerated by CIA Director George Tenet. Tenet repeatedly used the remotely known state secrets privilege and claims of statutory privilege (50 USC. 403-3(c) (6)) to derail legal discovery and pressure the courts to dismiss legitimate constitutional cases. Prior to Tenet's actions, the privilege had only been used with significant discretion and for real reasons of national security. The original intent was to protect the most "sensitive military missile technology secrets and imagery satellite technology." It is now being used to cover up CIA negligence, criminal activity and constitutional violations. From 2001 to 2002 alone, the Bush administration used the privilege to block lawsuits 39 times.

By abusing the state secrets privilege, the CIA has exerted tyrannical control over injured or aggrieved employees, contractors and even families of CIA officers who are not employed by the organization. The CIA's Office of General Counsel (OGC) uses "security procedures" to manipulate the legal system and its regulations, and routinely obstructs the legal process, delaying legitimate legal cases against them. In documented case after case, the plaintiff is subjected to intimidation and retaliation.

CIA OGC, Office of Security (OS), Office of Inspector General (OIG) and Office of Medical Services (OMS) officials continually conspire in RICO-like fashion to bring reprisals against the plaintiffs and, on many occasions, violate federal statutes and regulations. The plaintiffs are, as a matter of the OGC's strategy, faced with significant delays, mounting financial costs and psychological and emotional distress (some plaintiffs have later been diagnosed with Post Traumatic Stress Disorder). Most plaintiffs, intimidated, exhausted and financially drained, simply give up. In reality, the fox has total control over the hen house - and the "farmer" (the judicial branch).

Dominating the Legal Process

The CIA completely dominates the federal legal process in its favor. In reality, the Agency, as the defendant in legal proceedings, even has control over selecting the lawyers the plaintiffs use. As an example, only after a storm of adverse publicity did the CIA stop immediately offering its internal lawyer list as an approved source for employee counsel. However, the list still exists and is referred to regularly in less than public settings. Attorneys on the list are faced with a serious conflict of interest. Because the lawyer is now subject to CIA security pressures, this jeopardizes his or her motivation to litigate aggressively against the Agency.

The Agency mandates that plaintiff attorneys must be granted an Agency security clearance even before they can meet with their clients. No employee under CIA cover may discuss the case, even if it involves unclassified issues, with any uncleared public attorney; including cases of criminal activity. The truth is, uncleared attorneys can legally represent Agency clients, using an alias for their names and litigating without using classified information. The clearance process for attorneys representing Agency employees only involves a simple name trace for criminal activity and can be done in less than 24 hours.

The reality is the CIA will intentionally take up to a year or more in some cases to grant this basic clearance. In past cases, this delay by the CIA has caused plaintiff employees to miss their legal deadline for filing their legal complaint. In addition, based on its own policy, and no federal statute, the CIA may withdraw an attorney's clearance at will and without stating the reason. The cause could simply be the plaintiff's counsel had built a solid case against the organization. In some cases, the Agency has not informed the attorneys their clearance has been revoked, setting them up for accusations of "security violations."

The CIA OGC employs a large staff of attorneys, who are on the Agency's payroll. There are more than 100 full-time OGC attorneys in the Agency. As many as eight attorneys can be assigned to defend the Agency against a claim filed by an employee, while the employee has, initially, none or, once cleared, one or at most two attorneys. Agency attorneys, since they work for the organization, have nothing to lose for practicing obstruction and can prolong a case filed by a federal employee for years. If an OGC attorney leaves, another simply takes their place, continuing the delays.

These delays are a part of the Agency's strategy it uses on a regular basis. In addition to this, once the plaintiff's legal action is filed in court, the CIA's cadre of attorneys are joined by Department of Justice lawyers and their staffs. This seriously out-guns the plaintiff's attorney, over-saturating their time on the case and significantly increasing the legal expenses for the plaintiff. In these cases, the CIA knows exactly what it is doing. This has worked countless times in the past. In reality, no regulation exists limiting the number of attorneys a plaintiff may employ in their case. The Agency significantly limits the plaintiff's right to choose counsel and allows itself, as the defendant, to select who the plaintiff's counsel will be and whether or not that attorney will be cleared and able to work on the plaintiff's case.

To exert tyrannical control over the judicial process and the constitutional freedoms of Agency employees, their families and federal contractors, the CIA uses the following well documented tactics:

☐ As a mandate for receiving a clearance, the CIA demands lawyers representing Agency employees sign a CIA secrecy agreement. The Agency uses the secrecy agreement to control opposing counsel, court documentation and attorney-client information

☐ The CIA uses the clearance and secrecy agreement to force opposing attorneys to hand over to the Agency all complaints, briefs and motions before filing them in court. It also prevents opposing counsel from publishing "either by work, conduct or any other means" all court papers or information they plan to release to the public. The CIA reserves the right to redact any information it deems unsuitable from the documents. This gives the CIA complete control over and forewarning of all plaintiffs' court documents. This is an unchallenged, open door to abuse. The Agency ignores an existing Executive Order (EO 12,958, 1.8(2)) which provides guidelines for document classification and prohibits the classification of information only because it is embarrassing to the government

☐ The CIA uses the secrecy agreement and internal security procedures to coerce and intimidate lawyers. In documented cases, the CIA sent its security officers to warn opposing attorneys they had committed "security violations" by not submitting all attorney-client communication through the Agency. Lawyers are led to believe they have violated national security, and the insinuation is made they may have committed a crime

☐ The CIA will coerce the judge to force the plaintiff's counsel to file its legal complaint under seal, further restricting open access to the information and thereby adding the threat of contempt of court and jail time if counsel does not comply with CIA security rules

☐ Claiming the need for secrecy, the CIA insists on control of all information related to the suit and demands it must be stored in an Agency building. The CIA "screens" all information prior to transporting it. In addition, the Agency makes the decision which information the attorney is allowed to see and escorts him or her while the information is reviewed. All notes taken by the attorney are reviewed and, if the Agency deems it necessary, confiscated before the attorney leaves the facility. This amounts to total control of and access to privileged attorney-client information in any suit against it. This includes the opposing attorney's notes, drafts and any other document used in the suit. The CIA demands the attorney only use Agency safes and computers for all information related to the case, then withholds them from the attorney for months

☐ The CIA routinely uses obstruction and delay tactics that work in its favor. In some suits brought against it, the Agency took years to move forward with the case. Because it employs a large staff of OGC attorneys the Agency has nothing to lose and everything to gain by delaying a case. These delays increase the financial and emotional strain on the plaintiff and his or her attorneys

☐ The CIA denies attorney's access to potential witnesses for the plaintiff and withholds the identities of its witnesses. This is a direct violation of federal rules of discovery. Using secrecy, the Agency can claim it has evidence, when none actually exists

☐ Even in cases where the plaintiffs win, the CIA delays awards to plaintiffs and attorneys are forced to litigate to recoup fees. ██████████████████ the settlement agreement was signed by all parties, and the Agency canceled the settlement two days later

☐ Federal district courts refuse to order the CIA to disclose information in suits brought against it. Total deference is made by courts to the Agency, allowing it to decide what is and is not a matter of secrecy and national security

☐ The CIA regularly invokes secrecy to deny access to evidence. Most, if not all, information requested via discovery is withheld

☐ As an example of the CIA's abuse of privilege, citing the

National Security Act of 1947 (requiring the Agency to protect sources and methods), the CIA labels any evidence that may reveal wrongdoing as a "source" or a "method," to ensure it is concealed from the media or public exposure

☐ If it appears the Plaintiff may prevail against the CIA, or the CIA's actions may become public, the Agency will invoke the state secrets privilege and coerce federal judges to shut the case down entirely. Intimidated because of their lack of expertise in intelligence matters, or lack of effort to educate themselves on the intelligence issues involved, federal judges routinely bow to CIA pressure and invoke the privilege

☐ After invoking the State secrets privilege, the CIA requests closed-door sessions with the federal judge without opposing attorneys or the plaintiffs being present. Former CIA DCI Tenet used this tactic on several occasions, claiming the plaintiffs and their attorneys, all of whom had clearances, did not have the "need to know." This is a violation of the basic constitutional rights of the plaintiffs. In this way, all opponents of the CIA are totally excluded from the judicial process

☐ Using the Privilege as a sword instead of a shield, the CIA will heavily black out court documents, books and articles regarding cases where the privilege has been used to conceal civil cases brought against it ██████████████ ███████████████

☐ CIA employees are not advised that, as a condition of employment and by signing the secrecy agreement, they are giving up their right to a jury trial and, if they are injured or killed while on duty, they or their loved ones are obstructed from suing for damages. Thousands of contractors across the US sign these agreements, not knowing their rights have been taken away.

Shadow Strategy

The CIA invokes the state secrets privilege knowing federal district judges will automatically uphold it without review of the evidence. This is rubber stamped in the appellate courts. The CIA demands the case be sealed, permanently concealing case information from Congressional review and public disclosure. CIA strategy moves the case permanently into the judicial system. Congressional inquiries into misuse of the privilege to conceal constitutional violations are ignored. The CIA claims the case is now a completed, sealed, legal matter under the purview of the judicial branch, and no longer available for review by Congressional representatives. Because these cases have been sealed, the number of times the privilege has been used by the CIA to conceal evidence is unknown.

Although Congress has ultimate authority to proceed further and demand information regarding judicial use of the Privilege and reform it, most representatives are reluctant to move past the CIA's obstruction. The effort is too difficult, time consuming and will receive strong resistance from the executive branch, most notably the CIA. At the time of this writing, Congressman Jerold Nader (D-NY) is working for reform of the Privilege. In June 2012, Nadler introduced the State Secrets Protection Act [HR5956]. The purpose of the bill is "to provide safe, fair, and responsible procedures and standards for resolving claims of state secrets privilege." The bill requires federal courts to independently assess the validity of the government's assertion of the state secrets privilege. It prevents the courts from simply deferring to the claim without reviewing the evidence. The bill requires courts to consider introducing non-privileged substitutes for privileged evidence. This would make it possible for cases to proceed to adjudication even when claims are made that certain pieces of information or evidence are privileged. It would also make it more difficult for the CIA to assert case information is classified, when in reality it is not.

President Obama and Attorney General Eric Holder have issued statements indicating their intent to reform the privilege; to prevent abuses that have occurred in the past. At the time of this writing, these reforms have not taken place. ██████████

██████████████ identities and case facts are hidden in secret.

.

We all want to stop the war on terror. We all want terrorists brought to justice and terrorism neutralized. But, we must constantly monitor government's increase in power and make sure it does not use the war on terror to take away our freedoms. If it does, we will lose the war on terror also, giving up the very freedoms terrorist organizations seek to destroy.

Unknown Use of the State Secrets Privilege

It is critical that Americans understand how current use of the state secrets privilege affects their rights personally. Unknown to most of us, the privilege has been used hundreds of times – against American citizens. This does not include the cases which have been sealed - and remain unknown. It is especially true regarding the government's use of the privilege from 2001 until now.

Tens of thousands of Americans work for private government contractors, both large and small. Executive Order 10865 provides for the classification of several corporate activities involved in soliciting or winning government business. This includes bidding on contracts, contract awards, negotiations, contract performance and contract terminations. Because the information corporate personnel access as part of their normal duties is now classified, thousands of citizens fall under government secrecy laws or must sign a government secrecy agreement to continue their jobs; not knowing their rights have been taken away. The federal government established the National Industrial Security Program (NISP) to protect information disseminated to private contractors. This allowed government control of information, and those with access to it, routinely used by US corporations, small businesses and private citizens, and ushered in the use of the state secrets privilege in private industry, against American citizens. The Constitutional importance of this cannot be overstated.

In October 2011, the intelligence community report to congress revealed that 4.8 million US citizens hold security clearances for access to classified information. Each of these citizens is required to sign a government secrecy agreement, placing them under the shadow of the state secrets privilege.

US corporations with government contracts or access to government information now invoke the state secrets privilege against their own employees when lawsuits are brought against them. These lawsuits include assault, battery, racial discrimination, fraud, breach of contract, libel, patent infringement, toxic exposure, negligence and personal injury. Once the corporation claims the privilege to suppress evidence or request dismissal of the case, the government makes the decision whether or not the privilege applies. If the suit affects the government, risks exposure of its information or could reveal government malfeasance, the privilege will be upheld. Government claims of the privilege on behalf of the corporation are almost never reversed. The federal district courts automatically uphold it with no review of the evidence and the appeals courts follow suit.

I cannot stress enough how critical this issue is. Use of the state secrets privilege against American citizens to conceal government or corporate negligence is one of the most egregious violations of our Constitution in the last fifty years.

As I wrote earlier, this all began with the crash of an Air Force B-29 Superfortress bomber over Waycross, Georgia, on October 6, 1948, which killed nine of the thirteen men aboard. As I learned later in the investigation, four men either jumped too low or their chutes fouled in the aircraft. Five others plummeted to their death. One of these men was Albert H. Payla, an RCA engineer. Albert Payla was seated in the cockpit of the plane, which was buried on impact. Since February, 2000 his daughter, Judith Payla Loether, has been engaging in a heroic fight to expose the fraud behind the creation of the state secrets privilege. Loether was able to locate the unclassified B-29 accident report detailing the B-29 crash - on the Internet. This report was the central document used by the government to officially recognize the state secrets privilege, and deny the widows of the RCA engineers their rights.

In *Unites States v. Reynolds*, the district court and the Third Circuit upheld the widow's constitutional rights and ruled in their favor because of the government's refusal to release the Air Force report, allowing for just and fair proceedings to continue. This was, without a doubt, the constitutional approach. Supreme Court Chief Justice Vinson chose not to do so. Using his own definition of the scope of individual rights and basing his decision on an Air Force claim that was a fraud, i.e., claiming the accident report was secret when in reality was not, Vinson created a new constitutional doctrine based on his own tangled reasoning - and expanded the power of the executive branch to resemble that of a monarchy.

On February 26, 2003, lawyers Wilson Brown and Jeff Almeida, representing several families who lost fathers, and in one case a husband, in the crash of the B-29, filed a petition with the Supreme Court requesting it reconsider its landmark 1953 decision in *US v. Reynolds*.

Referring to the Air Force accident report, the lawyers wrote, "Indeed they are no more than accounts of a flight that, due to the Air Force's negligence, went tragically awry. In telling the Court otherwise, the Air Force lied. In reliance upon that lie, the Court deprived the widows [the three original plaintiffs] of their judgments. It is for this Court, through issuance of a writ of error *coram nobis* and in exercise of its inherent power to remedy fraud, to put things right... *United States v. Reynolds* stands as a classic 'fraud on the court,' one that is most remarkable because it succeeded in tainting a decision of our nation's highest tribunal."

On June 23, 2003, in a shocking decision, the Supreme Court refused to hear the petition to reopen the 1953 *US v Reynolds* case, despite its basis on fraud. It issued a one-sentence ruling:

"The motion for leave to file a writ of error *coram nobis* is denied."

This decision occurred within the same time period, 2001 – 2009, that the Bush administration and the CIA used the state secrets privilege to shut down lawsuits, brought by US citizens, against the executive branch – more than any other time in US history. It unilaterally upset the Constitutional balance of powers, making the judiciary an arm of the executive branch; and gave the executive branch unbridled power to silence lawsuits against it.

While writing this chapter I interviewed Judith Palya Loether regarding her story. Judy is an American who has felt the shock and pain of the state secrets privilege being used to cover up the truth, at the expense of her mother, three grieving widows and five little children. She made the following statement:

Judith Palya Loether.
Fought a heroic battle
to expose the fraud
behind creation of the
state secrets privilege.
(Photo courtesy of Judith Palya Loether)

"I grew up understanding that my father had been killed in a B-29 when I was seven weeks old, leaving my mother with three small children. He had been testing secret equipment that he developed for the government as a civilian contractor. I understood that my mother had been involved a lawsuit because of the crash and I knew she had won some money as a result of that lawsuit.

More than 50 years after my father's death, and with a lot of research, I finally came to know *exactly* what happened. I learned what my father saw and heard during his last minutes alive. I saw where his body came to rest and read about what it looked like. I read about the pilot turning off engine number 4 instead of the burning engine number 1. The engineer cut the fuel to engine number 2 instead of engine number 1. The mechanics had not installed heat shields as directed, and the plane needed special permission to fly that day because of its mechanical problems. The crew had not flown together before and the civilians had not been instructed how to get out of the plane in an emergency. But more shocking, and far more disturbing, I also learned what my America did to my mother in the Supreme Court of the United States so that the executive branch of the government could have a privilege.

I came to understand that my mother had not won her case, she had lost it, and it was a case that had gone all the way to the Supreme Court. The widows had won in the Federal Court and in the Federal Appellate Court. But the government chose to challenge the decision all the way to the Supreme Court, where the widows lost and received a settlement. In the now famous case *US v Reynolds* 345 US 1, the government told the Justices of the Supreme Court that the Air Force Accident Report, withheld from the Federal Court, revealed information about the secret equipment on the plane that was SO secret it would jeopardize national security if even a judge saw it. The Justices bought this lie and reversed the lower court decision in the favor of the government. I knew the government's statement to be a lie. I HAD that now declassified report in its entirety and the ONLY mention of that secret equipment was just that . . . "the secret equipment was removed from the plane [wreckage]."

Later I learned how the government had a purpose in their appeals. It was not to save them the $250,000.00 judgment for the three widows and their attorneys. It was to get the State Secrets Privilege. Still today I visualize a government building conference room in around 1951, where some big wigs are deciding to get an Executive privilege into case law by lying in the Supreme Court. This was not some cement factory the government was plowing under, it was my mom, three grieving widows and five little children. Is this *my* America? Truth, Justice and the *American* Way? Harry Truman was President then. He had to know about this power play for the President of the Unites States and all those heads of departments under him. He was "the buck stops here" guy remember? You know, that's all about taking responsibility.

I decided to sue the government. I wanted the People to know that the government lied, in the *Supreme Court of the United States* and did injury to my mother, me, my brothers and the other families with *malice aforethought*. I thought the Justices would be shocked. A small part of me thought that when the President heard about it he might call to apologize. Well, yeah, wasn't I awfully naïve? I thought my country usually did the right thing, this is AMERICA. But in my journey I have come to understand so much. This country is NOT about Truth and Justice. This country is not about WE the People."

Government bureaucracy always moves towards increase in power. Today, it is doing so using the state secrets privilege, with increasing frequency, to expand its control - and protect its own negligence. The founding fathers trumpeted the need to resist this inherent tendency of government, with eternal vigilance. Despite the fraud and unconstitutional ruling behind the creation of the state secrets privilege on March 9, 1953, dramatic abuse of the privilege continues today, routinely violating the rights of American citizens. As the saying goes, "Enough is enough."

The time for reform of the state secrets privilege has come.

Author in front of
a sign that says it
all. Government abuse
of secrecy leads back
to Waycross, Georgia
in 1948.

(Photo courtesy of the author)

Plaque placed at the site of the B-29 crash by Judith Payla Loether,
daughter of Albert H. Payla, an RCA engineer killed in the crash.
The plaque and its location have remained largely unknown to most
Americans. (photo courtesy of the author)

Author at the site where the B-29
Superfortress went down. The site
was previously farmland.

(photo courtesy of the author)

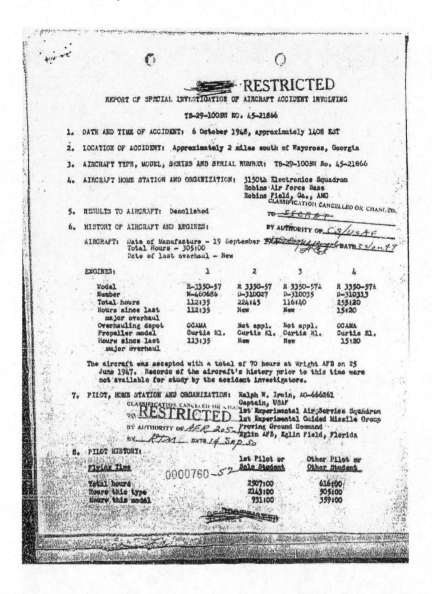

Copy of the Air Force's accident report. The Air Force originally claimed the document was classified. This was the basis of the Supreme Court decision *United States v. Reynolds*. Later it was determined there was no classified information in the document and the crash was the result of negligence. Despite the fact that the Supreme Court decision officially recognizing the state secrets privilege was based on fraud, the privilege remains today. Overt examination reveals it has been used approximately fifty times. In reality, the Privilege has been used *at least four hundred times*. This does not include the number of cases that have been sealed; hidden from Congress and the public. (photo courtesy of the author).

Photo of the B-29 crash site in 1948.
(Photo courtesy of Judith Palya Loether)

Photo of the cockpit's point of impact, B-29 crash site in 1948.
(Photo courtesy of Judith Palya Loether)

Albert Palya, RCA engineer.
(Photo courtesy of Judith Palya)

Elizabeth Palya, Albert Palya's
widow, with her daughter Judith
Alberta Palya, one month after
the B-29 Crash.
(Photo courtesy of Judith Palya)

Chapter 26
Tyranny - The Story of an American Family

"The only foundation of a free constitution is pure Virtue, and if this cannot be inspired into our people in a greater measure than they have it now, they may change their rulers and the forms of government, but they will not obtain a lasting liberty. They will only exchange tyrants and tyrannies." —John Adams

Following is the manuscript I submitted to the CIA for pre-publication review. ████████████████████████████
██

deleted several pages that were blacked out entirely.

██
██
██
██
██
██
██
██
██
██
██
██
██
██
██
██
██
██
██

In an important First Amendment case, United States Court of Appeals, Fourth Circuit decision; **UNITED STATES of America, Appellee, v. Victor L. MARCHETTI** (Nos. 72-1586, 72-1589) ruled:

"35. Because we are dealing with a prior restraint upon speech, we think that the CIA must act promptly to approve or disapprove any material which may be submitted to it by Marchetti. Undue delay would impair the reasonableness of the restraint, and that reasonableness is to be maintained if the restraint is to be enforced. We should think that, in all events, the maximum period for responding after the submission of material for approval should not exceed thirty days."

The CIA did not return my manuscript for six months, despite several requests.

In addition, this was a violation of Executive Order 12958, as amended by Executive Order 13292, which forbids the CIA from blacking out unclassified information simply because it is embarrassing to the Agency.

Following is the actual manuscript I submitted to the CIA for prepublication review. It includes CIA blackouts of public, open source information, readily available in public records. In keeping with my CIA Secrecy Agreement, below is the CIA's approved, blacked out version of our story.

"The story you are about to read is true. I am a former career Officer of the Central Intelligence Agency (CIA). During my career at the Agency, I functioned as a Staff Security Officer, Protective Agent for the Director of Central Intelligence, Chief of Training for the CIA police force, ███████████████████████████████, Counterintelligence Investigator, Counter Terrorism Center Training Officer and Polygraph Examiner. I was a Category I employee. Because of my previous employment with the CIA, I must abide by my duty to protect CIA sources and methods. I owe much of my career training to the CIA, have many fond memories of my tenure there and have many close friends who still work in the organization. In addition, the goal of this writing is to abide by any ███████████████ oversight regarding the following information.

Although, there are no direct intelligence sources or methods, or specifics of ██████████ ██████████, discussed in this manuscript, I have been careful to protect the true names of CIA employees, locations and any other information, the majority of which is overt, that could jeopardize the Agency or my former co-workers. Thus, I do not discuss my employment status (during my career I have also been assigned to several other government agencies), specific locations, true names of individuals or any other organizations involved. I use pseudonyms for all individuals discussed in this book, their positions and the names of all locations involved. The only true names used in the pages that follow are members of my immediate family and the former Director of the CIA, George Tenet. Because this account involves those I love the most, my wife and children, it is a story that must be told.

It was a beautiful sunny summer day in the Plains, Virginia. My wife, three children and I had purchased a home just behind Great Meadows, home of the International Gold Cup races. Life was good. My wife and I spent precious amounts of family time together with our children in learning exercises, field trips, etc. My children were the most important thing in my life. Several years before, I had been diagnosed with serious kidney disease and initially, was given six weeks to live. My kidneys had disintegrated and did not show up on X rays. I was bleeding internally. My mother, a skeptic at the time, asked her close friend and a small group of Christians to pray. The doctors took additional X rays, and learned that my kidneys were back. They could not explain what had happened. It was a clear medical miracle. My kidney tests became normal. However, doctors told me that, because of the drugs and radiation I had been exposed to, I would never have children. They were wrong. My wife and I had three. Because of this, Lorena and I loved our children more than life itself. These were days of love, loyalty and laughter.

During our time in the Plains, I was ordered by the organization I worked for to take an assignment as the Executive Officer at a ██████████ My wife was reluctant to move ██████████ and leave the life she loved behind. In the end, we chose duty over preference. We sold our house, packed our things and moved to our new surroundings. I had been directed by the Chief ██████████ ██████████ so I could take over the responsibility of responding to emergencies. I learned later that another reason ██████████ wanted me to ██████████ was so that he could sneak off late in the evening, spend the night with his secret mistress, and not be responsible for anything that could occur in his absence. Although I knew this, I dutifully complied.

███████████████████████████████████████
███████████████████████████████████████
███████████████████████████████████████
███████████████████████████████████████
███████████████████████████████████████
███████████████████████████████████████
███████████████████████████████████████
███████████████████████████████████████
███████████████████████████████████████
███████████████████████████████████████
███████████████████████████████████████
███████████████████████████████████████
███████████████████████████████████████
███████████████████████

Upon seeing ████████████ I made a request to ████████ to ██████████████████████████████ Although he had promised to do so ██████████████████████ the request was ignored. I made several more requests which were ignored as well. My verbal requests to ███████ were met with sarcasm and claims that ████████████ could not afford it.

During my tenure ██████████ I found several significant security lapses and unreported criminal activity. Because of the nature of ██████████ I was ordered not to report these past ██████████

███████████████████████████████████████
███████████████████████████████████████
███████████████████████████████████████
███████████████████████████████████████
███████████████████████████████████████
███████████████████████████████████████
███████████████████████████████████████
███████████████████████████████████████
███████████████████████████████████████
███████████████████████████████████████
███████████████████████████████████████
███████████████████████████████████████
███████████████████████████████████████

During this time ▮▮▮▮▮▮▮ abruptly retired and left the facility. He was replaced by the new Chief ▮▮▮▮▮▮▮ was also joined by ▮▮▮▮▮▮ ▮

▮▮▮▮▮▮ and ▮▮▮▮ denied there was a problem and did nothing.

After

several requests, ███████and ████████████refused, claiming it was not necessary.

Because of the seriousness of the situation, I, as the Executive Officer, made the request myself to ████████████████████ ████████████████To our relief, I located ███████████████

██

██

██

██

██

██

██

██

██

██

██

██

████████████████████████████████

Following the visit of ████████████████ I documented his comments and provided the information to ████████ Within hours, I received an emergency call from ████████ He advised that there had been a "terrible mistake," and that ████████████had found nothing. I responded that he was mistaken. The following day, ████████ delivered a memorandum to me from ████████stating that ████████

██

████████████████████We were shocked. This was an obvious fabrication. Unknown to ████████ and ████████ we had taped the conversation with ████████ We became convinced that, for some reason, the ████████████████████████████████was being covered up; at high levels. We prepared ourselves accordingly and began to document everything.

██

██

██

██

██

██
████████████████████.

██
██
██
██
██
██
██
██
██
██
██
██
████████████████████████████.

██
██
██
██
██
███████████████████.

I again requested that ████████████████████████████
have ████████████████████████ The request was refused. I finally
had enough. Subsequently, I sent a message back to headquarters in
Washington documenting ██████████████████████████████
██
██████████████████████████ A response came back
ordering ██
███████████████████████████████took us into his office, ordered
us █████████████████ to use a government credit card for expenses
███████████████████We requested that he put his orders to use the credit
card in writing. He refused, feigning being offended that we did not trust
him. He later lied to investigators and claimed he had ordered us not to
use the card. ████████████████████████████████

Once again, I demanded that ████████████████ and
██████████████████have ████████████████finally conceded and gave
me permission to ████████████████████████████ I did so, and

the date for ███████████████ was set. My wife and I again felt a sense of relief. Finally, we would find out, from an impartial source, what

██
██
████████████████████████████████.

    Finally, the date of ████████████████ was upon us. My wife and I were excited about the prospect of finding out what ████████████████████████████ The day before ██████████ was to take place, I called ████████████████████████████ to confirm the appointment. To my surprise, I was advised that ████████████████████had called and cancelled ██████████ I was livid. I called ████████████████and was advised that ██████████████ had scheduled ████████████████████████████████████
████████████████████████████

    ██
██
██
██
██
██
██
██
██
██
██████████████████████████████
██
██
██
██

██████████████████████████████████████Compliant, we sat at the dining room table for the interview. As ██████████████████████ opened his notebook to begin the questioning, we asked if he would mind if we taped the interview. He abruptly refused, advised that he did not do taped interviews, closed his notebook and left the house. He later reported, in official traffic, that he had interviewed ████████████████ and the results were favorable.

██
██
██
██

After the ██
████████████████████████████ were issued in a report. I was called to a
tense meeting ██advised
that ██
████████ I requested a copy of the ████████████████, which
████████████████████████handed over.

Following the meeting, I sent ████████████████, all open
source and unclassified, to a ████████████████████████████
████████ I also sent the ████████████████to a ████████████
████████████████████████████ Both issued reports, in writing, stating
that there ████████████████████████████████████ I issued a lengthy
report calling the organization ████████████████████ erroneous
and documenting the errors. We had the official documentation we
needed. I sent ████████████ to Washington. My wife and I hoped
that the organization would now listen. We were gravely mistaken. The
documents were ignored.

███
███
███
███████████████████████████████████ .

"A nation that is afraid to let its people judge the truth and falsehood in an open market is a nation that is afraid of its people."
—John F. Kennedy

███
███
███
███
████████████████████████████████ I filed an official, internal grievance. For a Category I Officer, filing a grievance was inconceivable. Although you were a top performer, your career would be forever tainted because you had rocked the boat. I had to choose between my career and my family. My family won.

The internal grievance I filed within the organization was extensive, documenting the chronology of events surrounding, what I now knew, ████████████████████████ and the erroneous procedures and findings of the organization's ███████████████ The redress I requested in the grievance was a second, objective ████████████ ███████████████████████████████ The majority of the document was unclassified. As a classifying authority, I appropriately marked each paragraph unclassified relating to ██████████████ ████████████████████████████To protect the identities of ███████personnel mentioned in the document I dutifully classified the overall report. Legally and with proper approval, paragraphs marked as unclassified can be removed from the document for the appropriate release. I sent the document through protected, official channels to headquarters.

Four weeks transpired after my filing of the grievance and I heard nothing. I contacted the office that was to receive the grievance and was advised that they had not received any correspondence from me. Livid, I located the grievance officer responsible for my office ████████████████████████ Since I was scheduled to travel to headquarters on official business the next week, I requested a meeting.

The appointment was scheduled for the day following my arrival.

On my visit to Washington, I checked into a local hotel regularly used by other officers of my organization. Early the second morning, I traveled to the organization's outer building to meet with the grievance officer. Prior to meeting with her, I visited the mail registry to inquire if they had received the package I had sent them. They advised they had not. While I was there, I noticed an envelope addressed to the grievance officer from the officer who was the subject of the grievance. I smelled a rat. That morning, I met with the grievance officer and presented her with ██ ██ ██ ██She acted shocked at seeing ██████████████████████ ██████████████████████████████ She advised that she would look into the situation. I felt a great sense of relief. However, again, that relief was to be shattered. I returned to my hotel room to find the door standing slightly open. As I always do, I had double checked the door, making sure it was locked, before I left for my meeting. Someone had been in the room. I checked with the front desk to see if the maids had cleaned the room. The hotel manager advised that the maids had not cleaned the rooms yet and no one from the hotel had been in that room.

During my visit to headquarters, I requested a meeting with the main office of the internal mail registry. I had the registry official, ███████████ check to see what had happened to my grievance correspondence. ███████████ entered the internal mail tracking system and located my package, tracking it ███████████ to the mail registry. To my and ███████████ surprise, the package was transported to headquarters, arrived; then disappeared. ███████████ was dumfounded. I asked him what that meant. He responded that the package had been lost and would probably never be recovered.

When I returned to my office back ███████████ I noticed that the boxes containing my personal records had been searched. Whoever did it did not even bother to close the boxes properly. A close friend in the building advised that he had seen ███████████Executive Administrator going through my desk. I knew the game had begun.

"When we assumed the Soldier, we did not lay aside the

Citizen." —George Washington

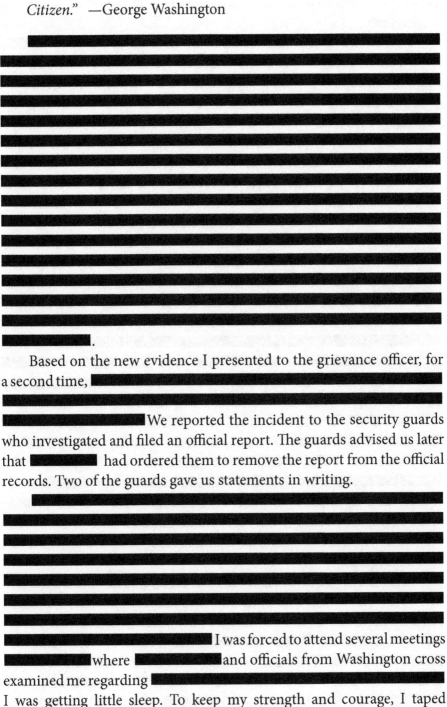

Based on the new evidence I presented to the grievance officer, for a second time, ██

██We reported the incident to the security guards who investigated and filed an official report. The guards advised us later that ████████████ had ordered them to remove the report from the official records. Two of the guards gave us statements in writing.

████████████████████████████████████ I was forced to attend several meetings ████████████where ████████████and officials from Washington cross examined me regarding ████████████████████████████ I was getting little sleep. To keep my strength and courage, I taped verses from Psalm 37 (in the Bible's Old Testament) inside my meeting notebook. When accusations were levied against me and meetings became stressful, I opened the notebook and read the verses. They gave me strength.

███.

██
██
██
██
██
██
██
██
██
██
██
██
██
██.

██
██
██
██

████████████████████████████████.

████████████████████████ security guards, who we had befriended because of my new support for their staff and their mission, began to confide in us that they had been ordered to conduct surveillance on ████████████████████████████████ The security guards, several of whom ██████████████████, confided in us, partly in hopes getting assistance with the ██ ████████████████████.

After these events, to bring some humor to a terrible situation, as our family drove through the ████████████ check point (knowing the guards were ordered to keep ████████████ under surveillance), we wore joke eye glasses and mustaches; as a comic way of letting ████████████ know we knew what he was up to. The guards appreciated the humor.

██
██
██
██
██

I began to curse and swear. I turned around and looked towards ███████████ ██████████████████████████ The thought crossed my mind to ████████████████ punch him in the nose. As I turned to do so, my conscience got the best of me. It was like a small voice inside said, "Kevin, you know you can't do that, it is against what you believe." Then, I also realized; that is exactly what they wanted me to do. The idea was to place me under enough pressure, so I lost my temper, brand me as security risk and use it in their defense ████████████ I was not going to let that happen. Instead, I drove my wife and the kids back to ███████████, took a long walk and prayed. The next year was one of constant discipline and self control. I could not have done it without the support of my wife and my faith.

.We thought it could not get any more bizarre, but it did.

Looking ahead, I put in a request for a new assignment at headquarters as a Polygraph Examiner. I was accepted into the program. I was ordered to move my family back to Washington. As we drove out ▮▮▮▮▮▮▮▮ I asked one of the guards, a friend of our family's, if I could borrow his radio one last time. With a smile, he handed it to me. Knowing that ▮▮▮▮▮▮ was monitoring our ▮▮▮▮▮▮▮ movements and the radio communications, I contacted ▮▮▮▮ The dispatcher responded. I requested that the dispatcher, "Please advise Mr. ▮▮▮▮▮ that Elvis has ▮▮▮▮▮▮▮" The guards found it hilarious. We will miss them. They were good to our family and to ▮▮▮▮▮▮

Late one evening, as our family drove from the hotel on our journey back to Washington, we noticed that a vehicle had been following us for several miles. Because it was late, there were very few other vehicles on the road. As we progressed down the four lane highway, I altered my speeds in order to see if the vehicle was indeed correlating with our movements. The vehicle did the same. I slowed the car down to 10 miles an hour. The vehicle did the same. Then the driver of the vehicle turned off the headlights and continued to follow us in the dark. My wife and the kids became terrified. At this point, I increased our speed to 70 miles per hour. The vehicle did the same. Now, absolutely convinced we were being followed, I accelerated to 90 miles per hour. The dark vehicle did the same. I increased our speed to over 100 miles per hour and, once again, the vehicle did the same. Now knowing that there was a potential danger to our family, I waited for an exit. When one appeared, I drove as if we were going to pass it, then, at the last minute, took the exit rapidly. The vehicle did not make the exit. I drove a circuitous route through the little town; then pulled off in a dark parking lot where we waited. My wife and the kids were frantic. After waiting 30 minutes, we pulled back onto the freeway. We never saw the vehicle again.

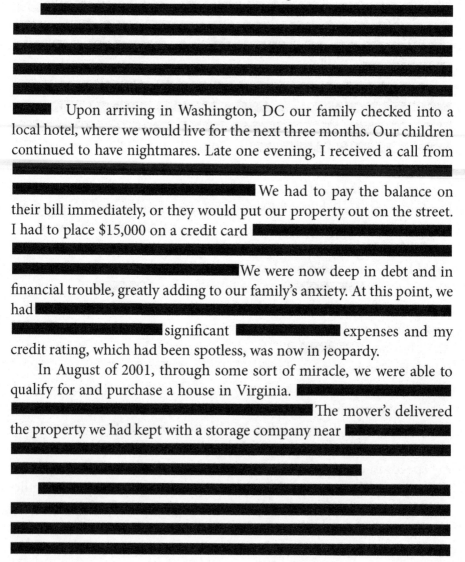

Upon arriving in Washington, DC our family checked into a local hotel, where we would live for the next three months. Our children continued to have nightmares. Late one evening, I received a call from

We had to pay the balance on their bill immediately, or they would put our property out on the street. I had to place $15,000 on a credit card

We were now deep in debt and in financial trouble, greatly adding to our family's anxiety. At this point, we had

significant expenses and my credit rating, which had been spotless, was now in jeopardy.

In August of 2001, through some sort of miracle, we were able to qualify for and purchase a house in Virginia.

The mover's delivered the property we had kept with a storage company near

██
██
██
███████████████████████

Several months later, as we entered our new house late in the evening after church, we opened the door to find our Labrador Retriever asleep in her cage by the door. We had gotten her to keep the house secure while we were gone. She was a watchdog and was never asleep when we arrived, especially right by the entry door. I had to shake her to wake her up. As we went upstairs, I found the ████████████████████ ██ ████████████████████████████████████The lock to the entry door was broken. We felt as if we were under a bizarre assault by some sort of organized monster.

> "The judicial power ought to be distinct from both the legislative and executive, and independent upon both, that so it may be a check upon both, as both should be checks upon that."
> —John Adams

After the litany of break-ins to our house, our family being surveilled, being followed and the corrupt activity of organization ████████████

I was called to several meetings in the organization where I was cross examined over the information contained in my grievance and the findings of ████████████████████████ I gracefully and professionally stuck to the truth. It was clear that headquarters was in an uproar over the documents and ████████████that had just hit their offices. They were also terrified of the case reaching the news media.

I sought out the grievance office again, requesting help. My phone calls and e-mails were not returned. I was advised later by an internal source that a reporter had contacted the organization's Inspector General's Office about ████████ and was demanding an interview with me by name. Apparently, I was difficult to locate, because the reporter never contacted me.

I was given a temporary office in the organization's outer security building. I kept documents from ███████ in the cabinet above the desk. I secretly trapped the closed cabinet with a magnetic strip. If the cabinet was opened the magnetic strip would be ajar. Upon my return to the office one afternoon, I checked the strip. It was out of place. Someone had been in the cabinet.

In Washington, I took on my assignment as a polygraph examiner. I received an award for preventing an attempted penetration of the organization by a foreign intelligence service. This did not matter; I had awakened the sleeping monster that had no tolerance for being exposed ███████████It was a strange feeling to walk through the halls of the organization I once loved, with the knowledge that they now knew ████████████████████████ My grievance had exposed their bogus ███████████████and they knew it. I knew my movements were being monitored. I knew how they were doing it. I used to be them. I was called and advised that I was under "Administrative Investigation." I was brought to several meetings where I was interrogated by several organization officials regarding the credibility of my grievance. I was accused of misusing the credit card ██████████████ordered us to use during ████████████

Knowing that my movements and e-mails were all being monitored and an attempt was being made to find a way, or create a way, to accuse me of anything that would damage my credibility ████████████ I submitted a surprise letter of resignation. Knowing they would accuse me (I used to be one of their CI interrogators) of resigning to hide something, I documented the effective date as 30 days later. It was slightly humorous. After laying the resignation letter on my supervisor's desk, I went in to conduct a polygraph test on a Subject. As I was conducting the test, I could hear the feet of my managers bumping up against the wall as they all crowded around the two-way mirror, watching me do the test and planning their next move.

Immediately afterward, I was called in to a meeting. When I advised I had resigned because of ███████████████████ they all feigned ignorance, claiming they knew nothing about ███████ I had grown tired of an organization that promotes lying as a way of doing business. I advised them that they better find resolution quickly because my wife and son, who were civilians and not employees of the organization, were about to contact the news media. That caused a firestorm of internal attempts to block our family from going public with what had happened.

Just after my resignation letter was submitted, I went to my organization's credit union, where I had excellent credit, and requested a "hardship loan." This loan was designed to lower the interest rates on member's car and signature loans and reduce the financial strain on the member. The application was completed and the loan was approved. When we received the loan paperwork, the organization's credit union had INCREASED the interest rate on all the loans and the payments had gone up significantly. Incensed, I paid a visit to the credit union office. The credit union manager advised that the person that handled our loan no longer worked there and there was nothing he could do. Subsequently, I called the credit union loan department and asked the representative to check our internal records. He responded that he was shocked by what he saw. He had never seen the interest rate on a loan be processed to be higher, instead of lower. He commented, "This looks like some sort or retribution." I tape recorded the conversation, which is legal in the state of Virginia.

I continued to demand that ██████████████████be allowed to review my personnel folder and my internal grievance. Several of these requests were refused because they claimed the document was "classified," even though ███████ had the necessary clearances. I continued to turn up the heat internally, letting them know that I knew how to press it through the system. Finally, the organization's legal office agreed to arrange a meeting at headquarters for ██████ to review the grievance document. The day soon came when I met ███████████████at the headquarters building. We were escorted to the legal office by a young legal employee who kept popping her knuckles as we rode up the elevator. I knew by her behavior that she knew the significance of our case. Negative stress has to leak out somewhere; many times it is through the hands.

As we entered the legal office, we were place in a small "interview room" with no windows. After waiting for over thirty minutes, an organization attorney entered the room, presenting to me what she claimed was my grievance. It was a single page document in someone else's handwriting. My document was written on a computer and was circa 15 pages long. I became incensed and backed to woman against the door demanding to see the real grievance. ████████████████ gently advised me to calm down and that they would handle it. The legal representative departed and was replaced by another official who claimed they did not have a copy of my original document and would have to do some "checking." The meeting was ended. ████████████ were visibly nervous and shocked by the events they had just witnessed.

Following the meeting, I again demanded that my attorneys and I be allowed to see the real grievance. I pressed the organization to produce it. Again, the organization scheduled a meeting at headquarters where they would let only ████████████see the document. I met ████████████at headquarters and, because I had escort privileges, escorted him to the legal office. We were again placed in a small "interview room." ████████████ was presented with the real grievance and my personnel file. He now knew my internal background. For him, it was a genuine eye opener. We were left sitting there for an hour. Finally, ████████████and I decided we had had enough. We got up, exited the room and advised the secretary that we were leaving the building. As we walked down the external hallway, two legal representatives ran from the legal office shouting, commanding us to stop and demanding that we could not leave. ████████████ advised that the meeting was over and no one was going to treat him or his client that way. I demanded, for the fourth time, that ████ ██ ████████████████ It had been a year since the request had been made ████████████████████████████████████ The representatives feigned ignorance regarding my previous requests, which were made to their office. ████████████ subsequently advised them that the meeting was over and we were leaving the building. I escorted ████████████ to his car and we said goodbye.

I arrived back at my office to find four organization representatives waiting for me. They demanded that I sign documents admitting to misusing a government credit card and to insubordination. They also demanded that I report immediately to the headquarters building ████
██

██████████████████████████████████I respectfully refused. I advised them that I knew exactly what they were doing. I was escorted out of the building and placed on "Administrative leave." ████████ became alarmed that the organization was trying to use its power to have us silenced by accusing us of security violations or being a threat to "National Security." I resigned from the organization effective immediately, to fight the battle with no internal controls over my actions. The organization immediately called and ordered me to report to headquarters to answer questions "about my travel records." This was a typical organization threat I had seen them use before to intimidate employees. I told the representative on the phone to convey to the official personally from me to, "Pound sand." The organization's legal office subsequently called ████████ and claimed that I had used profanity and refused to be cooperative. I must admit, that was a good feeling.

Immediately after my resignation, I requested that the cash amount, minus the withdrawal penalty, of my retirement be distributed to me. Our family needed it to survive. Several weeks went by, with no response. I called the OPM official responsible for these disbursements. She advised that she had been ordered by my organization not to provide me with the funds. This is a violation of federal law. I tape recorded the conversation. I called my organization's security department and demanded to know why they had done this. The representative on the other end of the line advised that they had withheld the funds ████████████ I tape recorded that conversation. I called the OPM representative back and advised her that withholding my retirement funds was a violation of federal law and, she better consider that over my organization's threats. I had the check in two weeks.

████████████████████began receiving threatening letters accusing them of "security violations" and commanding them not to exchange correspondence with our family unless it went through the organization. The organization's attorneys ordered them not to communicate ████████with anyone until they received a computer and safe from the organization. Despite ████████repeated requests, two years went by and the organization never provided these. We began to see that the organization had set up a complex internal system designed to make sure ██████████████were never made public. We learned that it had used this process to silence ████████against it several times in the past. However, we had collected signed letters from ████████

employees exposing this, ███████████████████████
████████████████████████████ of organization officials confirming
their actions. We were not going away.

A few months later, we learned from press reports that
███████████████had examined the organization's false ███████████
report and issued us a detailed report regarding the errors it contained
had ███
██

███████████████████

██

██

██████████████████████████ The only thing that kept us going was our
faith.

██

██
██
██
██
██
██
██
██
███████████████████

██
██
██
██
██
██
███████████████████

██
██
██

"Fear not, I will help thee." Isaiah 41:13

Late one evening, as I lay in bed next to my wife, I reached the end of my own strength. It had been five years. I was mentally and physically exhausted. With tears running down my cheeks, I raised my right hand to heaven and prayed. I told the Lord that I did not have any more strength left to defend my family. I could not go on anymore without His help. I asked Him to take my right hand. I fell asleep holding my hand in the air.

The next morning, still devastated, I sat in our living room and randomly opened the Bible, hoping to find strength. The verse I read jumped off the page. I had opened to Isaiah 41:10-13: "Fear thou not; for I am with thee: be not dismayed; for I am thy God: I will strengthen thee; yea, I will help thee; yea, I will uphold thee with the right hand of my righteousness. Behold, all they that were incensed against thee shall be ashamed and confounded: they shall be as nothing; and they that strive with thee shall perish. Thou shalt seek them, and shalt not find them, even them that contended with thee: they that war against thee shall be as nothing, and as a thing of nought. FOR I THE LORD THY GOD WILL HOLD THY RIGHT HAND, SAYING UNTO THEE, FEAR NOT; I WILL HELP THEE."

Three months later the Director of the organization, ███████████████, resigned in public shame. The resignation was on the front page of the major newspapers. The internal investigator in the organization refused to continue with the "Administrative Investigation," two of the organization officers that had cross examined me had left the organization. Later, I was given the job of Program Manager over a major US government Antiterrorism Program, making a salary almost twice what I was making before.

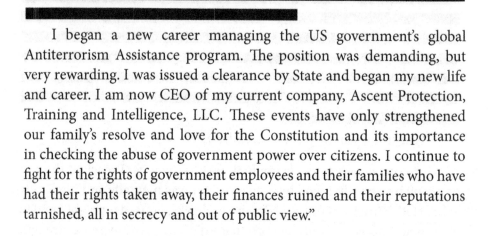

I began a new career managing the US government's global Antiterrorism Assistance program. The position was demanding, but very rewarding. I was issued a clearance by State and began my new life and career. I am now CEO of my current company, Ascent Protection, Training and Intelligence, LLC. These events have only strengthened our family's resolve and love for the Constitution and its importance in checking the abuse of government power over citizens. I continue to fight for the rights of government employees and their families who have had their rights taken away, their finances ruined and their reputations tarnished, all in secrecy and out of public view."

– End of the blacked out version of the story –

The author and his ▇▇▇▇▇▇▇▇▇▇
(Photo courtesy of the author)

Our story is a tragic example of the power the CIA uses to circumvent the Constitution and how far it will go to conceal its mistakes and negligence. ████████████████████████

████████████████████████████████████

████████████████████████

Before the creation of the CIA by President Harry S. Truman, the soon to be Secretary of State Dean Acheson Stated:

> *"I considered it very important to this country to have a sound, well-organized intelligence system, both in the present and in the future. Properly developed, such a service would require new concepts as well as better training and more competent personnel...it was imperative that we refrain from rushing into something that would produce harmful and unnecessary rivalries among the various intelligence agencies. I told Smith (Director of the Bureau of the Budget) that one thing was certain—this country wanted no Gestapo under any guise or for any reason. I had the gravest forebodings about this organization and warned the President (Truman) that as set up neither he, the National Security Council, nor anyone else would be in a position to know what it was doing or to control it."*
>
> —Secretary of State, Dean Acheson

Truman administration
Secretary of State, Dean Acheson

Apparently, President Truman regretted what the CIA had become. In a December 22, 1963 op-ed in *The Washington Post*, Truman wrote:

> "For some time I have been disturbed by the way CIA has been diverted from its original assignment. It has become an operational and at times a policy-making arm of the Government. This has led to trouble and may have compounded our difficulties in several explosive areas.
>
> But there are now some searching questions that need to be answered. I, therefore, would like to see the CIA be restored to its original assignment as the intelligence arm of the President, and that whatever else it can properly perform in that special field—and that its operational duties be terminated or properly used elsewhere.
>
> We have grown up as a nation, respected for our free institutions and for our ability to maintain a free and open society. There is something about the way the CIA has been functioning that is casting a shadow over our historic position and I feel that we need to correct it.
>
> The most important thing ... was to guard against the chance of intelligence being used to influence or to lead the President into unwise decisions."

Harry S. Truman,
December 22, 1963

This article by Truman was later was excised by the paper. *Why did the Post remove it?* Was it because of the "shadow" the CIA was casting over our historic position on freedom? Based on first-hand experience, this author is convinced this shadow is darker than ever before in US history.

Chapter 27
Summary

Writing a book about the CIA is unique challenge. Every word in every line of the manuscript must be approved by the CIA before it can be released, even to a publisher. The author must vet and edit his or her own work for much of the journey. It is a significant burden that can take months of back and forth approvals and disapprovals, until the skirmish is finally over. Some publishers are afraid of taking on the CIA by producing a book that calls the actions of the Agency into question. This was especially true regarding *From the Company of Shadows*. In this book, much of my writing has exposed activities the CIA has engaged in that are embarrassing and call into question its adherence to the Constitution. Running a manuscript by the CIA for approval is like submitting a crime report to the burglar before it is filed. It is not an easy task. So, every word that has made it into this book is precious. I am certain some of the information is like concentrated lemon juice; causing the reader to pucker a little. Restrictions of secrecy have prevented me from expanding further. So, I finish this discourse with a kind of embattled satisfaction and a strange sense of camaraderie with members of the CIA Pre Publications Review Board. I am sure they grew tired of addressing the myriad of changes I submitted over several months. I must thank them all for allowing me to present the information found in this book.

The role of intelligence in the function of the US government and national security cannot be overstated. It is vital to the protection of our precious freedoms. There are foreign countries, global terrorist organizations and religious and political philosophies that are determined to destroy the United States and the democratic way of life. Secrecy is an important part of defending this freedom, through US intelligence operations. It plays a critical role in the protection of our foreign agents, who are placing their lives on the line for our democracy and to protect the dedicated men and women who risk their lives as members of our armed forces.

We must understand that secrecy contains within itself an inherent power that is difficult to control, because of its very nature. And secrecy can bring with it certain vulnerabilities. It can prevent real oversight to restrain its misuse, cover up significant operational errors and the resulting damage to national security, hide negligent activity from healthy scrutiny and conceal deficiencies that can lead to significant damage, including the loss of life. This power exists within the CIA and its misuse has been evident.

The CIA has made many honorable and courageous contributions to our nations' protection, some of which I was a part of while I was there, accomplished by men and women whose sacrifice will never be publicly known. But, as a system, it has become out of control and overstepped the constitutional balance of powers designed to keep it in check and accountable to our democratic system of government. We must remain ever vigilant to keep the CIA and the secrecy it wields in check; in the same fashion we hold other government agencies accountable.

The enduring power of democracy is in its freedom, openness and accountability to the people which it serves. When a government or organization shields itself from openness, accountability and oversight, it circumvents the bedrock of democracy and weakens its ability to protect individual freedoms.

Democracy is the most successful form of government in world history. It must be protected at every turn, including from organizations within its governing system that hide from its processes. Our Constitution is the result of corporate political genius, and perhaps the result of divine providence. I am convinced it is both. It is my sincere hope that the reader heeds the warnings given in this book regarding the abuse of secrecy in our democracy.

Epilogue

My family was devastated by our government's abuse ███████████████████████. I have since married my best friend and gained a wonderful new life on a farm in South Georgia. I continue to work as a consultant and subject matter expert in intelligence, anti terrorism, executive protection and as a freelance journalist. My wife is teaching me to be a farmer; something quite a bit more challenging than what I did for a career. But, she is good at it, and I have the sore muscles to prove it. I am learning the complexities of successful farming from a local neighbor, Harvey. Harvey is the master and I am the grasshopper. Through all of this, I have gained a new perspective on life. It includes these simple lessons:

- Sue, my current wife, and I now live on a little farm in the Southeast. I spend my time living my life's dream, experiencing the fullness of nature, growing our own food, writing, lecturing and teaching. All things have a tendency to work out for the good

- The events I went through taught me the greatest lesson in life. True success is having peace of mind and heart no matter what is going on around you. Happiness is the absence of worry

- Always, in the back of my mind is the thought that it is our Constitution that makes us what we are as a people

- Too many people take for granted the freedoms we have in America. If we neglect to fight to keep them, we will lose them

- Early in the mornings, Sue and I watch the rising of the sun. God's creation goes on whether man notices it or not. True meaning in life is only found by those who diligently seek it

- Sue is a Master Gardener. I have learned so much from her love for plants, flowers and vegetable gardens. As the saying goes, "Gardening is a way of showing you believe in tomorrow"

- Each step in learning the ways of organic farming is like a science experiment. It has been fascinating. At first, my type-A personality could not handle it. The more I learned, the more I realized just how complex and scientific farming really is. This formerly high speed CIA agent missed it for two decades

- Contrary to popular belief, the Agrarian life is exciting and full of pleasant surprises. It's no wonder the farmers in our area live to be in their late 80s and 90s

- Rarely have we seen communities that are so close, so giving and so reliant on each other. I suppose this is the way we were meant to live

- Each step in our organic, off the grid gardening "experiment" has been as fascinating and fulfilling as anything I have ever done

- The events of the past ten years have begun to fade, slowly. Memories will stay; both bad and good. We can replace the bad ones with new, bright experiences. It just takes time

- Starting over is not easy, especially when you are used to going at a hundred miles an hour. It literally took me months to slow down. I realized I had become an adrenaline junky

- Parenting was the joy of my life. My kids still remain my greatest love. Kids are something you can take with you, if your goal is heaven

- Riding Harleys is our love. We are both in our 50s. The feeling of freedom you get on a motorcycle and the measure of risk involved keeps you young. As the joke goes, now we can see why dogs stick their heads out the windows of moving cars

- Invariably, the memories of the past ten years try to come back and haunt me. I have faced serious risk in my career; from terrorists, spies and criminals. Here is the greatest lesson. Most of our problems are between our ears. It is not what has happened to you that counts; it's how you handle it

- Virtue comes from true moments of reflection. Our society has become so busy with paying bills, sitting in traffic, listening to iPods, blasting music in our cars and hosting parties that we have drowned out the time we need to meditate and think about what really matters in life. It has deeply affected our morality

- In the tough times I have learned that only three things matter: Faith, family and friends

- Lessons are difficult aspects of life. But they are necessary. They teach us to appreciate the people we have in our lives and to cherish all that we have been given, regardless of the amount

- Every one of us will have challenges. It is the stuff of life

- Get into life with all the "gusto" you can. Breathe the air up in the mountains. Watch the sunrise over a pond. Stand in the rain. Lie in the sun on the beach and listen to the children play. Take all of it in. There is such a short time to enjoy it

- Every person in your life is important. Be tender to babies, have fun with children, respect and learn from the aged. Love your family, accepting their faults. Be true to your friends and someone they can trust with their secrets. After all, life is about people. It is about giving

The author and Sue on their Harleys

The author, his wife Sue and "Preacher Crane," who performed the wedding service. Preacher Crane, a state trooper, was armed - so they had to get married (kidding)

(Photo courtesy of the author)

The author, his family and his wife.

(Photo courtesy of the author)

The author and his second family

(Photo courtesy of the author)

The author and his friends in the motorcycle ministry
"2nd Thief"

(Photo courtesy of the author)

He that raises a large family does, indeed, while he lives to observe them, stand a broader mark for sorrow; but then he stands a broader mark for pleasure too. —Benjamin Franklin

"And you shall know the truth, and the truth shall make you free."
—John 8:32

Constitutional Foundation

To fully understand the legal foundation of the Constitution and the intent of those who framed it, one must become familiar with the writings of the men that engineered the most important legal document in history. It is also important to be well versed in the legal decisions that have been handed down since the Constitution was ratified. When you read these quotes, the extent to which the current United States government has departed from these principles will become glaringly obvious. The only hope for our country is a populace movement that demands a return to these principles as a matter of law, enforced by the people.

> *"Be not intimidated, therefore, by any terrors, from publishing with the utmost freedom whatever can be warranted by the laws of our country; nor suffer yourselves to be wheedled out of your liberty by any pretenses of politeness, delicacy, or decency. These, as they are often used, are but three different names for hypocrisy, chicanery, and cowardice. "*

—John Adams

Legal Decisions

Down v. Bidwell, 182 US 244 (1901)

"It will be an evil day for American Liberty if the theory of a government outside supreme law finds lodgment in our constitutional jurisprudence. No higher duty rests upon this Court than to exert its full authority to prevent all violations of the principles of the Constitution."

Elrod v. Burns, 427 US 347; 6 S. Ct. 2673; 49 L. Ed. 2d (1976)

"Loss of First Amendment Freedoms, for even minimal periods of time, unquestionably constitutes irreparable injury."

Boyd v. United, 116 US 616 at 635 (1885)

Justice Bradley, "It may be that it is the obnoxious thing in the mildest form; but illegitimate and unconstitutional practices get their first footing in that way; namely, by silent approaches and slight deviations from legal modes of procedure.....It is the duty of the Courts to be watchful of the Constitutional rights of the Citizens, and against any stealthy encroachments thereon. Their motto should be Obsta Principiis."

Gomillion v. Lightfoot, 364 US 155 (1966)

"Constitutional 'rights' would be of little value if they could be indirectly denied."

Mallowy v. Hogan, 378 US 1

"All rights and safeguards contained in the first eight amendments to the federal Constitution are equally applicable."

Miranda v. Arizona, 384 US 426, 491; 86 S. Ct. 1603

"Where rights secured by the Constitution are involved, there can be no 'rule making' or legislation which would abrogate them."

Sherar v. Cullen, 481 F. 2d 946 (1973)

"There can be no sanction or penalty imposed upon one because of his exercise of constitutional rights."

Simmons v. United States, 390 US 377 (1968)

"The claim and exercise of a Constitutional right cannot be converted into a crime"…"a denial of them would be a denial of due process of law."

Cannon v. Commission on Judicial Qualifications, (1975) 14 Cal. 3d 678, 694

"Acts in excess of judicial authority constitute misconduct, particularly where a judge deliberately disregards the requirements of fairness and due process."

Olmstad v. United States, (1928) 277 US 438

"Crime is contagious. If the Government becomes a lawbreaker, it breeds contempt for law; it invites every man to become a law unto himself; it invites anarchy."

Owen v. City of Independence

"The innocent individual who is harmed by an abuse of governmental authority is assured that he will be compensated for his injury."

US v. Lee, 106 US 196, 220 1 S. Ct. 240, 261, 27 L. Ed 171 (1882)

"No man in this country is so high that he is above the law. No officer of the law may set that law at defiance, with impunity. All the officers of the government, from the highest to the lowest, are creatures of the law and are bound to obey it."

"It is the only supreme power [Constitution] in our system of government, and every man who, by accepting office participates in its functions, is only the more strongly bound to submit to that supremacy, and to observe the limitations which it imposes on the exercise of the authority which it gives."

Duncan v. Missouri, 152 US 377, 382 (1894)

"Due process of law and the equal protection of the laws are secured if the laws operate on all alike, and do not subject the individual to an arbitrary exercise of the powers of government."

Giozza v. Tiernan, 148 US 657, 662 (1893)

"Undoubtedly it (the Fourteenth Amendment) forbids any arbitrary deprivation of life, liberty or property, and secures equal protection to all under like circumstances in the enjoyment of their rights... It is enough that there is no discrimination in favor of one as against another of the same class. And due process of law within the meaning of the [Fifth and Fourteenth] amendment is secured if the laws operate on all alike, and do not subject the individual to an arbitrary exercise of the powers of government."

Truax v. Corrigan, 257 US 312, 332

"Our whole system of law is predicated on the general fundamental principle of equality of application of the law. 'All men are equal before the law,' 'This is a government of laws and not of men,' 'No man is above the law,' are all maxims showing the spirit in which legislature, executives, and courts are expected to make, execute and apply laws. But the framers and adopters of the [Fourteenth] amendment were not content to depend... upon the spirit of equality which might not be insisted on by local public opinion. They therefore embodied that spirit in a specific guaranty."

42 USC 1983 – Availability of Equitable Relief Against Judges

"Nowhere was the judiciary given immunity, particularly nowhere in Article III; under our Constitution, if judges were to have immunity, it could only possibly be granted by amendment (and even less possibly by legislative act), as Art. I, Sections 9 & 10, respectively, in fact expressly prohibit such, stating, "No Title of Nobility shall be granted by the United States" and "No state shall…grant any Title of Nobility." Most of us are certain that Congress itself doesn't understand the inherent lack of immunity for judges."

Cooper v. Aaron, 358 US 1, 78 S. Ct. 1401 (1959)

"Any judge who does not comply with his oath to the Constitution of the United States wars against that Constitution and engages in acts of violation of the supreme law of the land. The judge is engaged in acts of treason."

"The U. S. Supreme Court has stated that "no state legislator or executive or judicial officer can war against the Constitution without violating his undertaking to support it."

Marbury v. Madison, 5 US (2 Cranch) 137, 180 (1803)

"…the particular phraseology of the Constitution of the United States confirms and strengthens the principle, supposed to be essential to all written constitutions, that a law repugnant to the Constitution is void, and that courts, as well as other departments, are bound by that instrument."

"In declaring what shall be the supreme law of the land, the Constitution itself is first mentioned; and not the laws of the United States generally, but those only which shall be made in pursuance of the Constitution, have that rank."

"All law (rules and practices) which are repugnant to the Constitution are VOID."

"Since the 14th Amendment to the Constitution states "No state (jurisdiction) shall make or enforce any law which shall abridge the rights, privileges, or immunities of citizens of the United States nor deprive any citizen of life, liberty, or property, without due process of law,…or equal protection under the law," this renders judicial immunity unconstitutional."

Scheuer v. Rhodes, 416 US 232, 94 S. Ct. 1683, 1687 (1974)

"The US Supreme Court stated that "when a state officer acts under a state law in a manner violative of the Federal Constitution, he comes into conflict with the superior authority of that Constitution, and he is in that case stripped of his official or representative character and is subjected in his person to the consequences of his individual conduct. The State has no power to impart to him any immunity from responsibility to the supreme authority of the United States."

United States v. Chadwick, 433 US I at 16 (1976)

"It is deeply distressing that the Department of Justice, whose mission is to protect the constitutional liberties of the people of the United States, should even appear to be seeking to subvert them by extreme and dubious legal argument."

Elmore v. McCammon (1986) 640 F. Supp. 905

"..the right to file a lawsuit pro se is one of the most important rights under the Constitution and laws."

Juliard v. Greeman, 110 US 421 (1884)

"Supreme Court Justice Field, "There is no such thing as a power of inherent sovereignty in the government of the United States...In this country, sovereignty resides in the people, and Congress cannot exercise power which they have not, by their Constitution, entrusted to it. All else is withheld."

Constitutional Quotes

"The judicial power ought to be distinct from both the legislative and executive, and independent upon both, that so it may be a check upon both, as both should be checks upon that."
—John Adams

"The means of defense against foreign danger historically have become the instruments of tyranny at home."

—James Madison

"When People fear their government, there is tyranny. When government fears their people, there is liberty."

—Thomas Jefferson

"In every stage of these Oppressions We have Petitioned for Redress in the most humble terms: Our repeated Petitions have been answered only by repeated injury. A Prince, whose character is thus marked by every act which may define a Tyrant, is unfit to be the ruler of a free people."
—Addressed to King George III, Declaration of Independence

"Be not intimidated, therefore, by any terrors, from publishing with the utmost freedom whatever can be warranted by the laws of our country; nor suffer yourselves to be wheedled out of your liberty by any pretenses of politeness, delicacy, or decency. These, as they are often used, are but three different names for hypocrisy, chicanery, and cowardice."
—John Adams

"Congress shall make no law respecting an establishment of religion, or prohibiting the free exercise thereof; or abridging the freedom of speech, or of the press; or the right of the people peaceably to assemble, and to petition the Government for a redress of grievances."
—US Constitution: Amendment 1

"It is as much the duty of Government to render prompt justice against itself in favor of citizens as it is to administer the same between private individuals."
—Abraham Lincoln

"I am for....freedom of the press and against all violations of the Constitution to silence by force, and not by reason, the complaints or criticisms, just or unjust, of our citizens against the conduct of their agents."
—Thomas Jefferson

"A nation that is afraid to let its people judge the truth and falsehood in an open market is a nation that is afraid of its people."
—John F. Kennedy

"it is essential that the public be informed concerning the activities of government. "[in] no case shall information be classified in order to conceal violations of federal law, inefficiency, or administrative error, to prevent embarrassment to a person, organization, or agency; to restrain competition; or to prevent or delay the release of information that does not require protection in the interest of national security."
—Ronald Reagan

"Happy is it when the interest in which government has in the preservation of its own power, coincides with a proper distribution of the public burdens, and tends to guard the least wealthy part of the community from oppression!"
—Alexander Hamilton

"*The very word 'secrecy' is repugnant in a free and open society; and we are as a people inherently and historically opposed to secret societies, to secret oaths, and to secret proceedings.*"
—John F. Kennedy

"*For too long, judges have allowed the government to hide its mistakes behind claims of national security.*"
—Barry Siegel

"*The only foundation of a free Constitution is pure Virtue, and if this cannot be inspired into our People in a greater Measure than they have it now, they may change their Rulers and the forms of Government, but they will not obtain a lasting Liberty. They will only exchange Tyrants and Tyrannies.*"
—John Adams

Liberty cannot be preserved without a general knowledge among the people, who have a right...and a desire to know; but besides this, they have a right, an indisputable, unalienable, indefeasible, divine right to that most dreaded and envied kind of knowledge, I mean of the characters and conduct of their rulers.
—John Adams

"*When we assumed the Soldier, we did not lay aside the Citizen.*"
—George Washington

"*Because power corrupts, society's demands for moral authority and character increase as the importance of the position increases.*"
—John Adams

"*Fear is the foundation of most governments.*"
—John Adams

"Liberty cannot be preserved without general knowledge among the people."
—John Adams

"Our Constitution was made only for a moral and religious people. It is wholly inadequate to the government of any other."
—John Adams

"Power always thinks it has a great soul and vast views beyond the comprehension of the weak."
—John Adams

"Power always thinks... that it is doing God's service when it is violating all his laws."
—John Adams

"There is danger from all men. The only maxim of a free government ought to be to trust no man living with power to endanger the public liberty."
—John Adams

"All tyranny needs to gain a foothold is for people of good conscience to remain silent."
—Thomas Jefferson

"Books constitute capital. A library book lasts as long as a house, for hundreds of years. It is not, then, an article of mere consumption but fairly of capital, and often in the case of professional men, setting out in life, it is their only capital."
—Thomas Jefferson

"Educate and inform the whole mass of the people... They are the only sure reliance for the preservation of our liberty."
—Thomas Jefferson

"Enlighten the people generally, and tyranny and oppressions of body and mind will vanish like evil spirits at the dawn of day."
—Thomas Jefferson

"Every government degenerates when trusted to the rulers of the people alone. The people themselves are its only safe depositories."
—Thomas Jefferson

"Experience hath shewn, that even under the best forms of government those entrusted with power have, in time, and by slow operations, perverted it into tyranny."
—Thomas Jefferson

"I am mortified to be told that, in the United States of America, the sale of a book can become a subject of inquiry, and of criminal inquiry too."
—Thomas Jefferson

"I have sworn upon the altar of God, eternal hostility against every form of tyranny over the mind of man."
—Thomas Jefferson

"I know of no safe depository of the ultimate powers of the society but the people themselves; and if we think them not enlightened enough to exercise their control with a wholesome discretion, the remedy is not to take it from them but to inform their discretion."
—Thomas Jefferson

"I own that I am not a friend to a very energetic government. It is always oppressive."
—Thomas Jefferson

"I tremble for my country when I reflect that God is just; that his justice cannot sleep forever."
—Thomas Jefferson

"My reading of history convinces me that most bad government results from too much government."
—Thomas Jefferson

"No government ought to be without censors; and where the press is free no one ever will."
—Thomas Jefferson

"Nothing can stop the man with the right mental attitude from achieving his goal; nothing on earth can help the man with the wrong mental attitude."
—Thomas Jefferson

"Nothing is unchangeable but the inherent and unalienable rights of man."
—Thomas Jefferson

"One man with courage is a majority."
—Thomas Jefferson

"Our country is now taking so steady a course as to show by what road it will pass to destruction, to wit: by consolidation of power first, and then corruption, its necessary consequence."
—Thomas Jefferson

"Our greatest happiness does not depend on the condition of life in which chance has placed us, but is always the result of a good conscience, good health, occupation, and freedom in all just pursuits."
—Thomas Jefferson

"*Rightful liberty is unobstructed action according to our will within limits drawn around us by the equal rights of others. I do not add 'within the limits of the law' because law is often but the tyrant's will, and always so when it violates the rights of the individual.*"
—Thomas Jefferson

"*The God who gave us life, gave us liberty at the same time.*"
—Thomas Jefferson

"*The natural progress of things is for liberty to yield and government to gain ground.*"
—Thomas Jefferson

"*Timid men prefer the calm of despotism to the tempestuous sea of liberty.*"
—Thomas Jefferson

"*We hold these truths to be self-evident: that all men are created equal; that they are endowed by their Creator with certain unalienable rights; that among these are life, liberty, and the pursuit of happiness.*"
—Thomas Jefferson

"*Whenever the people are well-informed, they can be trusted with their own government.*"
—Thomas Jefferson

"*Where the press is free and every man able to read, all is safe.*"
—Thomas Jefferson

"*The sacred rights of mankind are not to be rummaged for among old parchments or musty records. They are written, as with a sunbeam, in the whole volume of human nature, by the hand of the divinity itself; and can never be erased.*"
—Thomas Jefferson

"*There is a certain enthusiasm in liberty, that makes human nature rise above itself, in acts of bravery and heroism.*"
—Thomas Jefferson

"*They who can give up essential liberty to obtain a little temporary safety deserve neither liberty nor safety.*"
—Benjamin Franklin

"*Arbitrary power is most easily established on the ruins of liberty abused to licentiousness.*"
—George Washington

"*Government is not reason; it is not eloquent; it is force. Like fire, it is a dangerous servant and a fearful master.*"
—George Washington

"*If the freedom of speech is taken away then dumb and silent we may be led, like sheep to the slaughter.*"
—George Washington

"*A popular government without popular information or the means of acquiring it, is but a prologue to a farce, or a tragedy, or perhaps both.*"
—James Madison

"*A well-instructed people alone can be permanently a free people.*"
—James Madison

"*All men having power ought to be distrusted to a certain degree.*"
—James Madison

"*Despotism can only exist in darkness, and there are too many lights now in the political firmament to permit it to remain anywhere, as it has heretofore done, almost everywhere.*"
—James Madison

"Do not separate text from historical background. If you do, you will have perverted and subverted the Constitution, which can only end in a distorted, bastardized form of illegitimate government."
—James Madison

"I believe there are more instances of the abridgement of freedom of the people by gradual and silent encroachments by those in power than by violent and sudden usurpations."
—James Madison

"If Tyranny and Oppression come to this land, it will be in the guise of fighting a foreign enemy."
—James Madison

"It is a universal truth that the loss of liberty at home is to be charged to the provisions against danger, real or pretended, from abroad."
—James Madison

"Liberty may be endangered by the abuse of liberty, but also by the abuse of power."
—James Madison

"The advancement and diffusion of knowledge is the only guardian of true liberty."
—James Madison

"The essence of Government is power; and power, lodged as it must be in human hands, will ever be liable to abuse."
—James Madison

"The happy Union of these States is a wonder; their Constitution a miracle; their example the hope of Liberty throughout the world."
—James Madison

"*The people are the only legitimate fountain of power, and it is from them that the constitutional charter, under which the several branches of government hold their power, is derived.*"
—James Madison

"*The truth is that all men having power ought to be mistrusted.*"
— James Madison

"*To the press alone, chequered as it is with abuses, the world is indebted for all the triumphs which have been gained by reason and humanity over error and oppression.*"
—James Madison

"*We are right to take alarm at the first experiment upon our liberties.*"
—James Madison

"*Where an excess of power prevails, property of no sort is duly respected. No man is safe in his opinions, his person, his faculties, or his possessions.*"
—James Madison

"*Wherever there is interest and power to do wrong, wrong will generally be done.*"
—James Madison

Is it worth the struggle to return our government to a true Constitutional democracy? President Teddy Roosevelt said it best:

> *"It is not the critic who counts; not the man who points out how the strong man stumbles, or where the doer of deeds could have done them better. The credit belongs to the man who is actually in the arena, whose face is marred by dust and sweat and blood; who strives valiantly; who errs, who comes short again and again, because there is no effort without error and shortcoming; but who does actually strive to do the deeds; who knows great enthusiasms, the great devotions; who spends himself in a worthy cause; who at the best knows in the end the triumph of high achievement, and who at the worst, if he fails, at least fails while daring greatly, so that his place shall never be with those cold and timid souls who neither know victory nor defeat."*

We should never forget the most basic principles of our democracy. If we do, it will be to our peril. To guard our freedoms from the encroachment of a voracious government we must be ever vigilant; preventing our busy schedules and the distractions of life from draining our courage and resolve.

The Author

Notes:

1. Barry Siegel, Claim of Privilege, Harper Perennial, 2008.

2. Louis Fisher, In the Name of National Security; unchecked Presidential power and the Reynolds case, University Press of Kansas, 2006.

3. Laura K. Donohue, The Shadow of State Secrets, University of Pennsylvania Law Review, 2005 – 2012.

4. Steven Emerson, Jihad Incorporated, Prometheus Books, 2006.

5. Steven Emerson, American Jihad, Free Press, New York, 2002.

6. Charlie Savage, Takeover: the Return of the Imperial Presidency, Back Bay Books, 2007.

CPSIA information can be obtained
at www.ICGtesting.com
Printed in the USA
BVOW09*1431100717

488556BV00002B/11/P